The Star of Higher Knowledge:

The Five Guiding Mysteries of Esoteric Christianity

RON MACFARLANE

Published 2015 by
Greater Mysteries Publications
Mission, BC, Canada

Cover Design: Ron MacFarlane

Printed in the United States of America

ISBN:
ISBN-13: 978-0994007735
ISBN-10: 0994007736

DEDICATION

This esoteric Christian publication is lovingly dedicated to
our elder brother and saviour, Jesus-Immanuel,
for being the first of our human life-wave
to hypostatically unite with God the Son
through the intercession of the Solar-Christos,
and thereby re-open the door
to eternal paradise.

CONTENTS

THE STAR
OF HIGHER
KNOWLEDGE

INTRODUCTION

Background on Esoteric Christianity

THE STAR OF HIGHER KNOWLEDGE: The Five Guiding Mysteries of Esoteric Christianity, as the title indicates, presents information on the mysteries of Christianity from a perspective separate and distinct from mainstream Christian theology. This is not to say that the viewpoint taken here is at odds or disagrees with traditional Christian theology. Rather the contrary. Though much of the information presented here may be entirely new to (or substantially different from) traditional Christian theology, it is not meant to disparage or denigrate, but instead to reinforce, to complement and to expand.

From the very beginning of his teaching ministry on earth, Christ-Jesus presented the mysteries of Christianity in two fundamentally distinct ways. To his inner circle of disciples; that is, to those who had advanced spiritual preparation and knowledge, Christ-Jesus could teach openly, directly and comprehensively. To the general, less-educated public, however, he needed to teach more figuratively, illustratively and simply. As described in scripture:

Then the disciples came and said to him, "Why do you speak to them [the general public] in parables?" And he answered them, "To you it has been given to know the secrets of the kingdom of heaven, but to them it has not been given … This is why I speak to them in parables, because seeing they do not see, and hearing they do not hear, nor do they understand." (Matt 13:10, 13)

To those with "greater" advancement and prior knowledge, Christ-Jesus could go into "greater" depth and detail regarding his mystery knowledge. For this reason, these particular wisdom-teachings have been termed "the greater mysteries of the Son." To those with "less" education and prerequisite understanding, Christ-Jesus went into "less" detail and complexity regarding his mystery knowledge. For this reason, these particular wisdom-teachings have been termed "the lesser mysteries of the Son."

"Greater" and "lesser" in this case certainly do not imply "superior" and "inferior." All mysteries of the Son, since they are suffused with divinity and proceed from the highest reality, are equally fathomless and enlightening. Whether greater or lesser, the sacred mysteries of Christ-Jesus have the power to positively and completely transform us—bodily, psychologically and spiritually.

After the death, resurrection and ascension of Christ-Jesus into the heavenly realms, his twofold method of conveying the mystery-teachings of the Son became more formalized and institutionalized. St. Peter was chosen to establish a universal *religion* and *theology* in order to preserve, guard and promulgate the lesser mysteries of Christianity. Since these lesser Christian mysteries were openly and publically available to mankind in general, they can be collectively termed, "outer" or "exoteric" Christianity.

St. John the Beloved was similarly entrusted by our Saviour to establish a universal *philosophy* and *theosophy*[1] in order to preserve, guard and promulgate the greater mysteries of Christianity. Since the greater Christian mysteries were selectively and privately available only to advanced disciples with prior initiatory training, they can be collectively termed, "inner" or "esoteric" Christianity.

Exoteric and esoteric Christianity were intended by Christ-Jesus to be complementary and mutually-beneficial mystery-teachings, similar to the preparatory high school teachings and the successive university teachings of today. Sadly throughout Christian history, corrupt, intolerant and politically-powerful authorities within the universal Church of St. Peter have violently rejected any teaching not conforming to their own narrow, distorted and falsified interpretation of Christianity. Consequently, esoteric Christianity in its various historical forms—such as the Knights of the Holy Grail and the Fraternity of the Rose Cross—were forced underground, becoming guardedly-veiled and shroudedly-secretive in order to survive.

Understandably, for the past 2000 years, the various expressions of esoteric Christianity have remained deeply hidden from public view. Whenever possible, however, fragments of the greater mysteries of the Son were carefully and safely divulged to general mankind in order to assist with necessary Christian development.

Moreover, up until the late-nineteenth century, the lesser mysteries of Christianity, as conveyed by the exoteric Church of St. Peter, were intellectually sufficient for most believers. Profound mysteries such as the Holy Trinity, the Logos-Word and universal creation were dogmatically considered to be revelatory "matters of faith" that were beyond rational consideration and logical comprehension. As such, for many centuries there was little public or theological interest to intellectually pursue these mysteries.

By the late-nineteenth century, however, violent persecution by corrupt Church officials had largely disappeared and general humanity was intellectually open and advanced enough to consider some of the greater mysteries of esoteric Christianity.

Fortunately, by the end of the nineteenth century, the intellectual and spiritual development of mankind necessitated the gradual release of hidden information concerning the greater Christian mysteries. Authentic sources of esoteric Christianity began to increasingly (and carefully) share their wealth of mystery-knowledge with the general public. The Anthroposophical Society, founded in 1912 by Austrian philosopher and esotericist, Rudolf Steiner (1861-1925), is one such significant expression of modern-day esoteric Christianity.

The Divine Trinity According to Exoteric Christianity

Esoteric Christianity fully agrees with exoteric Christian theology that the Trinity of divine persons: Father, Son and Holy Spirit, is incapable of being logically deduced by natural reason alone. Esoteric Christianity nevertheless strongly maintains that once revealed this "mystery of mysteries" *is* capable of logical demonstration. According to Western Christian theology:

> The mystery of the Most Holy Trinity is the central mystery of Christian faith and life. It is the mystery of God in himself. It is therefore the source of all the other mysteries of faith, the light that enlightens them. It is the most fundamental and essential teaching in the 'hierarchy of the truths of faith'... The Trinity is a mystery of faith in the strict sense, one of the 'mysteries that are hidden in God, which can never be known unless they are revealed by God' ... To be sure, God has left traces of his Trinitarian being in his work of creation and in his Revelation throughout the Old Testament. But his inmost Being as Holy Trinity is a mystery that is inaccessible to

reason alone. (*Catechism of the Catholic Church*; paragraphs 234, 237)

Moreover, conventional Christian belief asserts that the mystery of the one God existing as a relationship of three divine persons—the Father, the Son and the Holy Spirit—was first revealed by Christ-Jesus. As recorded in scripture:

> And Jesus came and said to them, "All authority in heaven and on earth has been given to me. Go therefore and make disciples of all nations, baptizing them in the name of the Father and of the Son and of the Holy Spirit." (Matt 28:18, 19)

Even though the mystery of the Trinity, from the very beginning, was understood to be beyond unaided human reason to completely comprehend, the early Church still endeavored to clarify and understand this central article of faith. By the fourth century, numerous Church councils and synods had articulated a clear dogma of the Trinity primarily as a defense against recurrent, unsound ideological conjecture (heresy). The Athanasian Creed (c.500 AD) is one of the best and most enduring articulations of Trinitarian belief, and states (in part) the following:

> And the catholic faith is this: That we worship one God in Trinity, and Trinity in Unity; Neither confounding the Persons; nor dividing the Essence. For there is one Person of the Father; another of the Son; and another of the Holy Spirit. But the Godhead of the Father, of the Son, and of the Holy Spirit, is all one; the Glory equal, the Majesty coeternal. Such as the Father is; such is the Son; and such is the Holy Spirit. The Father uncreated; the Son uncreated; and the Holy Spirit uncreated. The Father unlimited; the Son unlimited; and the Holy Spirit unlimited. The Father eternal; the Son eternal; and the Holy Spirit eternal. And yet they are not three eternals;

but one eternal. As also there are not three uncreated; nor three infinites, but one uncreated; and one infinite. So likewise the Father is Almighty; the Son Almighty; and the Holy Spirit Almighty. And yet they are not three Almighties; but one Almighty.

So the Father is God; the Son is God; and the Holy Spirit is God. And yet they are not three Gods; but one God. So likewise the Father is Lord; the Son Lord; and the Holy Spirit Lord. And yet not three Lords; but one Lord. For like as we are compelled by the Christian verity; to acknowledge every Person by himself to be God and Lord; So are we forbidden by the catholic religion; to say, There are three Gods, or three Lords. The Father is made of none; neither created, nor begotten. The Son is of the Father alone; not made, nor created; but begotten. The Holy Spirit is of the Father and of the Son; neither made, nor created, nor begotten; but proceeding.

So there is one Father, not three Fathers; one Son, not three Sons; one Holy Spirit, not three Holy Spirits. And in this Trinity none is before, or after another; none is greater, or less than another. But the whole three Persons are coeternal, and coequal. So that in all things, as aforesaid; the Unity in Trinity, and the Trinity in Unity, is to be worshipped.

Though there have been a few additional insightful contributions to Trinitarian belief throughout the centuries (St. Thomas Aquinas' "psychological theory of the Trinity," for example), the doctrine of the Trinity has fundamentally remained unchanged for the past 1600 years. Moreover, outside of Western Christian theology, there are really no other reliable sources of information concerning the Trinity.

The Divine Trinity According to Esoteric Christianity

Regarding the Trinity of divine persons, the sources of esoteric Christianity have been publically silent on this particular mystery for the past 2000 years. This was most certainly due to the fact that the lesser mysteries of the Trinity, as delineated by exoteric Christian theology, were intellectually sufficient for most believers during that time. Moreover, the Trinity has been traditionally regarded as a matter of faith revealed in scripture, and not a mystery that was knowable by unaided human reason, or that was capable of logical demonstration once revealed. Consequently, there was little intellectual interest with Christian theologians in particular, and humanity in general, to delve deeper into the Trinitarian mystery in a logical or philosophical way.

While not providing much in the way of new or additional insight into the mystery of the Trinity, recent sources of esoteric Christianity have at least openly supported exoteric Christian doctrine concerning the Trinity. Anthroposophist Rudolf Steiner, for instance, has stated in a lecture given in Dornach on 30 July 1922:

> [I]t was an ancient dogma that the Father is the unbegotten begetter, that the Son is the one begotten by the Father, and that the Holy Spirit is the one imparted to humanity by the Father and the Son. This is not some kind of arbitrarily asserted dogma but rather the wisdom of initiation living in the earliest Christian centuries ... One must understand the Father, the Son, and the Holy Spirit if one would understand the teaching concerning God concretely and in a genuine way ... Whoever beholds the cross on Golgotha must at the same time behold the Trinity, for in reality Christ shows and makes manifest the Trinity in all the ways he is interwoven with the earthly evolution of humanity.

Other lesser-known sources of esoteric Christianity have quietly introduced Trinitarian concepts that diverge from traditional Christian theology. In *The Aquarian Gospel of Jesus the Christ* (1980), for example, Levi H. Dowling wrote the following:

> Before the worlds were formed all things were One; just Spirit, Universal Breath. And Spirit breathed, and that which was not manifest became the Fire and Thought of heaven, the Father-God, the Mother-God. And when the Fire and Thought of heaven in union breathed, their son, their only son, was born. This son is Love whom men called the Christ. Men call the Thought of heaven [the Mother-God] the Holy Breath. (Section III, Chapter 9: 15–18)

The Greater Mysteries of the Trinity Now Revealed

Thankfully today, established largely on the spiritual-scientific foundation of anthroposophy, the greater mysteries of the Trinity—out of the hidden sources of esoteric Christianity—can begin to be openly conveyed and intellectually understood in clear, logical concepts. While some of the greater mysteries of the Trinity revealed in this way will undoubtedly be met with some initial opposition from mainstream Christian theologians, they are in no way intended as criticism or diminishment of traditional Trinitarian doctrine. It will be recognized over time that these greater mysteries of esoteric Christianity positively complement and spiritually enhance the lesser mysteries of Church theology.

According to esoteric Christianity there is only one ultimate reality—God. Moreover, the nature of the one God is "spirit," or infinite and eternal mind. The spirit-mind of God is comprised of two fundamental characteristics: being and knowing. The mutual interaction of "divine being" and "divine knowing" eternally generates a third fundamental characteristic—"divine self-awareness." Together these divine mental characteristics comprise the complete "personhood" of God.

Since the spirit-nature of God is one and indivisible, each of the three fundamental characteristics of the divine mind share in the personhood of God. Consequently, they are infinitely more than lifeless, spirit-principles; they are living spirit-persons. The distinct person of "supreme being" is esoterically termed the "Heavenly Father." The distinct person of "all-knowing" is esoterically termed the "Holy Mother." The distinct person of divine self-awareness is esoterically termed the "Eternal Son."

As divine persons, then, the eternal interactions of the Heavenly Father, the Holy Mother and the Eternal Son are not impassive and impersonal. Rather, the intimate mutuality and unitive relationship of the three divine persons is impelled by divine love. "Divine love" is synonymous with "spirit" and "absolute, infinite mind." In other words, divine love is the spirit-nature of God.

The divine love that unites the Heavenly Father (supreme being) with the Holy Mother (all-knowing) continuously generates the Eternal Son (divine self-awareness). The infused parental love of the Eternal Son impels him to create, to reflect divine love back to the Heavenly Father and the Holy Mother. The Trinity, then, is a loving relationship of three divine persons whose unity constitutes the one life of God.

When understood correctly, the esoteric Trinity of Heavenly Father, Holy Mother and Eternal Son is not a radical departure from the familiar, traditional doctrine of the Trinity. In esoteric Christianity, the divine person of all-knowing—the Holy Mother—is synonymous with the Holy Spirit. Even in conventional theology, the Holy Spirit—as the spirit of truth—is associated with divine wisdom and knowing. For a more detailed understanding of the Trinity from an esoteric Christian perspective, please refer to *The*

Greater Mysteries of the Divine Trinity, the Logos-Word and Creation.

The Logos-Word as Understood by Exoteric Christianity

Very much a part of the traditional doctrine of the Trinity, as professed in exoteric Christianity, is the concept of the Logos (or Word). This is because the Logos-Word is regarded as being entirely synonymous with God the Son; it is seen simply as an arcane Greek term that is sometimes used to identify the "second person" of the Trinity, the Son. Moreover, since Christ-Jesus is theologically regarded as the incarnation of God the Son, the Logos is also logically synonymous with Christ-Jesus. As succinctly stated by Justin Martyr in the second century:

> We have been taught that Christ is the first-begotten of God [the Son], and we have declared Him to be the Logos of which all mankind partakes. (First Apology 46)

The Logos-Word as Understood by Esoteric Christianity

Up until now, information about the Logos-Word coming from sources of esoteric Christianity has been publically scant, limited and often imprecise. Nevertheless, it is clear from this meager information that the Logos-Word, as understood by esoteric Christianity, differs somewhat from traditional Christian theology. Most noticeably is the esoteric understanding that the Logos-Word is not synonymous with the divine person of the Son, but instead is the first-born creation of God. As described in *The Secret Doctrine of the Rosicrucians* (Magus Incognito; 1949):

> The Logos, a being intermediate between God and the World, is diffused through the world of the senses. The

Logos does not exist from eternity like God, and yet its genesis is not like our own and that of all other created beings. It is the First-Begotten of God, and is for us imperfect beings almost as a God. Through the agency of the Logos, God created the World.

More specifically, the Logos-Word is the highest mental concept created in the mind of God; it is God's "self-concept"—what the divine nature conceives itself to be. Since the one God cannot logically create a second God, the Logos-Word is not equal to the infinite and eternal God, but is instead a finite and temporal creation. Nevertheless, as the foremost idea in the absolute mind of God, the Logos-Word is a mental reflection of the divine nature, "created in the image and likeness of God."

Analogous to our own psychological experience as human beings where our individual self-concept is born out of our personal self-awareness, it is likewise with God. The self-concept of the Logos-Word—the "Universal I AM"—is born out of the divine self-awareness of the Eternal Son. As such, the Logos-Word is a conscious being, infused with the life of the Creator. The Logos-Word is the "original man," the Kabbalistic "Adam Kadmon," the lord of the universe.

The Esoteric Explanation of Universal Creation

As the mental image or reflection of God, the Logos-Word also mirrors the Trinitarian nature of its divine Creator. In this case, however, it is not a Trinity of divine persons, but a triplicity of universal principles. The reflection of the Heavenly Father within the Logos-Word manifests as the "universal masculine principle of will." The reflection of the Holy Mother manifests as the "universal feminine principle of wisdom." The divine person of the Eternal Son is mirrored in the Logos-Word as the "harmonizing principle of universal love." The cosmic principle of triplicity is further exemplified by the three great manifestations within the Logos-Word: universal mind, universal energy and universal matter.

For mainstream Christianity, the sole source of written information concerning the creation of the universe and all the life-forms within it (including mankind) is the ancient Hebrew Book of Genesis. Much of the information conveyed in Genesis is allegorical and poetic, not literal or factual. As such, the Genesis "story" is obviously not a scientific or historical account of universal creation.

The esoteric Christian information regarding universal creation, however, strives to be scientifically and historically accurate, even though much of this information is gathered by supersensible means. Esoteric Christianity recognizes an ultra-rarified, superphysical medium termed, "akasha." Akasha pervades the entire cosmos, and even the most subtle vibratory motions within the universe, such as human thought and feeling, are impressed upon this supersensitive medium. Moreover, these impressions are enduringly retained for cosmic aeons of time. Simply described, then, akasha is "Nature's cosmic memory"—the stored recollections of the Logos-Word.

Regarding the creation of the universe, sufficiently-trained spiritual scientists are able to clairvoyantly access or "read" the akashic "records" and, thereby, obtain detailed information of the primordial past-history of the universe. The information obtained in this way demonstrates that the universe has had a much longer history than modern science supposes. Moreover, the universe has experienced a number of cosmic contractions and expansions, esoterically termed "Days and Nights of Manifestation." These cosmic oscillations are not mechanical or purposeless; but instead are the astronomical "sleeping" and "waking" periods of the Logos-Word.

As a result of these numerous cosmic vacillations, the

Logos-Word has increasingly awoken to its divine origin as the self-concept, the I AM, of God the Son. In the process, the Logos-Word has also individualized itself into countless life-forms and beings—from sub-atomic particles to super-celestial seraphim; thereby experiencing companionship, gaining a wealth of rich knowledge, and sharing the life-giving love of the triune God.

Our own solar system has likewise undergone four lengthy planetary periods of contraction and expansion in order to reach the developmental stage of today. In Rosicrucian terminology they are known as: (1) the Ancient Saturn Period, (2) the Ancient Sun Period, (3) the Ancient Moon Period and (4) the Present Earth Period of planetary manifestation. Moreover, three additional developmental periods are destined to occur in the future before our system reaches its apogee of planetary completion: (5) the future Jupiter Period, (6) the future Venus Period and (7) the future Vulcan Period.

Within each of these large planetary periods of development, seven smaller evolutionary cycles have been clairvoyantly identified. Within the present Earth period, five of these cycles have been reached: (1) the Hyperborean Age, (2) the Polarian Age, (3) the Lemurian Age, (4) the Atlantean Age and (5) the Age of Western Civilization (the age we are currently in). The following two cycles are only destined to take place thousands of years from now (since each age lasts 15,120 years, the length of a Platonic "great year").

Unfortunately, further details are outside the discussion focus of *The Star of Higher Knowledge*. For more wondrous, awe-inspiring details of cosmic creation as understood by Christian esotericism, please refer to *The Greater Mysteries of the Divine Trinity, the Logos-Word and Creation* (by this author) and *An Outline of Esoteric Science* (by Rudolf Steiner; 1997).

CHAPTER 1

THE MYSTERY OF THE SOLAR-CHRISTOS: THE REGENT OF THE SUN

1.1   The Solar-Christos and the Universal Hierarchy of Being

The Solar-Christos as the Central Celestial Figure in Human Evolution

EVEN THOUGH MOST world religions recognize and acknowledge the general existence of superphysical beings, such as angels and archangels, there is scant, specific detail about individual celestial beings. The Bible, for example, does mention the angel Gabriel (who appeared to the virgin Mary prior to the conception of Jesus); the archangel Michael (who fought a war in heaven, and who continues to battle the Satanic dragon); and archangel Raphael (who provided safe journey, chased away a demon and performed a healing service in the Book of Tobit). As well, there is some brief mention of "fallen" angels: Abaddon (or Apollyon, the angel of the bottomless pit); Baal-zebub (or Beelzebul, the ruler of demons); and Satan (the devil, the adversarial dragon). Perhaps surprising to many, there is no mention of a fallen angel named "Lucifer" in the Bible. The Hebrew "star of the morning" mentioned in the Book of Isaiah (translated in Latin as "Lucifer") is clearly a historical reference to the despised Babylonian king, Nebuchadnezzar.

Various mystical and esoteric writings throughout the centuries have, however, provided a wealth of fascinating detail concerning specific superphysical beings; but this information is often confusing and contradictory. *A Dictionary of Angels: Including the Fallen Angels* (1994) by Gustav Davidson is, nevertheless, an excellent and fascinating compilation of Talmudic, gnostic, cabalistic, apocalyptic, patristic and legendary writings about superphysical beings.

The clearest, most reliable and extensive information concerning superphysical beings that is publically accessible today is the spiritual-scientific (or anthroposophical) research of Rudolf Steiner (1861–1925). As a highly-trained, esoteric Christian (Rosicrucian) initiate, Steiner was able to clairvoyantly perceive and conceptually convey profound and original information on the entire hierarchy of celestial beings. Out of his extensive and careful research, one particular superphysical being emerged as a crucial and central figure throughout mankind's entire evolutionary journey. That being is the superplanetary regent of the sun, the initiate leader of the archangelic sun-spirits, known esoterically as the "Solar-Christos."

The Solar-Christos, since the birth of humanity during the ancient Lemurian Age, has protectively guided, compassionately nurtured and superphysically supervised progressive human development. At critical instances of human development, he has even directly intervened to ensure that nascent mankind would not fall prey to powerful, inimical superphysical forces and beings. It is vitally important, therefore, that sincere and dedicated Christian esotericists acquire a clear understanding of, and a deep, heartfelt appreciation for, this steadfast and heaven-sent "friend of mankind."

Humanity and the Celestial Hierarchy

In an effort to better understand and appreciate the Solar-Christos, it is important to not only place him in the context of humanity, but also the context of the entire hierarchy of celestial beings. Currently, as the result of several cosmic Days of Manifestation (Manvantaras), the universal person of the Logos-Word is differentiated into countless beings and life-forms that reflect the divine life of the Trinitarian God. According to esoteric tradition (such as *The Celestial Hierarchy* of Pseudo-Dionysius), mainstream Christian theology (the writings of St. Thomas Aquinas, for example) and the anthroposophical research of Rudolf Steiner, there are nine distinct levels of beings (above humanity) that have developed self-conscious awareness (not including the Logos-Word and the divine Trinity). There have been, of course, different names given to each of these levels of being by the different religions, traditions and philosophies. The diagram of the celestial hierarchy in Figure 1 below includes the four most familiar designations: (1) Western theology, (2) Hebrew tradition,[2] (3) Greek tradition and (4) anthroposophy.

These nine levels of self-conscious being are not arbitrary, but are based on distinct and recognizable degrees of advancement. These divisions or levels of advancement are somewhat analogous to the various colours of the radiant light spectrum. Though each colour is essentially a difference in vibration, the colour red is obviously qualitatively different than the colour blue. The characteristics of an "archangel," then, are recognizably different than that of an "angel." Some of what the defining characteristics are for the various celestial beings will be further explained as we proceed.

THE TRIUNE GOD	WESTERN THEOLOGY	HEBREW TRADITION	GREEK TRADITION	ANTHROPOSOPHY
THE TRIUNE GOD	THE BLESSED TRINITY (INCLUDES)	YAHWEH	THEOS	THE TRINITY
THE WORD	THE WORD	MEMRA	LOGOS	THE CREATIVE WORD
FIRST HIERARCHY	SERAPHIM	CHAIOTH HA-QADESH	(SERAPHIM)	SPIRITS OF LOVE
	CHERUBIM	AUPHANIM	(CHERUBIM)	SPIRITS OF HARMONY
	THRONES	CHASHMALIM	(THRONES)	SPIRITS OF WILL
SECOND HIERARCHY	DOMINIONS	SERAPHIM	KYRIOTETES	SPIRITS OF WISDOM
	VIRTUES	MALACHIM	DYNAMEIS	SPIRITS OF MOVEMENT
	POWERS	ELOHIM	EXUSIAI	SPIRITS OF FORM
THIRD HIERARCHY	PRINCIPALITIES	BENE ELOHIM	ARCHAI	TIME SPIRITS
	ARCHANGELS	KERUBIM	ARCHANGELOI	SUN SPIRITS
	ANGELS	ISHIM	ANGELOI	MOON SPIRITS
	HUMANITY	BENEI-ADAM	ANTHROPOS	SPIRITS OF FREEDOM

Figure 1: The Universal Hierarchy of Being

In esoteric Christianity, the nine distinct levels of celestial beings are further organized into three major divisions, each of which includes three levels. The names given to these three major divisions are the "First Hierarchy," the "Second Hierarchy" and the "Third Hierarchy." The three levels of celestial beings in the First Hierarchy are the most advanced in cosmic creation, and therefore are the closest in God-consciousness. The three levels of celestial beings in the Third Hierarchy (though much more advanced than human beings) are not as advanced as the other two hierarchical divisions. Once again, the three major hierarchical divisions are not arbitrary. In this case, the principled reason for the groupings of three levels is because each hierarchical division reflects the Trinitarian nature of God: Heavenly Father, Holy Mother and Eternal Son.

Referring to Figure 1, and selecting the more familiar (and often biblical) names of Western theology, the First Hierarchy includes the seraphim, cherubim and thrones. The Second Hierarchy includes the dominions, virtues and powers. The Third Hierarchy includes the principalities, archangels and angels. It's also important to understand, when viewing Figure 1, that the various levels of celestial beings aren't literally stacked on each other like some gigantic, cosmic parfait. Instead, the various levels of celestial beings actually interpenetrate one another and pervade the same superphysical cosmic space, in a manner similar to the interaction of various forms of familiar energy. Pervading the space of a typical household room, for example, are radio waves, light waves, heat waves, sound waves, ultra-violet waves; as well as earth gravity and planetary magnetism. All these energies independently co-exist within the same space due to their differences in vibration. Similarly, angels, archangels and principalities can independently co-exist within the same superphysical space—without necessarily perceiving or affecting one another—because of their vibratory differences in development.

In connection with the celestial hierarchy of advanced beings, a Fourth and Fifth Hierarchy can also be delineated, which includes those life-forms which have not, as yet, acquired self-conscious awareness. These beings and life-forms are associated with physical existence, rather than with superphysical existence, and hence can be referred to as the "Terrestrial Hierarchies." Figure 2, below, diagrammatically illustrates their relative levels of development.

FOURTH HIERARCHY	HUMANS
	ANIMALS
	PLANTS
FIFTH HIERARCHY	MINERALS
	ATOMIC PARTICLES
	SUB-ATOMIC PARTICLES

Figure 2: The Terrestrial Hierarchies

Identifying Characteristics of Celestial Being

One obvious identifying characteristic of the entire hierarchy of celestial beings is that all forms of advanced life are invisible to physical sight. Nevertheless, even without clairvoyant perception, these superphysical inhabitants can still be indirectly perceived through their effects in the physical world (similar to the scientific study of invisible energy). What physical science postulates as the "natural laws of the universe," for instance, are most often the physical effects of superphysical beings.

Since progressive, evolutionary advancement is usually a slow, gradual and arduous cosmic process, the most highly-advanced celestial beings have been in existence much longer than less-advanced beings. In fact, the thrones, cherubim and seraphim of the First Hierarchy came into existence prior to our current evolutionary Day of Manifestation. They were already advanced, self-conscious beings well before the primal-germ of mankind's physical body was even established.

The various levels of the celestial hierarchy can also be understood as evolutionary steps on a cosmic ladder of attainment, progressing from self-consciousness to God-consciousness. Thrones will in time become cherubim; angels will advance to archangels; and human beings will eventually become angels—that is, with a noteworthy and crucial difference. Since evolutionary development is ever-upward, the future levels of attainment will necessarily be more advanced than the present-day ones. In other words, humanity's future, angel-like level of development will be more advanced than the present-day angels. Likewise, when the present-day animal kingdom attains a human-like level in the future, they will be superior to present-day human beings.

Cosmic evolution, then, is an ever-ascending spiral of advancement with each higher level unfolding increased consciousness, life and being. In this way, individual life-forms are slowly perfected, which in turn contributes to the total enrichment of the Logos-Word—wonderfully demonstrating the wise, old saying: "As the rose adorns itself, so it adorns the entire garden."

As beings and life-forms progress in advancement, their conscious awareness, degree of life and sense of being gradually expand outwardly to cosmic proportions. While human consciousness, life and being is essentially confined to the earth (and planetary vicinity, through space travel), the exalted consciousness, life and being of the cherubim and seraphim extensively embraces the entire Milky Way galaxy. Not surprisingly, then, expanded consciousness and being results in much wider spheres of influence and power, as well as increased cosmic responsibility and authority.

The Celestial Spheres of Activity

In order to help visualize and better understand the different spheres of activity associated with each level of celestial being, Figure 3 has been included below. In this case, the various spheres of activity are in relation to our present-day solar system. Moreover, the various spheres are arranged according to the Ptolemaic system. This ancient system, used throughout the Middle Ages, and still used in esoteric science today, positions the earth at the centre and is, therefore, also known as the "geocentric model" of the universe. Regarding the entire solar system, the Ptolemaic model only recognizes the earth, sun, moon and five "wandering" planets: Mercury, Venus, Mars, Jupiter and Saturn. In esoteric science, the celestial bodies of Uranus, Neptune and Pluto are not considered to be part of the original solar system, but are believed to have been acquired later in cosmic evolution. Consequently, they are not included as separate spheres of activity. Also significantly, in the Ptolemaic system the names for the planets Mercury and Venus are reversed. Venus is considered to be the planet closest to the sun, and then Mercury.

It should also be noted in regard to Figure 3, that the illustrated size of sun, moon, earth and planets obviously does conform to their actual relative sizes. Likewise, the distances between the illustrated spheres are certainly not in proportion to the actual relative distances between sun, moon, earth, and planets. Nevertheless, the diagram can still prove helpful in visualizing the spheres of activity for the various levels of celestial beings as viewed from the perspective of the earth.

While modern science considers a geocentric model of the universe, such as the Ptolemaic system, to be inaccurate and out-of-date, it is actually quite scientifically correct to place the earth at the centre of the universe—if one wishes to do so. In accordance with relativity theory, within an inflationary universe without physical boundaries, any place can be correctly designated as the "relative centre" of the universe—including the earth.

From the diagram in Figure 3, human beings are shown to be basically confined to the earth. Even though astronauts have occasionally travelled into space, they must take sufficient earth conditions with them in order to exist (such as air, water, food, warmth, and protective clothing). From an earth-centred perspective, the superphysical angels "live, move and have their being" in an invisible, etheric sphere of activity that extends from the earth to the moon. The powers (spirits of form) are able to superphysically exist within the entire sphere that extends from the earth to the sun. The thrones (spirits of will) are even able to extend their superphysical sphere of life, being and consciousness to the very edge of our original solar system; that is, to the orbital distance of Saturn. More remarkably still, the cherubim and the seraphim are advanced enough to be able to extend their sphere of life and activity beyond the confines of our solar system and into the far reaches of galactic space (what the ancients called the "sphere of the fixed stars"). Only the Logos-Word is able to consciously exist throughout the entire universe, from centre to circumference. And of course, beyond the cosmic sphere of the Logos-Word, only the Triune God exists.

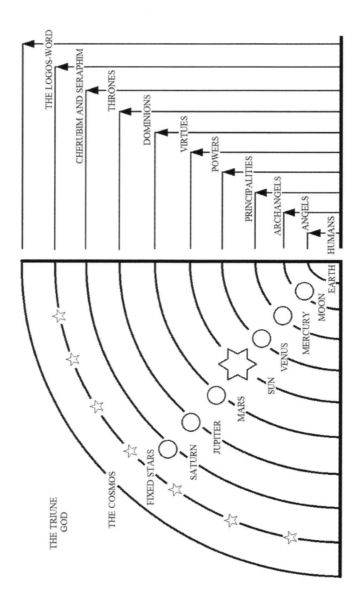

Figure 3: The Celestial Spheres of Activity

1.2 Vehicles of Expression and Degrees of Consciousness

Life-forms and Vehicles of Expression

In order for any life-form to function—to perceive, to act, to feel and to comprehend—on any cosmic realm of existence, it is necessary to have a "vehicle of expression": a form or a body composed of the substances and forces of that realm. Therefore, in order to completely function on the material plane of the physical world, a life-form must possess a vehicle of expression composed of solid, liquid and gaseous matter. Likewise, in order to completely function on the upper astral plane of the soul world, a life-form must possess a vehicle of expression composed of soul light, active soul force and soul life.

In the course of multiple cycles (Days) of cosmic evolution, vehicles of expression for most life-forms have become infused with vast natural wisdom, thereby becoming superlatively complex and organized. The human physical body, for example, is a masterpiece of cosmic design. Figure 4 (below) categorizes the nine vehicles of expression (as described in anthroposophical spiritual science) developed for use in each of the three realms of cosmic existence. These nine different vehicles are commonly arranged into three broad divisions: body, soul and spirit.

All vehicles of expression are composed of unique combinations of matter, energy and mind. Of course, the matter-substances, energy-forces and mental-materials of the soul world are at a much higher vibration than those of the physical world; hence body-vehicles of the physical world are much denser than the more tenuous vehicles of the soul world. Moreover, different life-forms will have quite differently developed vehicles as well. The etheric body of an angel is much different in form and activity than the etheric body of a human, an animal or a plant. The various life-forms will also possess different combinations of vehicles. Angels, for example, do not possess a physical body comprised of earthly solids, liquids and gases. They do, however, possess the other eight vehicles of expression, but their lowest one is an etheric body. Mineral-forms, on the other hand, are entirely comprised of solids, liquids and gases; they have no higher vehicles. Since minerals possess no internal etheric or astral vehicles, they exhibit no external characteristics of life, emotion or thought.

Body, Soul and Spirit

Esoterically, the designation "body" includes the physical body, the etheric body, and the astral body. It is customary in human language to describe these three vehicles of expression as bodies since each of them has a distinctly delineated form that is clearly perceptible to sensible and supersensible vision. This is because these three vehicles were the first to be developed in cosmic evolution and, therefore, have the longest history of refinement. The physical body was the first to evolve, then the etheric body, and after that, the astral body. Contrarily speaking, then, even though the physical body is composed of the coarsest materials and is, thereby, the lowest vehicle vibrationally, for those life-forms that have a physical body, it is actually the most highly developed of all the vehicles they possess.

For human beings, the three soul vehicles of sentient soul, intellectual soul and consciousness soul are still quite underdeveloped and, therefore, are far less organized and sharply defined. Esoterically, they are more correctly termed "sheaths" or "envelopes," rather than "bodies," for this very reason. Supersensibly, the soul vehicles appear as large, luminous, auric cloud-forms surrounding and interpenetrating the three lower bodies. While the three soul vehicles may be less distinct in form, they are still highly complex in movement and activity. To the supersensible observer, this complexity is perceived as purposeful, rapidly-changing colours, shapes and sounds. With life-forms much more advanced than human beings, such as powers, virtues or dominions, the three soul vehicles are highly formulated and can therefore by correctly described as "bodies" as well.

To adequately function in the celestial world, an advanced life-form requires the vehicles of spirit-self, life-spirit and spirit-body.[3] In this case, "spirit" must be understood to mean "spirit-like," since only the divine nature of God is truly spirit. With ordinary humanity, these vehicles exist in a germinal state of latency. They will only become fully developed far into the future. To supersensible perception, then, these formative spiritual "seeds" appear as diffuse aureoles of light surrounding and penetrating the human head. Highly-advanced human initiates, such as the twelve bodhisattvas, however, have already begun to unfold and to consciously use these celestial vehicles. Even higher life-forms such as thrones, cherubim and seraphim have presently perfected these spiritual vehicles for their supernally-advanced cosmic activities.

As previously mentioned, the various regions of cosmic existence (refer to Figure 1) are not rigidly separated and stratified, but instead mutually interpenetrate and influence one another throughout universal space. Likewise, the nine vehicles of expression that are composed of the substances, forces and mental impulses of these cosmic regions also interpenetrate and influence one another. In human beings, therefore, the etheric body does not exist apart from the physical body, but rather interpenetrates it, thereby infusing the physical form with the characteristic activities of life: movement, growth, metabolism and reproduction. As well, the astral body permeates both the etheric and the physical bodies, thereby instilling emotion, feeling and sensation in the human life-form. Once again, this mutual interaction is amazingly complex and organized. Though a detailed examination is far beyond the focus of this discourse, further information has been amply provided in the esoteric works of Rudolf Steiner, particularly *Theosophy* (1994) and *An Outline of Esoteric Science* (1989).

COSMIC REALMS OF EXISTENCE	INDIVIDUAL LEVELS OF EXISTENCE	VEHICLES OF EXPRESSION	SANSKRIT TERMS	DEGREES OF CONSCIOUSNESS
CELESTIAL WORLD [SPIRIT LAND]	SPIRIT	SPIRIT-BODY (THE HIGHER EGO (SELF))	ATMAN	DIVINE CONSCIOUSNESS
CELESTIAL WORLD [SPIRIT LAND]	SPIRIT	LIFE-SPIRIT (THE HIGHER EGO (SELF))	BUDDHI	COSMIC CONSCIOUSNESS
CELESTIAL WORLD [SPIRIT LAND]	SPIRIT	SPIRIT-SELF (THE HIGHER EGO (SELF))	MANAS	SPIRITUAL CONSCIOUSNESS
SOUL WORLD	SOUL	CONSCIOUSNESS SOUL (THE LOWER EGO (SELF))	KAMA-RUPA	SOUL CONSCIOUSNESS
SOUL WORLD	SOUL	INTELLECTUAL SOUL (THE LOWER EGO (SELF))	KAMA-RUPA	SELF CONSCIOUSNESS
SOUL WORLD	SOUL	SENTIENT SOUL (THE LOWER EGO (SELF))	KAMA-RUPA	WAKING CONSCIOUSNESS
SOUL WORLD	BODY	ASTRAL BODY	LINGA-SHARIRA	DREAM CONSCIOUSNESS
PHYSICAL WORLD	BODY	ETHERIC BODY	PRANA-JIVA	SLEEP CONSCIOUSNESS
PHYSICAL WORLD	BODY	PHYSICAL BODY	STHULA-SHARIRA	TRANCE CONSCIOUSNESS

Figure 4: Vehicles of Expression and Degrees of Consciousness

Vehicles of Expression and the Universal Law of Rhythm

As with all manifestations of the created cosmos, the various vehicles of expression are subject to the universal law of rhythm. As stated in *The Kybalion* (1949):

> Everything flows out and in; everything has its tides; all things rise and fall; the pendulum-swing manifests in everything; the measure of the swing to the right, is the measure of the swing to the left; rhythm compensates.

Consequently, all vehicles undergo rise and fall, fluctuation and alteration over time. Predictably, the higher the vehicle the more permanent and enduring it is.

The physical body, as we know from human experience, wears out quickly and becomes unusable in a relative short time. The etheric body is slightly more durable, but is also subject to deterioration and dissolution. While the astral body will endure the longest of the three bodies, it too will decline and dissipate in time. The soul vehicles, however, can endure for vast aeons of cosmic time. Collectively, then, the "soul" or the "lower ego" will continue to exist long after the three lower bodies have completely disappeared. Though the soul is also subject to the universal law of rhythm, this manifests as gradual renewal and transformation rather than overall disintegration and total reconstruction. Since they're the most "spirit-like" in nature, the celestial vehicles—collectively known as the "spirit" or the "higher ego" (though still in a condition of latency for most human beings)—exhibit an abiding condition of cosmic "timelessness."

Due to the cyclic decay of the physical, etheric and astral bodies, the human soul and spirit are required to alternate between periods when they indwell the lower vehicles, and periods when they exist external to the lower vehicles. While existing independently of the lower bodies in the soul and celestial realms, the human soul and spirit (under the wise direction of more advanced beings) are able to reconstruct new astral, etheric and physical vehicles for use on earth. The strong, evolutionary impulse to increasingly improve and unfold the various vehicles of expression—in order to expand the conscious awareness of the indwelling "real self," the spirit of God within—also necessitates repeated cycles of bodily incarnation and excarnation for the human soul and spirit. The process of rebirth, or reincarnation, then, is the means whereby the human soul and spirit (the lower and higher egos) perfect themselves over vast stretches of evolutionary time. Logically, a single incarnational experience (that is, one lifetime) is hardly sufficient to achieve cosmic perfection, to become "one with God."

Achieving Personhood

In order for a life-form to become a "person"; that is, a self-conscious, autonomous being endowed with free-will, it is fundamentally necessary to possess an independent "soul" and "spirit"—higher vehicles of expression that endure over time. Life-forms become "created persons" by reflecting divine spirit, the "real personhood" of God, within their soul and celestial vehicles. Unfortunately, as presently constituted, the physical, etheric and astral bodies are not refined and polished enough to adequately reflect the spirit-light of God. Therefore, any life-form that is restricted to these vehicles, such as minerals, plants and most animals, does not exhibit the consciousness of "self" that is required for basic personhood. The human stage of evolutionary development, then, is the first rudimentary manifestation of personhood in a life-form. All life-forms more advanced than human beings, naturally exhibit a more pronounced expansion of personhood, of "self."

In the case of human evolution, an individualized soul (the lower ego) was acquired by our animal-like ancestors during ancient Lemurian times.[4] Moreover, according to esoteric research, the indwelling ego was bestowed upon primeval humanity by the elohim (the powers, or the spirits of form). In an act of cosmic sacrifice, the elohim separated off a part of their own soul nature and infused this into the primitive lower bodies of the individual human life-forms on earth. With the gift of rudimentary self-consciousness, lowly human "creatures" had now become nascent human "persons."

The lengthy evolutionary acquisition of ego-consciousness by humanity was, of course, a very complex and detailed process, involving many other advanced beings as well. In *An Outline of Esoteric Science* (1989), Rudolf Steiner has provided a very thorough esoteric account, as indicated by the following:

> On earth, human beings became individualized soul beings. The astral bodies that the Spirits of Motion (Virtues) had poured into them on the [Ancient] Moon [condition of the earth] divided into sentient, mind [intellectual], and consciousness souls on earth. When their consciousness souls had advanced far enough to be able to shape bodies fit to receive them, the Spirits of Form endowed each of these with a spark of their own fire, kindling the I in each one ... From this point onward, human beings felt themselves to be independent entities in this world.

The Bible as well, though in a more general, allegorical manner, attributes human personhood to the activity of the elohim, as indicated by the following passage:

> [T]hen the LORD God [in Hebrew: "Yahweh Elohim"] formed man of dust from the ground, and breathed into his nostrils the breath of life; and man became a living being. (Gen 2:7; RSVCE)

External Vehicles of Expression and "Group-Egos"

Not only is it necessary that the soul and spirit vehicles be sufficiently developed in order for a life-form to acquire the self-consciousness of personhood, but these vehicles must indwell the lower three bodies. If the soul and spirit vehicles are external to the physical, etheric and astral bodies, then the life-form cannot manifest an individualized ego. Nevertheless, there will be an ego-self associated with that life-form; but it will belong to another, more advanced being, who acts outside the life-form as an "oversoul," or a "group-ego."

Such is the case with animals, for example. An individual animal (of whatever species) typically possesses a physical, an etheric and an astral body (along with some elementary elements of sentient soul in the higher animals). These interpenetrating bodies, however, are supersensibly surrounded by highly-developed soul and spirit vehicles that influence the lower bodies, but remain external to them on the higher planes of existence. With individual animal life-forms, the external soul and spirit vehicles belong to a higher, more advanced being who acts as a governing oversoul. Very often, the higher being provides the soul and spirit vehicles for all the animal life-forms of a particular species. The entire kingdom of cats, for instance, has the same animal oversoul who functions as a "group-ego" for each individual house cat, tiger, lion, panther and cougar. All experience acquired by the various cat-creatures does not disappear with bodily dissolution (death), but rather resides in the oversoul of the higher being. This accounts for what is commonly known as "instinct"; the innate wisdom possessed by individual animals. In other words, instinct is the wise guidance of a particular animal by the overseeing group-ego.

Even though individual animals do not manifest self-conscious awareness—they have no sense of "I am"—the overseeing group-egos associated with the various animal species do. Predictably, there are group-egos associated with the plant and mineral kingdoms as well. In the case of plants, the various group-egos provide encompassing astral bodies as well as external soul and spirit vehicles. Since the mineral kingdom only possesses a physical body, the group-egos of these life-forms provide enveloping etheric and astral bodies as well as soul and spirit vehicles.

According to anthroposophical research, the group-egos of plants and animals are special beings actualized by, and directly connected to, the dominions and virtues of the Second Hierarchy (refer to Figure 1). The group-egos of the mineral kingdom are special beings actualized by, and directly connected to, the thrones of the First Hierarchy.[5] As a consequence of being highly-advanced life-forms, the group-egos of the animal kingdom inhabit the upper astral plane; the group-egos of the plant kingdom inhabit the lower heavenly plane; and the group-egos of the mineral kingdom inhabit the higher heavenly plane.

The Vehicles of Expression and Their Relationship to Each Other

Prior to the attainment of individual egohood, human life-forms were entirely formed and developed by other, more advanced beings. The physical, etheric and astral bodies were originally gifted to humanity, as were the rudimentary self-conscious soul vehicles. Once individual egohood is acquired, however, the indwelling, individualized "human-self" also begins to slowly transform and perfect the three bodies that it now "possesses," that now "belong" to its existence. By "personalizing" the three bodies, the human-self develops the three soul vehicles: the astral body is transformed into the sentient soul, the etheric body is transformed into the intellectual (or mind) soul, and the physical body is transformed into the consciousness soul (see Figure 5 below).

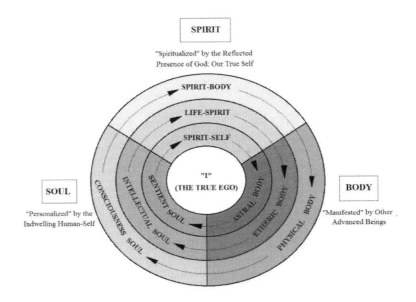

Figure 5: The Vehicles of Expression and Their Relationship to Each Other

Furthermore, by "spiritualizing" the three soul vehicles, the human-self is able to unfold the three spiritual vehicles: the sentient soul is transmuted into spirit-self, the intellectual soul is transmuted into life-spirit, and the consciousness soul is transmuted into spirit-body. In other words, spirit-body is a perfected, higher-vibratory refinement of the physical body. Likewise, life-spirit is a perfected, higher-vibratory refinement of the etheric body; and spirit-self is a perfected, higher-vibratory refinement of the astral body. It is equally correct to express these connections in reverse: the physical body is the imperfect, lower-vibratory manifestation of spirit-body; the etheric body is the imperfect, lower-vibratory manifestation of life-spirit; and the astral body is the imperfect, lower-vibratory manifestation of spirit-self. From this perspective, we can better understand that prior to our capacity to consciously unfold and develop the three spiritual vehicles, they already existed, but as the germinal ideas of soul, life and form on the higher heavenly plane of the celestial world.

Human beings as we are constituted today, therefore, possess nine vehicles of expression. Correctly understood, the true human ego is *not* a vehicle, but rather the self-reality of God that is *reflected* in each vehicle. The more perfect the vehicle, the greater the mirroring capacity to reflect the "I" of God—which each of us experiences as our true self. There is truly only one "I" in reality, and that is the selfhood of God. All life-forms, from the most basic sub-atomic particle to the most exalted heavenly seraphim, to a greater or lesser degree, reflect the personhood of God. In more familiar religious terms, the spirit of God reflected in each of us is our true spiritual self.

While there is only one divine "Self" in existence, that Self is individualized in every manifested life-form within the Logos-Word. However, life-forms that only incorporate physical, etheric or astral vehicles (such as minerals, plants and animals) do not *consciously* reflect the One Self—hence they do not exhibit self-conscious awareness. Only life-forms that incorporate an individualized soul vehicle (such as human beings) are consciously aware of an indwelling self.

To be clear, then, the real "I" within every self-conscious being never changes since it is a reflection of the one eternal spirit. However, the perception, understanding and awareness of this spiritual-self does certainly change depending on the reflective capacity of the various vehicles of expression. The more advanced the vehicle, the more perfect the embodiment of the spiritual "I."

The Sevenfold Arrangement of Vehicles

In esoteric literature, as with most mainstream religions, it is common to refer to the three distinct soul vehicles collectively as "the soul." Moreover, since the indwelling soul is characterized by self-conscious awareness, it is equally common to refer to this collective soul as "the ego." A less common, but more accurate term for the tripartite soul is "the ego-bearer," since the soul (as a vehicle) *reflects* or *bears* the true spiritual self.

By uniting the three soul vehicles into a single designation, it is also esoterically accurate to say that human beings possess seven interpenetrating vehicles of expression: (1) physical body, (2) etheric body, (3) astral body, (4) ego-bearer (soul), (5) spirit-self, (6) life-spirit, and (7) spirit-body. In other words, human beings possess three lower bodily vehicles; three higher spiritual vehicles, and an intermediary, tripartite soul vehicle.

The important reason for applying this sevenfold arrangement to human beings is that this conforms with the esoteric principle that all self-conscious life-forms, from human to seraphim, possess seven vehicles of expression: three higher vehicles, three lower vehicles, and a single intermediary vehicle. While this sevenfold arrangement is shared by all advanced beings, the particular vehicles that are included in the arrangement are quite different and depend entirely on the level of evolutionary advancement.

The angel-beings, for example, are at a degree of evolution one level above human beings since they attained self-conscious awareness (their "human" stage) during the previous Ancient Moon Period. Consequently, the densest vehicle of expression for ordinary angel-beings is the etheric body; they no longer require a physical body for their continued development. Since all beings from human to seraphim possess seven vehicles of expression, the angels have germinally unfolded a supernal vehicle one level higher than spirit-body, a vehicle imbued with cosmic will (refer to Figure 6 below).

THE PERSONS, PRINCIPLES, AND VEHICLES OF EXPRESSION	THE GREAT HIERARCHY OF BEING	THE LEVEL OF ORDINARY HUMANITY	THE LEVEL OF ORDINARY ANGELS	THE LEVEL OF ORDINARY ARCHANGELS	THE LEVEL OF ORDINARY PRINCIPALITIES
GOD THE FATHER	THE TRIUNE GOD				
GOD THE SON					
GOD THE MOTHER					
UNIVERSAL WILL	THE LOGOS WORD				
UNIVERSAL LOVE					
UNIVERSAL WISDOM					
COSMIC WISDOM	SERAPHIM				
COSMIC LOVE	CHERUBIM				
COSMIC WILL	THRONES				
SPIRIT-BODY	DOMINIONS				
LIFE-SPIRIT	VIRTUES				
SPIRIT-SELF	POWERS				
EGO-BEARER	PRINCIPALITIES				
ASTRAL BODY	ARCHANGELS				
ETHERIC BODY	ANGELS				
PHYSICAL BODY	HUMANS				

Figure 6: The Seven Vehicles of Expression and Hierarchic Levels of Advancement

In the case of archangelic-beings, since they attained self-conscious awareness (their human-like stage) during the Ancient Sun Period, they are two levels above human beings in evolutionary advancement. Consequently, their densest vehicle is the astral body; they no longer require a physical body or an etheric body for their continued development. For archangels, therefore, their seventh vehicle extends two levels higher than humanity's highest vehicle (spirit-body), and is a germinal vehicle imbued with cosmic love.[6]

While Figure 6 only details the sevenfold vehicle arrangement for humans, angels, archangels and principalities, the chart can also be similarly used for the other advanced beings. Also in regard to Figure 6, it is important to note that the term "vehicles of expression" does not correctly apply to the Logos-Word. The three divisions of universal will, universal wisdom and universal love are more correctly understood to be *principles* of expression. The "I" (ego-self) of the Logos-Word is reflected in these three principles: (1) the father-principle (universal will), (2) the mother-principle (universal wisdom), and (3) the son-principle (universal love).

Though it is not diagrammatically obvious in Figure 6, the Logos-Word also exhibits a sevenfold division to its nature. Since the universal principles are direct reflections of the divine persons, the universal principles can be regarded as the three lower "bodily forms" of the Logos-Word; while the divine persons can be regarded as the three, higher "spiritual perfections" that the Logos-Word continually strives to unfold. The vibrational dividing line between creation and Creator, the thin veil of spirit-like substance that separates the created universal being from the eternal level of God, is therefore understood to be the seventh, intermediary integrant of the Logos-Word.

When contemplating the categories in Figure 6, it is also important to understand in reference to the Triune God, that neither "vehicles" nor "principles" correctly apply to the divine nature. The distinctions of divine will, divine wisdom and divine love are properly understood to be divine *persons* of expression. Obviously the "rule of seven" does not apply to God since there is nothing beyond the divine "Three." Moreover, by diagrammatically arranging the divine persons into three vertical levels is not to suggest, of course, that one person of God is higher or superior to another, since all are co-equal. Nevertheless, God the Father is here placed on the first level in the Triune God category since this divine person is characterized by the centripetal contraction (or "densification") of the divine nature. God the Mother is therefore placed on the third level in the Triune God category since this divine person is characterized by the centrifugal expansion (or "rarefaction") of the divine nature. And of course God the Son has been categorically placed in the middle since this divine person is characterized by the harmonious balance and mutuality of the divine nature.

1.3   Yahweh-Elohim and the Mystery of the Moon

Progressive Beings and Regressive Beings

Within the general populations of all advanced beings there are those individuals who progress ahead of their companions, and those individuals who lag behind. As a general rule, the progressive beings often become pioneering leaders and forerunners for the general population, while the developmentally-delayed beings usually become adversaries and antagonists of the general population. As a familiar example, reference is often made to "fallen angels," referring to those angel-beings who have developmentally lagged behind, and who act as adversaries towards their angelic companions. What is shattering, however, is to esoterically discover that even beings as highly advanced as the cherubim and the seraphim have individuals within their ranks who lag behind and who act in opposition to the others. One would logically expect that such supernal beings close to God would act in spiritual unity; but surprisingly, such is not the case. Thankfully, however, the omniscient, underlying direction of the universe is able to transform "oppositional" activity into positive development.

One particular example of the "cooperative merger" of

progressive beings and oppositional beings is the activity of the spirits of motion (virtues) on earth. The normally developed virtues have been responsible for many, broad civilizing and religious impulses that continue from age to age, such as Buddhism. As well, the offspring of the normally developed virtues function as the group-souls of the animal kingdom. Adversarial virtues, however, have been responsible for establishing the various racial forms of humanity. Both kinds of virtues, then, have significantly contributed to the overall development of humanity on earth, though they don't necessarily act in complete unison with each other.

There has also been an ages-long conflict between two opposing classes of dominions (spirits of wisdom) that has profoundly impacted humanity, and the entire solar system. Progressive dominions, and their regressive counterparts, both inhabit the superphysical sphere of the sun. Due to their high advancement, the progressive dominions are able to pour out life-giving, supersensible light from their invisible domain on the sun. This supersensible sunlight is, of course, entirely invisible to physical sight. It is the oppositional activity of the regressive dominions of the sun that vibrationally reduces this supersensible sunlight to sense-perceptible sunlight. Since these regressive dominions carry or "bear" supersensible sunlight down into the physical realm, they are esoterically termed, "light-bearers" or "Luciferic-beings." As explained by Rudolf Steiner:

> [T]he fixed stars as directed by the Spirits of Wisdom, are not physically visible, they do not shed physical light. Physical light can only be shed if there is something underlying it which serves as a bearer to the light, when light is, as it were, held captive through a bearer. For a fixed star [such as our sun] to become visible, something more is necessary than the mere presence of Spiritual Beings of Wisdom at work there. It is necessary that in this fixed star Luciferic Beings should work, who resist

the mere substance of Wisdom and permeate it with their own principle ...

The fixed star [of the sun] would not be visible if it had not within it, in addition to the Spirits of Wisdom who have progressed normally, those who have not attained their goal, who remained at a lower stage, either at the stage of the Spirits of Motion [virtues] or that of the Spirits of Form [powers]. Thus we have to recognize the backward Spirits of Wisdom who have not attained their goal, as light-bearers in the lightless spiritual substance of the fixed star. Now, if we are clear as to the fact that from the fixed stars, from our own sun, physical light only reaches us because the normal Spirits of Wisdom have as companions those who have remained behind and who have become light-bearers:—Light—Lucifer—Phosphoros. (Lecture 10: *Spiritual Beings in the Heavenly Bodies and in the Kingdoms of Nature*)

These same regressive spirits of wisdom (dominions) are also responsible for the abnormal mineralization of gold in the earth. Normally, mineral-substance is precipitated on earth by etheric forces directed by the progressive spirits of motion (virtues) associated with each planet. This mineral-substance is then externally held together or compressed by the astral forces of the progressive spirits of wisdom on the sun; and then given crystalline shape by the spirits of form (powers). So arose the mineral-substance of lead from Saturn, tin from Jupiter, iron from Mars, copper from Venus and mercury (quicksilver) from Mercury. The other minerals arise from various planetary combinations—except for gold and silver.

Due to their incomplete development, the regressive spirits of wisdom on the sun are unable to pour out mineral-compressing astral forces like their progressive companions. Instead, they abnormally pour out etheric mineral substance from the sun-centre instead of from a planetary-centre. The mineral gold, since it is abnormally developed by regressive, Luciferic dominions on the sun, is therefore an agitating, powerfully-disruptive element to progressive earth evolution. Once again, in the words of Rudolf Steiner:

> The Luciferic Spirits, the Spirits of Wisdom of the Second Hierarchy who have not gone through their development with the rest—instead of sending astral streams from the sun to the mineral, send etheric streams to the earth. This resulted in a certain basic substance being formed, which received its inner-being, not from the planets but directly from the sun; and this mineral is *gold*. Gold is that Luciferic mineral which as regards its inner-being is not influenced etherically by the planets, but by the sun. (Ibid)

The Luciferic Formation of the "Eighth Sphere"

The retrograde spirits of wisdom have also been the instigators of a far more insidious threat to earth evolution than the mineralization of Luciferic gold. The foremost leader of these renegade light-bearers—the being known esoterically as Lucifer—has been instrumental in attempting to establish a separate, abnormal planet within the solar system. During the Lemurian age, when the atavistic moon forces were being spun off from the earth, Lucifer and his regressive companions (including abnormal spirits of form) intervened at the periphery of the etheric lunar sphere. Similar to the other instances of planetary densification that were initiated by abnormal spirits of form, the Luciferic-beings likewise undertook to densify a separate lunar globe by covertly siphoning off attenuated mineral substance from the earth.

Within the normal, etheric lunar envelop surrounding the earth, then, was planted the abnormal seed of a retrograde,

Luciferic planet. Since progressive evolution characteristically develops in periods or cycles ("spheres") of seven, this planetary aberration has been esoterically termed, the "eighth sphere," to indicate its abnormal status. Notice of this mysterious, esoterically-guarded eighth sphere was first brought to public awareness in Theosophical literature, particularly by A.P. Sinnett in *Esoteric Buddhism* (1918). Unfortunately, Sinnett's book also popularized the inaccuracy that the eighth sphere *is* the physical moon, when in fact our present moon was purposely established to *counteract* the dangerous effects of the eighth sphere.

The dangerous threat posed to earth evolution by the counterfeit existence of the eighth sphere is that Lucifer and his rebellious companions, not only intend to unlawfully materialize a renegade planet, but they plan on populating this planetary aberration with etherically hijacked human souls (particularly after death). To assist them in this nefarious plan, the Luciferic spirits of wisdom have also elicited the cooperation of certain regressive spirits of form (powers); most notably, the being known esoterically as Ahriman (or Satan). As payment for his cooperation, Ahriman-Satan would acquire the densified corpse of planet earth that would remain after the eighth sphere has siphoned off a large portion of the finer etheric and mineral substances. He and his companions would subsequently rule a world populated by soulless, human-like creatures, and any other coarsified life-forms able to survive there. As further elaborated by Rudolf Steiner:

> Into our Fourth Sphere [of the earth], therefore, there has been instilled a sphere that is really a Moon-sphere, but is filled with Earthly substantiality and is therefore a bogus creation in the Universe. To the seven Spheres, an Eighth, created in opposition to the progressive Spirits, has been added. The necessary consequence of this is that the Spirits of Form must do battle on the Earth for every

morsel of substantiality capable of mineralisation, lest it should be wrested from them by Lucifer and Ahriman and borne into the Eighth Sphere … Lucifer and Ahriman strive unceasingly to draw from the Earth's substances whatever they can snatch, in order to form their Eighth Sphere which then, when it is sufficiently advanced, will be detached from the Earth and go its own way in the Cosmos … Needless to say, the Earth would then pass over to [the future evolutionary period of] Jupiter as a mere torso … Therefore we ourselves are involved in the battle. Lucifer and Ahriman battle against the Spirits of Form, with the aim of wresting mineral substance from us everywhere. (Lecture 5 given in 1915; published in *The Occult Movement in the Nineteenth Century*)

Yahweh-Elohim and the Solar Rescue Mission

Such a deviant scenario would clearly thwart the lawful, evolutionary mission of the earth. To prevent such a terrible earthly disaster from occurring, the progressive beings of the sun—particularly the spirits of wisdom, spirits of motion and spirits of form—united forces to neutralize the threat of the eighth sphere. Their combined solution was to dispatch an elite rescue team of progressive beings from the sun to the actual etheric lunar sphere itself. The leader of this "tactical solar unit" is the exalted being referred to in ancient Hebrew scripture as "Yahweh-Elohim."

Nowadays, Yahweh-Elohim (or Jehovah) is commonly understood to be the sacred name of the supreme God. In esoteric Christianity, however, Yahweh-Elohim is understood to be one of the progressive spirits of form (powers) who normally reside in the superphysical sphere of the sun. Moreover, according to Rosicrucian wisdom, Yahweh-Elohim is a very unique and special being. He is actually an angel-being who, through initiatory development, has advanced three levels higher than the ordinary angels to the level of a power.[7] As such, his foremost vehicle of expression reaches up as high as the universal wisdom-principle of the Logos-Word (please refer to Figure 7). Consequently, Yahweh-Elohim is the chief representative of the mother-principle (the reflection of the Holy Mother-Spirit of God) for all the beings of the third hierarchy. Needless to say, he is the highest initiate of the angelic kingdom and its foremost leader.

Because of his unique development, Yahweh-Elohim was ideally suited to lead the lunar rescue mission to earth. Due to his advanced initiatory development, he was capable of operating at a number of different levels, from angel to elohim. Furthermore, by spiritually uniting with the six solar spirits of form who act as planetary-egos for our system, Yahweh-Elohim was able to function as the representative conduit for even more exalted beings, such as the progressive spirits of motion (virtues) and the progressive spirits of wisdom (dominions).[8]

By sacrificially transferring their superphysical residence from the circumference of the sun to the perimeter of the moon (that is, the etheric lunar sphere that envelopes the earth), Yahweh-Elohim and his companions (certain spirits of motion and spirits of wisdom) were able to establish a colony of progressive sun-spirits in the vicinity of the earth. From here they could authoritatively counteract the harmful activities of the rebellious Luciferic-beings. Most importantly, Yahweh-Elohim and his solar compatriots were able to effectively block the germinal formation of the rogue eighth sphere by establishing a counter-sphere in its place—our present moon. As a powerful spirit of form, Yahweh-Elohim was able to accrete super-dense (lifeless) matter into a solid globe at the circumference of the etheric lunar disk where the rebellious spirits of form had hollowed out the eighth sphere.

The ultra-compressed orb of the moon forcefully resists any further planetary amassing of rarified material that is illicitly siphoned off from the earth.

Our present moon, then, under the direction of Yahweh-Elohim, now exerts a positive influence on earth evolution. Moreover, from the solid fortress of the moon, Yahweh-Elohim and his elite corps of solar peacekeepers have been able to effectively neutralize other Luciferic assaults on earth evolution. For instance, by directing etheric mineral-substance from the moon to the earth (as had also normally occurred from the other planets), the progressive forces of Yahweh-Elohim were able to precipitate silver as a metallic antidote to the Luciferically-produced gold and its disturbing influence.

Furthermore, even though our present moon has hampered the establishment of the evil eighth sphere, the regressive beings continue to stubbornly strive to materialize a renegade planet. They continue to illicitly extract rarefied earth substance, particularly from the thought-producing heads of human beings. Specifically, as a counter-measure to this Luciferic activity, Yahweh-Elohim and the progressive moon-beings established and regulated the reproductive forces of heredity. In so doing, the human physical form is more strongly anchored to the earth from generation to generation, thereby impeding the Luciferic siphoning of physical substance that properly belongs to human development.

Fortunately, due to the numerous counteractive activities of the Yahweh-Elohim forces (many of which have not been detailed here), the eighth sphere currently exists as a diffuse, shadowy etheric wasteland surrounding the earth, filled only with illusionary picture images and phantom, ghostly forms. Unfortunately, this bogus reality continues to have an undue influence on weak-minded and credulous individuals. Drug-use, New Age-style channeling, occult experimentation, religious cultism and illusory thinking are all Luciferic means to seduce the unwary individual into the counterfeit realm of the eighth sphere. Prolonged exposure to these aberrant and abnormal moon-forces detaches the healthy mind from normal earth-reality, and often leads to temporary or prolonged insanity—more appropriately termed, "lunacy" (from the Latin "luna" = moon). Thus far, no human soul has been permanently lost due, thankfully, to the preventative measures of Yahweh-Elohim and the progressive sun-beings in the realm of the moon.

The Angelic Kingdom and the Dark Side of the Moon

Since the angelic kingdom underwent their "human" stage of development (that is, their attainment of self-conscious awareness) during the Ancient Moon Period, they are also esoterically referred to as "moon-beings" or "lunar pitris." Not surprisingly, then, the angels have a natural affinity toward the etheric sphere of the moon. Moreover, as beings more advanced than humanity, their superphysical abode is above the earth, extending to the orbital circumference of the moon. From here they benevolently extend their range of influence down to the earth. Benevolently at least for the majority of the angels; some, unfortunately, did not complete their full development during the Ancient Moon Period, and therefore joined the ranks of the other regressive beings that have already been mentioned. Predictably, these regressive angels enlisted in the Luciferic rebellion that occurred during the Lemurian age, and have since been commonly referred to as the "fallen" or Luciferic angels. The progressive angels, however, joined forces with Yahweh-Elohim and his relocated solar companions.

From what can be diagrammatically inferred from Figure 3, beings more advanced than angels reside close to, on or around the sun; the less advanced beings reside further away from the sun. Furthermore, the more advanced beings have a more extensive, more powerful range of influence. For example, though the spirits of will (thrones) are supersensibly located in the vicinity of the sun, they can nevertheless extend their range of influence to the orbital distance of Saturn. Archangels, on the other hand, reside primarily in the supersensible space between the moon and the planet Venus (the ancient Mercury), and can only extend their range of influence to the distance of the earth.

In the case of the etheric lunar spheroid that surrounds the earth, half of it faces towards the sun while the other half faces away. Commonly speaking, the "dark side of the moon" refers to the spherical half of the solid moon that always faces away from the earth (even though this half receives equal sunlight in its orbit around the earth). Esoterically speaking, however, the dark side of the moon is the hemispherical half of the etheric lunar ellipsoid that is furthest away from the sun. Consistent with the general rule of planetary formation, the progressive angels are attracted to the half that is closest to the sun, while the regressive, fallen angels gravitate to the half that is further away from the sun—the dark side of the moon.

The dark side of the moon is also home to a very backward class of moon-beings who have been stunted in their developmental growth from previous planetary periods. Folk tales about "little green men" on the moon are quite supersensibly accurate. As described by Rudolf Steiner:

> One who is able to approach these things clairvoyantly knows that on their scene of action, the moon, these are beings in a certain respect similar to man, but that they are dwarfs in comparison, scarcely reaching the height of a six or seven year old child. Upon the moon, however, a particular opportunity is offered them for their activity … These dwarf-like beings can maintain an astral existence

within our world. (Lecture given in 1908; published in *The Influence of Spiritual Beings Upon Man*)

As briefly indicated here, under certain conditions (such as drug-use, insanity or upon falling asleep) these undeveloped moon-beings can astrally appear to human consciousness. The diminutive, green-coloured, large-headed, black almond-eyed "aliens" that are frequently encountered and described are not advanced UFO visitors from outer space; but instead are mischievous, developmentally-delayed beings from our own astral "moon-space."

Yahweh-Elohim and the "Goddess of the Moon"

Considering that Yahweh-Elohim, as leader of the progressive moon-forces, resolutely and powerfully protected earth evolution from the formidable assaults of the Luciferic-beings, it is quite understandable that ancient Hebrew culture portrayed this elohim as a tough, authoritarian, masculine figure. In the Judeo-Christian heritage, therefore, it is easy to forget that like all advanced beings, Yahweh-Elohim embraces the universal feminine-principle in his nature as well as the universal masculine-principle.

This essential gender duality is esoterically incorporated in the sacred "Tetragrammaton" (four letter word): Y H W H. The Hebrew letter Y is called "Yod" and is a masculine prefix. The remaining three letters, H W H, when joined together can mean "being" or "life." They can also be used to spell the proper name, "EVE"—the biblical "mother of all living" (Gen 3:20). The name Yahweh, then, can also be understood as "Yod-Eve," which better indicates a feminine counterbalance to the "tough-guy" persona of this mighty elohim.

Many other ancient cultures clairvoyantly intuited this feminine aspect to the "spirit of the moon," hence the popularity of moon goddesses. In Greek mythology, Phoebe, Selene, Artemis and Hecate were goddesses of the moon. In Roman mythology, Luna and Diana were the moon goddesses. Many of the female lunar deities were responsible for childbirth, fertility and a woman's reproductive cycle. Since the united company of Yahweh-Elohim did in fact establish and regulate the genetic forces of reproduction, many ancient cultures correctly attributed these life-giving forces to the moon.[9]

1.4   The Initiate-Leader of the Archangelic Sun-Spirits

The Solar-Christos as Regent of the Sun

Perhaps no other prominent celestial-being who is significantly involved in the life of our entire solar system and in human evolutionary survival is more hierarchically misunderstood than the "Solar-Ego" of the sun. To what hierarchical level of development does this exalted sun-being belong? Since supersensibly contacting, communicating and cooperating with a particular celestial-being very much depends on knowing who they truly are, it is critically important for esotericists to be accurate in their understanding. In this case, false knowledge concerning the "spirit of the sun" can lead us dangerously astray.

Even for the Christian esotericist who has made a thorough study of all the available written material concerning this exalted sun-being, it is still not easy to come to a comprehensive and satisfying understanding. Only through Rosicrucian inspiration is it currently possible to approach this being in a truly enlightened way. While a wealth of Rosicrucian information has certainly been made available through the anthroposophical research of Rudolf Steiner, it all appears contradictory and confusing without a unifying key.

For instance, we understand that this exalted sun-being was known as Vishva-Karman in the ancient Vedic culture,[10] as Ahura Mazdao by the ancient Persians and as Osirus[11] by the ancient Egyptians. Moreover, prior to these remote times, an important oracle centre dedicated to this sun-being even existed on the antediluvian continent of Atlantis. In the various Northern Mystery sites that were established after the Great Flood, initiates were also encouraged to contact this exalted being in the sphere of the sun when they astral-journeyed during the three-day temple sleep.

Humanity's association with the "regent of the sun" (by whatever name) was obviously much deeper than simply pagan sun-worship. Furthermore, as human beings became increasingly divorced from the supernatural realm and correspondingly entangled in the material world, the initiate-leaders of the various Mystery centres more fervently clung to the hope that one day the sun-king would descend to earth and bring spiritual light into the growing darkness of human life. In the Greek Mysteries this longed-for "saviour of the sun" was called "Christos," meaning "anointed one." The Hebrew word "mashiach" (from which is derived the English word, "messiah") also means "anointed one." The long-awaited Hebrew saviour, however, was believed to be an entirely human figure, quite unlike the anticipated supernatural saviour of the Grecian Mysteries.

In esoteric Christianity, then, it is important to understand that centuries prior to the birth of the world-saviour, Christ-Jesus, the Grecian Mysteries were preparing for the descent of the Solar-Christos, the great sun-being, as future saviour to the earth. Before examining if there is any connection between Jesus and the Solar-Christos, it is still necessary to determine more about the hierarchical position of the sun-king—where exactly does he fit in with the rest of the celestial-beings?

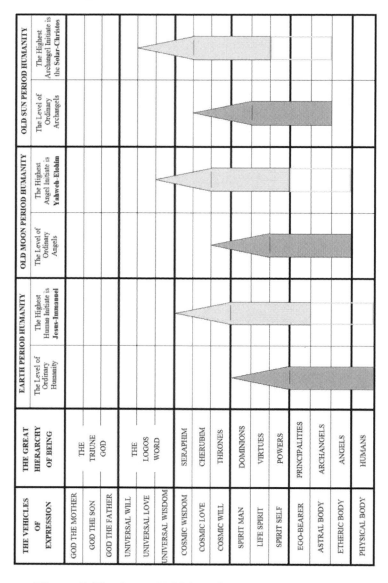

Figure 7: The Seven Vehicles of Expression and Hierarchic Levels of Advancement

The Solar-Christos as Spirit of Movement (Virtue)?

To begin, in a lecture given in 1908 (published in *The Influence of Spiritual Beings Upon Man*), Rudolf Steiner explained the term, "Mystical Lamb," in connection with the Solar-Christos—who he simply refers to as, "Christ":

> This Being is called the "Mystical Lamb," for Lamb and Aries are the same; therefore the description 'Sacrificial Lamb' or 'Ram' is given to Christ. Christ belongs to the cosmos as a whole. His I, his Ego, reaches to Aries and thus He becomes Himself the "Great Sacrifice," is related with the whole of mankind and in a certain sense the beings and forces present on the earth are His creations.

Just prior to this information, the following diagram was included:

```
                        Aries ....... 12th member  ⎫
                        Taurus .......11th member   ⎪
                        Gemini.......10th member    ⎪
                        Cancer ...... 9th member    ⎬  "Mystical
                        Leo .......... 8th member   ⎪    Lamb"
        7th Spirit-Man ........Virgo ......... 7th member ⎪
        6th Life-Spirit ........ Libra ........ 6th member ⎭
        5th Spirit-Self ....... Scorpio
        4th Ego ............. Sagittarius
        3rd Astral Body ..... Capricorn
        2nd Etheric Body ..... Aquarius
        1st Physical Body..... Pisces
```

As with all advanced beings, the Solar-Christos (as Christ, the Mystical Lamb) is here illustrated possessing seven vehicles of expression, in this case linked with the signs of the zodiac. But what is significant for our particular examination is the clear indication that his lowest vehicle is life-spirit. Referring to Figure 7, we can diagrammatically determine that the virtues (spirits of movement) are the celestial beings who have life-spirit as their lowest vehicle. From this, then, the Solar-Christos appears to be a being in advance of the elohim (spirits of form), but not as advanced as the dominions (spirits of wisdom).

The Solar-Christos as Spirit of Wisdom (Dominion)?

But in another instance, Rudolf Steiner repeatedly states that Christ, the Solar-Christos, is *not* a sun-spirit of motion (virtue) but rather a sun-spirit of wisdom (dominion), as evidenced from the following information:

> Hence it was possible to recognize as a fact that the sphere of this Sun-spirit of Wisdom is much more comprehensive than the sphere of the Spirits of Motion, for it now embraces the whole collective process of civilisation on earth. That which was designated in the language of the Holy Rishis as Vishvakarma, in that of Zarathustra as Ahura Mazdao, in the Egyptian (if one really understands what stands behind the name) as Osiris, and which we, in the fourth period of civilisation designate by the word "Christ," is that which has shone down through the portal of the Sun-spirit of Wisdom. I have never said that the Spirit of Motion alone shone through the Buddha, nor do I now say that the Sun-spirit of Wisdom alone shone through the Christ. He was the portal through which occult vision could be directed into infinite spheres, wherein are the Spirits of the higher hierarchies; but the portal was the Spirit of Wisdom, the Sun-spirit of Wisdom. As the sun is related to the planets, so is the Sun-spirit of Wisdom related to the Spirits of Motion who, on their part, express themselves in such

Spirits as the one who inspired Buddha. (Lecture 9 given in 1912; published in *Spiritual Beings in the Heavenly Bodies and in the Kingdoms of Nature*)

The Solar-Christos as Fire-Spirit (Archangel)?

In yet another instance, Rudolf Steiner has clearly stated that the Solar-Christos (the Christ-spirit) is not a virtue or dominion, but rather a "fire-spirit" or archangel. In a lecture given in 1906 entitled, "The Mystery of Golgotha," he presented the following information:

> What the spirits of the Moon were unable to give human beings could be given to them only by a single common, yet higher being, who had finished developing his humanity on the [Old] Sun, a spirit of fire [archangel]. Many such fire spirits had developed themselves on Old Sun and were sublime spirits on the Earth. One such fire spirit was called on to pour the essence of his being over all humanity. For the entire Earth there was one common spirit who could pour over all humankind and into its members the element of the spirits of the Sun (the fire spirits), which was Buddhi, or life spirit ... What entered into the physical, etheric, and astral bodies of Jesus of Nazareth is this entire fire spirit, the common source of the fire of the spirit in all human beings. This is the Christ—the only divine being—who is not present on Earth in this way in any other form. (Published in *The Christian Mystery*; 1998)

The Solar-Christos (Christ-Spirit of the Sun) as the Logos-Word?

If these three descriptions of the Solar-Christos aren't

contradictory and confusing enough for the intrepid Christian esotericist, Steiner has also given a fourth one to add to the frustration. In notes recorded from memory by Mathilde Scholl in 1906, Steiner is purported to have said, "Christ is the living Word" (published in *From the History and Contents of the First Section of the Esoteric School 1904–1914*; 1998). Did he here suggest that the Solar-Christos and the Logos-Word are the same being?

Do these four vastly different descriptions of the Solar-Christos (the Christ-being) indicate that Rudolf Steiner was himself unsure and confused regarding the hierarchic status of this sun-spirit, or is there some possible way of reconciling these four apparent differences?

Reconciling the Apparent Conflict of the Solar-Christos as Logos-Word

Firstly, when Rudolf Steiner was referring to the "living Word" or the "creative Word" he was not necessarily referring to the universal-being of the Logos-Word. In the statement recorded by Scholl (quoted above), Steiner went on to explain that he considered the living Word to be the microcosmic unity within the human being of all universal life—which he also equates with Christ-Jesus. Once again, as recorded by Scholl:

> All beings in nature come together in human beings, and form the Word in them. That is the human I—Christ Jesus. Humankind becomes Christ [as the Word] when it inwardly experiences that the whole world comes together within, unites inwardly. (Ibid)

Furthermore, in the same lecture where Steiner referred to Christ as a fire-spirit (archangel), he also explained that the "divine Word of creation" was the germinal life-spirit (buddhi) that originally hovered outside of the human soul. The actions of the sun-spirit, Christ, on earth enabled human beings to incorporate the life-spirit within themselves. In Steiner's own words:

> Through the deed of Christ on Earth, a predisposition was created in human beings for them to take into their Manas [spirit-self] what we call "Buddhi"... The possibility of receiving Buddhi begins with the appearance of Jesus-Christ on Earth. [St.] John called this the divine Word of creation. The divine Word of creation is this fire spirit, who poured his fire into human beings. (From the 1910 lecture entitled, "The Mystery of Golgotha"; published in *The Christian Mystery*)

It is quite obvious, then, that when Rudolf Steiner equates the Christ-spirit with the Word, he is clearly *not* stating that the Christ (an advanced sun-spirit) is the same being as the Logos-Word (the lord of the universe). Whether the Solar-Christos is an archangel, a virtue or a dominion, the fact remains that the Logos-Word existed long before any of the life-forms differentiated within his nature. Moreover, in the same way that being *united* with God does not mean that one is *identical* to God, being *united* with the Logos-Word does not mean that the Christ-being is *identical* to the Logos-Word.

Reconciling the Apparent Conflict of the Solar-Christos as Virtue and Archangel

Considering the remaining three apparent identity conflicts of the Solar-Christos, two can be satisfyingly resolved by referring to the information illustrated in Figure 7. What is here illustrated is the Rosicrucian teaching that the Solar-Christos (the Christ-spirit of the sun) is the highest initiate of the archangelic-beings (fire-spirits). In general, these beings attained self-conscious awareness (their human stage) during the Ancient Sun Period and currently have the astral body as their lowest vehicle of expression. The Solar-Christos, however, as their foremost initiate and spirit-leader, has advanced three levels higher than ordinary archangels.

In consequence, even though the Solar-Christos is an archangelic-being, he is able to operate at the level of a virtue (spirit of motion). When operating at the level of a virtue, the Solar-Christos has life-spirit (buddhi) as his lowest vehicle of expression, and his highest vehicle reaches up to the universal love-principle of the Logos-Word. Because of this exalted attainment, the Christ-spirit of the sun is the chief representative of the son-principle of the Logos-Word (the reflection of the Son-person of God) for all the beings of the Third Hierarchy. Once again, this deep supernal affinity with the threefold nature of the Logos-Word does not mean that the Solar-Christos is the same person as the Logos-Word.

Reconciling the Apparent Conflict of the Solar-Christos as Dominion

So if the Solar-Christos is an archangelic-being who is manifestly distinct from the person of the Universal Word, and who has attained the level of a virtue through initiatory development, why has the Rosicrucian-initiate Rudolf Steiner also referred to him as a spirit of wisdom (dominion)? In answer to this seeming contradiction, recall that Yahweh-Elohim and the six planetary powers on the sun were able to unite in a collective consciousness, and thereby operate at a level that was higher than each of their individual attainments. In fact, according to esoteric Christianity, the elevated collective consciousness of Yahweh-Elohim enabled his higher vehicles to be infilled with the inspirations of a virtue (spirit of motion)—more precisely, with the spirit-impulses of the Solar-Christos. Therefore, when Yahweh-Elohim disclosed his inner being to Moses as "I Am the I Am," it was actually the Christ-spirit of the sun who was making this self-declaration through the reflective nature of the planetary form-spirit of the moon.

Similarly, the Solar-Christos (in response to specific crucial events) has occasionally united in a collective consciousness with companion solar-virtues. This has enabled him to be temporarily infilled with the transcendent impulses of a spirit of wisdom (dominion). The archangelic-initiate of the sun, then, has not actually advanced to the level of a spirit of wisdom, but may be inspired by such a being under special circumstances. As a rule, initiate-beings don't advance more than three levels beyond their celestial peers for the simple reason that progressing too far in advance would disassociate and estrange them from their own evolutionary life-wave, similar to a bright student skipping too many grades in school.

The Solar-Christos as the Ego-Being of the Sun

Recall that within our solar system, there are eight original celestial bodies: sun, Mercury, Venus, earth, moon, Mars, Jupiter and Saturn. Also recall that there are seven spirits of form (elohim) who act as planetary-spirits: six of which superphysically reside in the sphere of the sun, and one of which (Yahweh-Elohim) resides in the periphery of the moon. It is obvious from this information that there is no spirit of form who acts as the ego-being of the sun. The reason for this, of course, is that the higher-vibrational status of the sun requires a more advanced being as its solar-spirit, a spirit of movement (virtue). As we are now esoterically informed, that spirit of movement is the Solar-Christos, the Christ-being of the sun.

As Rudolf Steiner has helpfully indicated, the spirits of movement and the spirits of form, even though they reside in the sphere of the sun, are entirely focussed outwardly on the planetary and lunar life of our solar system. Their own level of advancement is not sufficient to consciously direct the evolution of the sun itself; that is left to the spirits of wisdom, the thrones, the cherubim and the seraphim. As detailed in a lecture given in 1912:

> [O]nly those spiritual beings of the higher hierarchies from the seraphim down to the spirits of wisdom have a certain power over the nature of the sun; only they work for the development of the fixed star itself and its beings, whereas the spirits of motion and form can, so to speak, do nothing for the evolution of the beings of the fixed star itself. To them is apportioned the planets that surround the fixed star in the planetary system … Those spirits—the spirits of motion and the spirits of form—who are going through their evolution upon the fixed star itself are powerless to do anything for its evolution. They are not of sufficiently exalted rank. (Published in *Spiritual Beings in the Heavenly Bodies and in the Kingdoms of Nature*)

The Solar-Christos, then, in his individual responsibility as ego-being of the sun, is nevertheless focussed primarily on the welfare of humanity and the many other life-forms evolving throughout our planetary system. When collectively united with other dedicated virtues, he can also act under the guidance of the solar spirits of wisdom for the benefit of sun evolution as well.

The Initiate-Leader of the Principalities (Time-Spirits)

As the archangelic Solar-Christos (functioning as a spirit of movement) was able to inspire the angelic Yahweh-Elohim (functioning as a spirit of form), so has a lofty principality (functioning as a spirit of wisdom) been able to inspire and direct the Christ-spirit of the sun. The ordinary principalities of today attained self-conscious awareness (their human stage) during the Ancient Saturn Period and use the ego-bearer as their lowest vehicle. Their foremost initiate, however, has advanced to the level of a spirit of wisdom and uses the spirit-body as his lowest vehicle of expression. His highest vehicle reaches up to the universal will-principle of the Logos-Word. As such, the initiate-leader of the principalities is the chief representative of the father-principle of the Logos-Word (the reflection of God the Father) for all the beings of the Third Hierarchy. Since the principalities (the "humanity" of Ancient Saturn) are also referred to as time-spirits, their initiate-leader is esoterically known as "Chronos-Aeon," or more affectionately as "Father Time."

In other words, within the Third Hierarchy, the representative of the Holy Mother (Yahweh-Elohim) looks up to the representative of the Eternal Son (the Solar-Christos) for inspiration and guidance. The Solar-Christos, in turn, looks up to the representative of the Heavenly Father (Chronos-Aeon) for higher direction and advice. These three initiate-beings, then, faithfully reflect and represent the divine Trinity within the third hierarchy of evolving life.

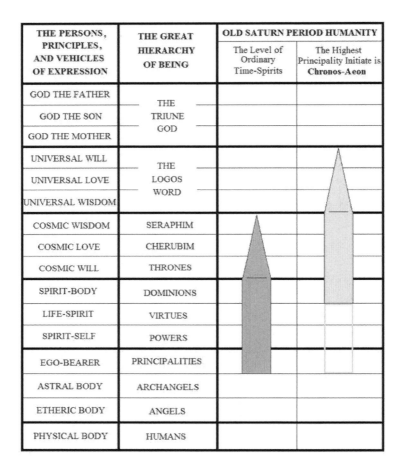

THE PERSONS, PRINCIPLES, AND VEHICLES OF EXPRESSION	THE GREAT HIERARCHY OF BEING	OLD SATURN PERIOD HUMANITY	
		The Level of Ordinary Time-Spirits	The Highest Principality Initiate is **Chronos-Aeon**
GOD THE FATHER	THE TRIUNE GOD		
GOD THE SON			
GOD THE MOTHER			
UNIVERSAL WILL	THE LOGOS WORD		
UNIVERSAL LOVE			
UNIVERSAL WISDOM			
COSMIC WISDOM	SERAPHIM		
COSMIC LOVE	CHERUBIM		
COSMIC WILL	THRONES		
SPIRIT-BODY	DOMINIONS		
LIFE-SPIRIT	VIRTUES		
SPIRIT-SELF	POWERS		
EGO-BEARER	PRINCIPALITIES		
ASTRAL BODY	ARCHANGELS		
ETHERIC BODY	ANGELS		
PHYSICAL BODY	HUMANS		

Figure 8: The Hierarchic Level of the Principalities and Their Highest Initiate

The Association of the Solar-Christos with Jesus of Nazareth

As indicated above, the Solar-Christos is benevolently and

comprehensively responsible for humanity and all life evolving on earth (as well as the other planets). Moreover, in esoteric Christianity, there is a deep, profound and abiding relationship between the Christ-being of the sun, and one particular human being—the man Jesus. But in order to delve meaningfully deeper into this important relationship, it is first necessary to esoterically reveal something of the "mystery of Jesus."

CHAPTER 2

THE MYSTERY OF JESUS:
HIGH INITIATE OR VIRGIN SOUL?

2.1   The Jesus Dilemma: Two Opposing Esoteric Conceptions

Who is Christ-Jesus? The Familiar, Exoteric Understanding

THE WIDESPREAD, commonly-accepted Christian belief today is that Jesus-Christ is the direct incarnation of the Word, who is God the Son, the Second Person of the Trinity. Moreover, he was miraculously conceived without a biological father through the action of the Holy Spirit. As such, he is considered to be one person with two natures: one human and one divine. His mother, Mary, had no other children and remained a virgin her entire life. The family lived in Nazareth and Jesus spent the first thirty years of his life at home doing carpentry work with his step-father, Joseph. At thirty years of age, Jesus was baptized by his cousin John in the Jordan River, whereupon the Holy Spirit alighted upon him and the voice of God declared that "This is my beloved Son, with whom I am well pleased."

This event signaled the start of Jesus' public ministry of teaching, healing and performing miracles, which lasted for about three years. Though innocent of any civil crime, Jesus was nevertheless arrested by the Jewish Sanhedrin for claiming to be the Messiah and the Son of God. Fearful of a civil uprising, the Roman governor Pontius Pilate reluctantly condemned Jesus to death. He died by crucifixion and was entombed for three days, after which time he arose from the dead in a glorified physical body and appeared to his disciples. Forty days after his bodily resurrection, Jesus ascended into heaven and disappeared from sight. To this day, he supernally abides with God the Father until he physically returns (the "Second Coming") at some unknown future date to pronounce a final judgement on the world. Since he overcame original sin and physical death, Jesus is regarded as the "Saviour" of humanity and the "Truth, the Life and the Way."

While the basic elements of the foregoing conception of Christ-Jesus are cordially agreed upon by most Christian denominations today, this was not always the case. In the early centuries of Christianity, there was searing debate and hostile disagreement as to the identity of Christ-Jesus and the details of his life. Several philosophical fringe theories developed to explain the nature of Christ-Jesus, which later came to be considered heretical by the Catholic Church. Some examples are the following:

(1) "Docetism": was a belief promulgated by many of the early Gnostic groups which held that Jesus was entirely divine (an "aeon") and not human in any way. He only appeared to have a human form by means of perceptual illusion.

(2) "Apollinarianism": was the belief that Jesus had a human body and a human soul, but not a human spirit; he had a

divine spirit instead.

(3) "Ebionism": was the belief that Jesus was fully human and not divine in any way; he was simply empowered and inspired by God on occasion.

(4) "Eutychianism": was the belief that Jesus had a single human nature that was a unique mixture of human and divine elements. This belief is equated with "Monophysitism."

(5) "Nestorianism": was the belief that Jesus had two separate natures that were not hypostatically united: one nature that was human, and one nature that was divine.

Who is Christ-Jesus? The Hidden, Esoteric Understanding

Numerous and novel conceptions of the nature of Christ-Jesus also developed within the esoteric traditions of East and West, not just in connection with conventional Christian ideology. Despite the variety, however, only two have stood the test of time as the most credible and compelling conceptions. Unfortunately, the obvious problem was that each of these two, equally-convincing esoteric conceptions, both bearing the weighty stamp of clairvoyant truth and investigation, was diametrically opposed to the other. The thorny dilemma for Christian esotericists, then, was how to reconcile these two radically different conceptions of Christ-Jesus; how was it logically possible that both conceptions were true? And if there was no way of reconciliation, which conception was the most correct?

The "Theosophical" Conception of Christ-Jesus

The one esoteric conception of Christ-Jesus, which gained

considerable esoteric familiarity due to its development and promotion by the Theosophical Movement, may be summarized as follows: Jesus was a highly-advanced human being who had attained his spiritual mastery over numerous prior incarnations on earth. Many of these incarnations were influential and historical figures, such as Zarathustra, the founder of the ancient Persian religion. Jesus was, and continues to be, a bodhisattva, a member of an exalted brotherhood of initiates who oversee the spiritual and cultural development of humanity.

As Jesus of Nazareth, he was born and conceived by natural means. Moreover, though Jesus was the eldest child, Mary his mother and Joseph his father had several other children as well. From the age of twelve to the age of thirty, Jesus travelled extensively throughout the Middle East, Asia and Europe, teaching and learning from the various mystic masters and initiates. Upon his return to Nazareth, he taught, healed and performed miracles throughout Roman Judaea before being arrested and condemned to death. After his death by crucifixion, he continued to incarnate as important personages throughout history. Esoterically, he is referred to as the "Master-Jesus."

A concise written description of this particular conception was provided by Levi H. Dowling (1844–1911) in *The Aquarian Gospel of Jesus the Christ* (1980):

> Jesus was an ideal Jew, born in Bethlehem of Judea. His mother was a beautiful Jewish girl named Mary. As a child Jesus differed but little from other children only that in past lives he had overcome carnal propensities to such an extent that he could be tempted like others and not yield … In many respects Jesus was a remarkable child, for by ages of strenuous preparation he was qualified to be an avatar, a saviour of the world, and from childhood he was endowed with superior wisdom and was conscious of the fact that he was competent to lead the [human] race into

higher ways of spiritual living … After his death, burial and resurrection he appeared in materialized form before the Silent Brothers in the temple of Heliopolis, in Egypt.

The "Mystical" Conception of Jesus-Christ

The other credible esoteric conception of Christ-Jesus that was more "quietly" promoted by various mystically-oriented individuals and groups may be summarized as follows: Jesus was a special being unique in human history in that he had *no* physical incarnations previous to his birth in Bethlehem by natural means to Mary and Joseph. As such, he was a completely "virgin soul," *without* numerous lifetimes of worldly knowledge and experience. Nevertheless, the pure, virginal soul of Jesus retained a cosmic oneness and deep compassion for all life that ordinary humanity had lost due to the Luciferic fall into matter that occurred during the Lemurian Age.

This Jesus did not have any natural brothers and sisters. Some accounts relate that he travelled between the ages of twelve and thirty, while others maintain that he remained close to home in Nazareth. After teaching, healing and performing miracles throughout Judaea for three years, he was arrested and crucified. Due to a holy and unblemished life, he was able to rise to supreme heavenly heights, and continues to assist struggling humanity from the higher planes of existence. A good summary of this alternate, mystical conception of Jesus has been provided by Yogi Ramacharaka in *Mystic Christianity or the Inner Teachings of the Master* (1935):

> The Mystery of the Life of Jesus forms the subject of some important Inner Teachings of the Mystic Fraternities and Occult Brotherhoods, and is considered by them to be the foundation of the other teachings … In

55

the first place we must remember that the soul of Jesus was different from the souls of other men. His was a "virgin birth"—not in the commonly accepted use of the term, but in the occult sense … His spirit had not been compelled to work through repeated incarnations, pressing forward for expression through humble and ignoble forms. It was free from taint, and as pure as the Fountain from which it flowed. It was a virgin soul in every sense of the term. This being so, it follows that it was not bound by the Karma of previous incarnations—as is the case with the ordinary soul. It had no entangling ties—it had no seeds of desire and action planted in previous lives, which were pressing forward toward expression in His life. He was a Free Spirit—an Unbound Soul … The Occult Teachings tell us that Jesus, after his final disappearance from before the eyes of His apostles, passed on to the higher planes of the Astral World … He retained the highest vehicle—the Spiritual Mind in its highest shade of expression—in order that as an entity He might labour for the [human] race.

As is evident from the foregoing descriptions, both of these conceptions of Christ-Jesus are esoterically compelling and strike a chord of deep, inner truth. But likewise, it is also clearly evident that they are fundamentally different. So how could each of them be true? One must be true and the other false. But which one?

For many centuries, Christian esotericists were logically impelled to accept one or the other conception, since there seemed to be no satisfactory way of accepting them both as historically true. Fortunately in our day, this is no longer the case. Thanks to the clairvoyant investigations and anthroposophical writings of Rudolf Steiner, the esoteric solution to this dilemma (previously safeguarded within the Rosicrucian Order) has been made publicly accessible.

2.2   The Anthroposophical Solution: The Two Jesus Individualities

The Two Jesus-Children Born in Judaea.

Without doubt, Rudolf Steiner's supersensible investigations into the life, nature and significance of Christ-Jesus are exceedingly complex, detailed and demanding. For the sincere seeker of truth, however, they are also a supernova of penetrating and illuminating spiritual light, and well worth the effort to comprehend and assimilate.

As startling and implausible as it first appears, Steiner's clairvoyant research of the akashic records has revealed (and confirmed the Rosicrucian teaching) that at the beginning of the Christian era, *two* historically significant individuals named Jesus were born about the same time in Judaea; *both* to parents named Mary and Joseph.

This fact becomes much easier to accept when it is understood that the Hebrew names for "Mary" (Miriam), "Joseph" (Yosef) and "Jesus" (Yeshua) were commonly-used names at that time. It would not be surprising, then, that numerous families included these names; similar to families today having a son named "John," with parents named "Mary" and "Joe." But much more important than shared family names is that one of these Jesus-individualities was a high-initiate with numerous prior incarnations throughout human history, while the other Jesus-individuality was a "virgin-soul" with no prior physical incarnations on earth.

The Initiate-Jesus Individuality

The esoteric information provided by Rudolf Steiner indicates that the initiate-Jesus was born to parents living in a house in Bethlehem. This particular Jesus-child (as indicated in the Gospel of Matthew) belonged to a hereditary stream descended from King David through his son, King Solomon. Consequently, anthroposophical writing often refers to this particular Jesus-child as the "Solomon-Jesus." In a previous important incarnation, the initiate-Jesus had been Zarathustra (Zoroaster), the original founder of the ancient Persian religion. Since this Jesus-individuality was the incarnation of a high-initiate, an adept, he is also known in esoteric circles as "Master-Jesus."

As a highly-advanced soul, the young Master-Jesus was able to express, unusually early in his childhood, all the prodigious talents and abilities that he had acquired from numerous prior incarnations. Because of this, the initiate-Jesus was an exceptionally intelligent and precocious child. As explained by Rudolf Steiner in a lecture given in 1911:

> This Zarathustra individuality, with all the great and powerful inner forces which in the nature of things he had brought over from earlier incarnations, had to incarnate in a body descended from the Solomon line of the House of David ... We are concerned therefore with a human body which did not wait until later years to work on these faculties, but could do so in a youthful, child-like and yet powerful organism. Hence we see the Zarathustra-individuality growing up in such a way that the faculties of the child developed comparatively early. The child soon showed an extent of knowledge which would normally have been impossible at his age. (Published in *From Jesus to Christ*, 1973)

As the reincarnated Zoroaster (whose name means "Golden Star"), the initiate-Jesus attracted the clairvoyant attention of Eastern masters, Persian magi, who traced the supersensible light of his astral ("star") body to the Bethlehem home several months after his birth. Shortly thereafter, the Zarathustra-Jesus child was taken to Egypt to escape the murderous intentions of King Herod. After Herod's death, the family safely returned to Judaea and eventually settled in Nazareth to raise an additional six children: four boys (named James, Joseph, Simon and Jude) and two girls (Mary and Salome).

The Virginal-Jesus Individuality

The second Jesus-individuality, born a few months after the first, was a special human being utterly unique in the history of earth evolution. Unlike the rest of humanity, this Jesus-individuality had no previous physical incarnations on earth. In esoteric terms, he was indeed a "virginal-soul." Immediately, two questions naturally come to mind: (1) how had this occurred, and (2) why?

According to Rudolf Steiner's supersensible research, when Yahweh-Elohim and the spirits of form bestowed the gift of a separate ego-bearing soul to ancestral humanity during the ancient Lemurian Age, two nascent human beings were protectively retained in a supersensible, paradisal condition (the unblemished, edenic state of all human life-forms prior to Luciferic interference and the resultant "Fall" into material forms on earth). By remaining in a pristine, angel-like condition, these two virginal-souls—one male and one female—still preserved an instinctive clairvoyant awareness of the supernatural world, and an innate sense of oneness with the living universe.[12]

Since these two virginal-souls were insulated from the materializing effects of the Luciferic-beings, they were not drawn into physical incarnation. As a result, they did not experience an increasing sense of separation from the natural environment around them as did their fellow human beings. By continuing to exist in this primordial, innocent condition, these two virginal-beings did not develop a strong, individualized sense of self; that is, a separate ego-awareness. Their sense of self was still intimately united with the entire cosmos (similar to the consciousness of spirit-self). While it would be esoterically accurate to say that these two virginal-beings did not possess an "ego," in the usual sense of the word, it would also be incorrect to think that they did not possess a sense of self, or that they were not distinct human "beings," but only "ego-less bodies."

As startling as this may sound to conventional Christian belief, then, not every human being "fell from grace" and became subject to "original sin." Two human beings actually remained in "paradise" long after the rest of humanity had been expelled from the "Garden of Eden." Consequently, to esoteric Christianity, these two virginal-beings are known as the "heavenly-Adam" and the "heavenly-Eve." The heavenly-Adam would later incarnate, for the first time, in the virginal Jesus-individuality. Likewise, the heavenly-Eve would later incarnate, for the first time, in the virginal Mary-individuality.

Some Pre-Incarnational, Earthly Activity of the Heavenly-Adam

Prior to his first physical embodiment, then, the heavenly-Adam existed supersensibly in an angel-like condition: he possessed an invisible, physical force-body; an etheric body; an astral body, and an "immaculate ego" (one free from original sin or Luciferic corruption). Though he was sheltered by higher beings, he was not insulated from superphysically interacting with the rest of humanity. In fact, certain mythological figures, as well as many critical developments in human evolution, can be traced to the supernatural actions of the heavenly-Adam.

Esoterically, the name "Immanuel," as recorded in the Gospel of Matthew, refers to the angel-like heavenly-Adam who would come to fulfill the Hebrew prophecies of a Messiah. Moreover, in ancient Greece, it was the angel-like Immanuel who spoke through the oracles at Delphi, and who came to be known in the Mysteries as the sun-god Apollo. As stated by Rudolf Steiner:

> Apollo is the angelic Being of whom we have spoken; he was a reflection projected into the Greek mind of the angelic Being who had in fact worked at the end of the Atlantean time and who had been permeated by the [Solar] Christ. This reflection was the Apollo who spoke wisdom to the Greeks through the mouth of the Pythia … The weakened form of the angel in whom [the Solar] Christ once dwelt is a healer on Earth, or for the Earth. For Apollo was never physically embodied, but he worked through the Earth-elements. (From a lecture in 1913; published in *Christ and the Spiritual World and the Search for the Holy Grail*, 2008)

In ancient India, it was the heavenly-Adam whose primordial cosmic-consciousness inspired the historical Krishna[13] to express such sublime wisdom as that recorded in the *Bhagavad Gita*:

> But beyond my visible nature is my invisible Spirit. This is the fountain of life whereby this universe has its being.
> All things have their life in this Life, and I am their beginning and end.
> In this whole vast universe there is nothing higher than I. All the worlds have their rest in me, as many pearls upon a string.
> I am the taste of living waters and the light of the sun and the moon. I am OM, the sacred word of the Vedas, sound in silence, heroism in men.
> I am the pure fragrance that comes from the earth and the brightness of the fire I am. I am the life of all living beings, and the austere life of those who train their souls.

And I am from everlasting the seed of eternal life. I am the intelligence of the intelligent. I am the beauty of the beautiful.

For my glory is not seen by all: I am hidden by my veil of mystery; and in its delusion the world knows me not, who was never born and for ever I am. (*The Bhagavad Gita*; translated by Juan Mascaro; 1962)

Pre-Incarnational Cooperation of the Heavenly-Adam with the Solar-Christos

The heavenly-Adam has also significantly contributed to fundamental human development at three critical times in the remote past. By uniting forces with the Solar-Christos—once during the Lemurian Age and twice during the Atlantean Age—disastrous injury to human development that would have resulted from Luciferic and Ahrimanic assailment was thankfully averted.

Since the heavenly-Adam throughout ancient times preserved an innate cosmic oneness, connection and affinity with all life, certain advanced beings—particularly the Solar-Christos—were able to effectively permeate his angel-like vehicles with their own consciousness and power. In the case of ordinary humanity, a strong personal ego would usually interfere and interrupt any external direction and control coming from a separate entity. Since this was not the case with the heavenly-Adam, the Solar-Christos could harmoniously guide and direct his actions without egotistical hindrance.

Such a uniquely intimate association was of mutual benefit for both beings. As experienced by the heavenly-Adam, when permeated by the Solar-Christos, his own consciousness, wisdom, power, ability and compassion were transcendently uplifted and expanded. In a very real sense, then, the heavenly-Adam could gaze out at the universe through the eyes of the exalted Sun-King, as well as temporarily act with his celestial power and authority. As for the Solar-Christos, by being able to permeate the vehicles of the heavenly-Adam, he was able to powerfully effect beneficial internal changes to the whole of humanity, and not simply to one human being. This is because a fundamental principle of evolutionary development establishes that whatever is progressively accomplished by one individual becomes the common property of all.

During the Lemurian Age, serious disorder would have occurred to human sense perception through the Luciferic impulses of separatism and self-centeredness if the heavenly-Adam had not willingly united with the Solar-Christos. By doing so, the superplanetary forces of the Solar-Christos were able to vertically align the supersensible human form of the heavenly-Adam, such that the head forces were directed and opened to the beneficial influences streaming down from the sun. These selfless, altruistic solar forces constructively transformed human sense perception, such that it *serves* human development and does not Luciferically hinder it.

In this crucial instance, the united participation of the heavenly-Adam and the Solar-Christos commonly bestowed on all humanity the power to stand upright, to vertically align the physical body between sun and earth. Without this proper alignment, humanity would have remained in an animal-like condition, and not able to develop true self-conscious awareness.

A second critical stage in human development occurred near the beginning of the Atlantean Age. According to the supersensible research of the akashic records by Rudolf Steiner, the harmonious interaction of the various internal organs of the human body was being disrupted by Luciferic and Ahrimanic interference. The separative and ossifying forces of these regressive beings, if left unopposed, would have destroyed the selfless unity of the body's organs, resulting in internal, biological discord. Once again, this was averted through the joint cooperation of the heavenly-Adam and the Solar-Christos.

One of the vital organs that would have been seriously affected at that time was the developing larynx. Thanks to the superplanetary intercession of the Solar-Christos working through the heavenly-Adam, human speech was able to properly develop. The power to speak, the ability to objectively communicate thoughts and feelings through the spoken word, was thereby bestowed on all humanity by the selfless actions of the Solar-Christos working within the superphysical human form of the heavenly-Adam.

In the latter part of the Atlantean age, the forces of Lucifer and Ahriman were targeted on the soul of primeval humanity, rather than on the physical body that was assaulted twice before. At that prehistoric time, the regressive powers were intent on separating and densifying the soul-forces of thinking, feeling and willing. Without the harmonious interaction of these three essential soul activities, humanity's inner life would be thrown into turmoil, and progressive development aborted. Fortunately, the powerful forces of the Solar-Christos, acting within the soul of the heavenly-Adam, once more intervened for the salvation of human evolution.

By guaranteeing the congruous interrelationship of the three essential soul-forces, objective human thinking was able to develop in a healthy way into the post-Atlantean age. The power to think, to independently formulate ideas in the mind that conform to objective reality, was thereafter imparted to all of humanity through this third sacrificial cooperation of the Solar-Christos and the heavenly-Adam in prehistoric times.

Apparent Contradictions regarding the Nature of the

Heavenly-Adam

In various lectures (and sometimes even in the same lecture), Rudolf Steiner has described the heavenly-Adam in a number of different ways: as "an Angel" or "having the form of an Angel"; as "an Archangel" or "having the nature of an Archangel."

For example, in a lecture entitled, "Pre-Earthly Deeds of Christ" (1914), he stated: "[T]hree times previously we have an Angel permeated with that [Solar-Christos] Impulse." Later in the same lecture he stated:

[I]n that old Lemurian epoch—but in etheric spiritual heights—the being who later became the Nathan-Jesus, and who otherwise would have had the form of an angel, took on human form (not of flesh, but a human etheric form). In the super-earthly region Jesus of Nazareth is to be found as an etheric angel-form.

Earlier in the same lecture, however, he also stated:

He who was later the Nathan-Jesus had been present in the three earlier events, but not incarnated as physical man; he lived in the spiritual worlds as a spiritual Being of the nature of the Archangels.

Furthermore, in another lecture entitled "The Four Sacrifices of Christ" (1914), Steiner additionally stated:

[T]oward the end of the Atlantean evolution, the third Christ event occurred. Once more the Christ Being ensouled Himself in an archangel.

While these various descriptions might at first appear confusing and contradictory, fortunately they can be esoterically resolved. Even though the heavenly-Adam has always belonged to humanity, by not taking physical embodiment throughout the ages, he had to exist in a superearthly, angel-like form, even though he wasn't technically an angel-being. However, because of his repeated sacrificial service to human evolution, and his devoted self-surrender to the Solar-Christos during three critical earthly events, the heavenly-Adam accelerated his own superphysical development to the level of an archangel. Even without physically incarnating, then, the heavenly-Adam had achieved a high level of initiatory advancement (please refer back to Figure 7 for diagrammatic illustration).

The Incarnation of the Heavenly-Adam as "Jesus-Immanuel"

According to Rudolf Steiner's esoteric research, when the heavenly-Adam was physically incarnated for the first time as the virginal Jesus-child, as "Jesus-Immanuel," he was born in Bethlehem to parents who had temporarily travelled there from their home in Nazareth to pay their taxes. The humble birth in a nearby cave went unnoticed by worldly attention except for some nearby shepherds who still retained a degree of atavistic clairvoyance and who could, thereby, perceive some of the celestial activity surrounding the special event. The paternal hereditary lineage of this second Jesus-child also descended from King David, but in this case through his son Nathan (as related in the Gospel of Luke). For this reason, in anthroposophical literature he is commonly referred to as the "Nathan-Jesus."

Also of great esoteric significance regarding the birth of the heavenly-Adam as Jesus-Immanuel is the fact that his young mother, Mary, was the first physical incarnation of the other virginal-soul sheltered from the Luciferic fall during the Lemurian Age—the heavenly-Eve. This esoteric discovery confirms the Catholic dogma of the "Immaculate Conception": that Mary, the mother of Jesus, was born without "original sin" (the negative effects of Luciferic interference). The dual embodiments of the heavenly-Adam as Jesus, and the heavenly-Eve as Mary, also shed great esoteric light on the further Catholic assertion that Jesus is the "new Adam" and Mary is the "new Eve." As stated in the *Catechism of the Catholic Church* (paragraph 411):

> The Christian tradition sees in this passage [from Genesis] an announcement of [Jesus as] the "New Adam" who, because he "became obedient unto death, even death on a cross," makes amends superabundantly for the disobedience, of Adam. Furthermore many Fathers and Doctors of the Church have seen the woman announced in the *Protoevangelium* as Mary, the mother of Christ, the "new Eve." Mary benefited first of all and uniquely from Christ's victory over sin: she was preserved from all stain of original sin and by a special grace of God committed no sin of any kind during her whole earthly life.

As an only child growing up in Nazareth, Jesus-Immanuel displayed no aptitude for intellectual learning; nor did he demonstrate any other worldly talents or skills. To external observation, he was instead a gentle, caring, simple-minded boy. He did, however, radiate an unusual and deep compassion for all life, as well as a mysterious healing presence. As described by Rudolf Steiner:

> Jesus of the Nathan line grew up with a deeply inward nature. He had little aptitude for acquiring external wisdom and assimilating facts of ordinary knowledge. But the depths of his soul were fathomless and he had a boundless capacity for love, because in his etheric body was contained the power that streamed down from the time when man had not yet entered into earthly incarnation, when he was still leading a Divine existence. This Divine existence manifested in this boy in the form of an infinite capacity for love. It was therefore natural

that he should have been ill-adapted for everything acquired by men in the course of incarnations through the instrumentality of the physical body, while on the other hand an untold warmth of love pervaded his inner life. (Lecture given in 1910; published in *The Gospel of St. Matthew*, 2003)

Tragedy Strikes Both Jesus-Families

At a certain point in time, in an obvious stroke of destiny, the two Jesus-families ended up living close to each other in Nazareth, where they met and regarded one another on quite friendly terms. The cordial interrelationship of the two families was brought even closer with a series of seemingly tragic events that began around the time the two Jesus-children turned twelve years old.

Just prior to this time, the father of Zarathustra-Jesus died, leaving the unfortunate mother with seven children to take care of on her own. But even more devastating for the widowed Mary was the sudden and unexpected death of the Zarathustra-Jesus boy at twelve years of age. The brilliant child that demonstrated such exceptional promise, recognized by the Magian priest-kings, unexpectedly wasted away from no apparent physical disease.

At the same time, the second Jesus-family in Nazareth also experienced some shattering and equally grievous events. Soon after the death of the Zarathustra-Jesus boy, Jesus-Immanuel began behaving uncharacteristically different than before. He began expressing profound intellection, as well as exhibiting skills and talents that he didn't previously possess, to the complete surprise and confusion of his concerned parents. One such incident has been faithfully recorded in the Gospel of Luke (2:42–51), which relates how the twelve-year-old Jesus suddenly went missing for three days only to be found in the temple in Jerusalem authoritatively discussing complex theological issues with the educated Jewish elders.

Soon after this radical and totally unexpected personality change in Jesus-Immanuel, tragedy struck the small Nazarene family as well—the premature death of the young mother Mary (the heavenly-Eve). Sadly, for a time both families were left to struggle with only one parent; that is, until another destiny-laden event occurred—the merging of the two single-parent households into one, large, blended family. Once again, this event appears at first to be historically outlandish, but on reflection it makes total practical sense. One family lacked a father, and the other a mother; each family was amicably familiar with the other; and both lived in close proximity to the other in the small community of Nazareth.

At a certain remarkable point in human history, then, there lived in Nazareth a mysterious Hebrew boy named Jesus, with an older step-mother named Mary and a natural father named Joseph, together with four step-brothers and two step-sisters. It was *this* Jesus-individuality who, at the age of thirty, became the long-awaited Messiah.

Before examining the supersensibly revealed (akashic) history of how and why Jesus-Immanuel became the promised Messiah, it is important to know about a third significant Jesus-individuality who lived about 100 years before Zarathustra-Jesus and Jesus-Immanuel.

2.3 A Third Jesus: The "Great Teacher" of the Essenes

The Historical Figure of Jesus-Pandira

A great deal of mystery, misinformation and misunderstanding surrounds yet another important historical Jesus-individuality—Yeshua ben Pandira—Jesus, son of

Pandira. Since accurate historical information is sorely lacking, it is fortunate that detailed supersensible research is available instead. What little historical information there is about this third Jesus is mostly contained in the Talmud, a collection of ancient rabbinic writings accumulated over a 700 year period from about 200 BC to about 500 AD.

From the Talmud we read that Jesus, the son of Pandira, lived around 100 BC, and that he was a student of Rabbi Yehoshua ben Perachiah. According to this account, Jesus-Pandira and his teacher escaped a general persecution of Hebrew rabbis by King Hyrcanus by fleeing to Alexandria in Egypt. After a decade in hiding, Jesus-Pandira and his teacher safely returned; but shortly thereafter, due to a misunderstanding between the two men, Jesus-Pandira broke away from his teacher and started his own Jewish sect. Unfortunately, his teachings were considered heretical and idolatrous by certain religious authorities, and even after gaining some assistance from his government connections, Jesus-Pandira was convicted, stoned and then hanged for his beliefs on the eve of Passover.

It is also recorded in the Talmud that Jesus-Pandira had five main disciples: Mathai, Nekai, Netzer, Buni and Todah, who were also tried and executed despite their clever theological defenses. The sect, however, had several other followers who continued the teachings for many years after the death of Jesus-Pandira, though it eventually disappeared after the destruction of the temple in 70 AD.

Regrettably, though not surprisingly, the figure of Jesus-Pandira has been used by various scholars (as well as esotericists) to deny the later historical existence of Jesus-Immanuel who became the Messiah. To the unbiased investigator, however, they are clearly separate historical individualities. Moreover, the Talmud account draws no connection between Jesus, son of Pandira and Jesus, son of Joseph.

Rudolf Steiner's akashic investigations, however, indicate that Jesus-Pandira was a highly-respected teacher belonging to the mystical order of Essenes, whose mission was to prepare for the immanent incarnation of the Messiah. Together with the Pharisees and the Sadducees, the Essenes ("Essenoi") were a third Jewish sect that had a large number of adherents throughout Judaea. They lived primarily in closed fraternal communities dedicated to asceticism, voluntary poverty, strict celibacy, rules of abstinence and religious devotion. But far more importantly, in regard to Jesus-Pandira, we are dealing with an individual who was inspired and directed by a bodhisattva-being—the one known in the East as "Lord Maitreya."

The Bodhisattva-Maitreya and Jesus-Pandira

Lord Maitreya is one of twelve bodhisattvas who form an exalted association of high-initiates known as the "Great White Brotherhood" or the "Mother Lodge of Humanity."[14] These twelve special individuals are responsible for the spiritual, cultural and material welfare of humanity throughout the ages. They take their inspiration and direction from a "hidden master," an invisible thirteenth member at the centre of their circle. The light of illumination at the heart of the twelve is none other than the regent of the sun—the Solar-Christos. In the words of Rudolf Steiner:

> If you were able to look into the great Spirit-Lodge of the twelve Bodhisattvas you would find that in the midst of the Twelve there is a Thirteenth—one who cannot be called a 'Teacher' in the same sense as the Bodhisattvas, but of whom we must say: He is that Being from whom wisdom itself streams as very substance. It is therefore quite correct to speak of the twelve Bodhisattvas in the great Spirit-Lodge grouped around One who is their

centre ... the Thirteenth is himself the Being of whom the others teach, whom they proclaim from epoch to epoch. This Thirteenth is He whom the ancient Rishis called Vishva Karman, whom Zarathustra called Ahura Mazdao. (Lecture from 1909; published in *The Gospel of St. Luke*; 1990)

Vishva Karman and Ahura Mazdao (as previously mentioned) were ancient names for the great sun-spirit, the Solar-Christos.

According to anthroposophical research and Buddhist tradition, Lord Maitreya is the bodhisattva next destined to become a buddha (about 3000 years from today), thereby succeeding Siddhartha Gautama in this position. By inspiring the teaching and directing the actions of Jesus-Pandira, the Bodhisattva-Maitreya played a crucial role in preparing for the promised Messiah. For instance, one of the five main pupils trained by Jesus-Pandira became the teacher of the writer of Matthew's Gospel:

> Spiritual-scientific investigation finds that after the death of Jeschu ben Pandira the teaching relating to the preparation of the blood for him who was to be the [Zarathustra] Jesus of St. Matthew's Gospel was propagated especially by [Jesus-Pandira's pupil] Mathai." (Lecture by Rudolf Steiner in 1910; published in *The Gospel of St. Matthew*)

Moreover, another of Jesus-Pandira's main disciples, Netzer, was instructed to establish a strict and secluded Essene community dedicated to the ancient Nazarite order. This community later became known as "Netzereth" or "Nazareth," the very location which later provided the esoteric atmosphere necessary for the special inner growth and soul development of Jesus-Immanuel, who would become the Messiah.

The manner in which an advanced individuality (such as

the Lord Maitreya) can properly employ and influence the various vehicles of another being (such as Jesus-Pandira) is an esoteric process that is unfamiliar to most people in today's materialistic culture. Since a similar process was involved in the supersensible cooperation of Jesus-Immanuel and the Solar-Christos, it is therefore important at this point to provide some basic understanding and clarification.

The Unlawful Use of Another's Vehicles: Spirit-Possession and Trance-Channeling

Many movie-goers and TV-watchers today are somewhat familiar with sensationalized scenes and depictions of what is known as "spirit-possession." The common understanding of this phenomenon is that a foreign entity (usually malicious or demonic) takes unwanted control; that is, "possession," of another person's mind and body. These instances are naturally regarded as abnormal, undesirable and psychologically harmful. Thankfully, authentic cases of spirit-possession are exceedingly rare today due primarily to the personal acquisition of a strong sense of self; that is, to the acquisition of firmly established ego-boundaries which act (subconsciously) as a defensive barrier to unwarranted psychic intrusion. Since true spirit-possession is a clear violation of an individual's free-will and inner sovereignty, such instances have damaging effects over time and are, therefore, esoterically considered to be "unlawful."

As well, there is a vague familiarity these days with what is known as "trance-channeling"; the practice whereby a suitably-skilled individual (the "channeller") lapses into a self-induced trance, which allows a discarnate entity (usually considered to be a more advanced being) to control the channeller's mind and body in order to dispense words of supermundane wisdom and advice. This New Age practice is really just a modernized version of the Victorian Age séance. While most instances of trance-channeling are simply fraudulent attempts to extract money from gullible believers, on the rare occasions when a channeller actually passes into a trance and speaks aloud, it is usually their own subconscious mind that is doing the vocalization. If an actual discarnate source is involved, it is rarely an advanced being, but almost always an inferior, mischievous astral-entity.

Both spirit-possession and New Age channeling result from an unnatural, unhealthy diminishment of sensory-awareness, rational thinking and ego-consciousness. Particularly with trance-channeling, the astral body and the ego-bearer are disengaged from the physical and etheric bodies. While this condition is similar to sleep, the dangerous difference is that the physical and etheric bodies of the trance-channeller, or the possessed-victim, are left open and unprotected.

During normal sleep, the somnambulant lower vehicles are permeated and protected by benevolent higher beings. In the case of possession or channeling, the situation is analogous to a car driver getting out of an automobile, leaving the doors open, the keys in the ignition and the engine running. A responsible citizen, on seeing this, will find the driver and safely help him or her back into the vehicle. The irresponsible passerby, on the other hand, will seize the illegal opportunity to climb in and take the unprotected vehicle for an illicit "joy-ride." Such is similarly the case with possession and channeling; no truly-advanced superphysical being will use such hazardous, unlawful methods to convey important wisdom and advice.

The Lawful Indwelling of Another's Vehicles

Unlike spirit-possession and trance-channeling, there are

positive instances where a more advanced, incorporeal being will lawfully and beneficially use another individual's bodily vehicles. In these lawful instances, there is no diminishment in the consciousness of the host-individual; in fact, quite the opposite. Not only is the host-individual entirely awake and aware, but their own consciousness is raised and expanded by the indwelling presence of the advanced entity. In other words, the ego-bearer and the astral body of the host-individual have not foolishly vacated or been forcefully ejected from their lower vehicles; but remain conjoined, interconnected and unimpaired.

Moreover, a strict requirement of lawful indwelling is that the free-will of the host-individual is not in any way violated, compromised or negated. The indwelling entity always has the fully-informed, free-will consent of the host-individual to use their various vehicles. On rare occasions, the more-powerful, high-vibrational indwelling of an advanced superphysical being may cause minor or serious damage to one or more of the host vehicles. Especially in these instances, it is crucially important that the host-individual is fully aware of these consequences, and is entirely willing to sacrificially accept them.

Various Levels of Lawful Indwelling

There are various levels of lawful indwelling, depending on the degree of penetration and permeation of the host-vehicles by the more advanced superphysical being (see Figure 9 below). For example, the indwelling entity might only penetrate to the level of the host-individual's astral body. A familiar esoteric term for this level of indwelling is "ensoulment." In other words, to be "ensouled" by a higher being, means that the level of indwelling extends only as far as the astral body. If the degree of indwelling extends even deeper, to the level of the etheric body, then "incorporation" is the term that is most often used. In other words, if the degree of penetration extends to the level of the etheric body, the indwelling entity is said to be "incorporated" in the host-individual.

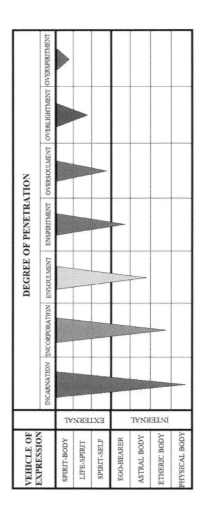

Figure 9: The Various Levels of Lawful Indwelling

If the indwelling entity were to extend the range of influence as deeply as the physical body, this would be termed an "incarnation." While this degree of penetration has certainly occurred throughout human history, it is not as common. As a general rule, it is the more exalted beings that have the superphysical strength to extend into the physical; but such powerful indwellings often run the risk of vibrationally shattering the denser host-vehicle.

To be "enspirited" by a superphysical-being is to have one's lower ego-awareness raised and expanded by the greater self-awareness of the indwelling entity. In other words, if the indwelling entity only penetrates to the level of the ego-bearer, then this would be termed, "enspiritment."

Since the three highest vehicles of expression: spirit-self, life-spirit, and spirit-body continue to abide in a latent, undeveloped condition for most people today, they are in a sense "above" or "outside" everyday human experience. The indwelling of these vehicles, therefore, is external; the advanced entity supersensibly envelopes the host-individual on the "outside." Expressed another way, the indwelling-entity is supersensibly "over" and "around" the host-individual. For this reason, appropriate terms of description for these levels of indwelling are "*over*soulment," "*over*lightment" and "*over*spiritment."

While these terms are here suggested and not universally acknowledged in esoteric literature, hopefully some such standardization in terminology will encourage more accuracy in certain details. For example, if a host-individual is said to be "oversouled" by a higher-being, it is here understood that the level of indwelling extends to the spirit-self. If the host-individual is said to be "overlighted" (rather than "overshadowed") by a higher-being, then it is here understood that the level of indwelling extends to the life-spirit. Thirdly, to be "overspirited" by a higher-being, is here understood to mean that only the spirit-body of the host-individual is indwelt.

Indwelling as an Evolutionary Factor in the Past

After first receiving the spark of self-conscious awareness during the Lemurian Age, new-born humanity was in a helpless, naïve and vulnerable condition. Protection, guidance and learning were benevolently provided by more advanced beings. In order to provide this evolutionary assistance to humanity, the advanced beings would indwell select individuals who would thereby act as wise leaders to families, tribes, clans, folk-groups and ethnic communities. Since primeval human bodies were more ethereal in the past and since ego-awareness was dim and undeveloped in the beginning, indwelling penetration easily extended down into the astral, etheric and physical human vehicles. As described by Rudolf Steiner in a lecture in 1909:

> Lemurian human beings were helpless; they could not manage their existence on earth; they did not know what they were here for. Heavenly beings, the [superphysical] inhabitants of [ancient] Venus [now called Mercury], who had an affinity with the physical body, now descended to those who dwelt on earth and permeated their soul substance … Even in post-Atlantean times, mankind had not advanced sufficiently to dispense with ensoulment from above. We have seen that in Lemurian times it took place through the fact that a Spirit of Personality [principality] permeated the physical body; in the Atlantean period the physical and etheric bodies were ensouled by archangelic beings; in post-Atlantean times the great leaders of humanity were ensouled by angelic beings who had descended into their physical, etheric and astral bodies. (Lecture 7; published in *Spiritual Hierarchies and their Reflection in the Physical World*; 1970)

Predictable, as humanity progressed and became more responsible for their own free-will decisions and development, indwelling by higher beings gradually decreased. Nevertheless, in crucial moments of human history (even into the present day) when heavenly assistance was required, higher beings continued to lawfully indwell the various vehicles of chosen individuals. Such was the case with Jesus-Pandira.

2.4   The Nazarene-Master: The Two Become One

The Indwelling of Jesus-Immanuel by the Bodhisattva-Zarathustra

While the unexpected death of the twelve-year-old Zarathustra-Jesus must have been a cruel and senseless tragedy for his loving family and for the magian priests who had expected great things from their re-embodied religious leader, later events were to positively prove otherwise. Supersensible investigation has revealed that after his premature death, the immortal soul of Zarathustra-Jesus did not sojourn in the upper astral and heavenly planes of existence, as is usual between incarnations. Amazingly instead, his discarnate ego-bearer immediately descended into the pliant vehicles of the twelve-year-old Jesus-Immanuel. Since Zarathustra-Jesus was also a bodhisattva-being, the indwelling process was similar to that of Jesus-Pandira by the Bodhisattva-Maitreya; the main difference being that usually the indwelling occurs later in life (between the ages of thirty and thirty-three).

The indwelling of the Bodhisattva-Zarathustra explains the radical transformation that suddenly occurred in the twelve-year-old Jesus-Immanuel. Once again, this indwelling was cosmically pre-planned as further necessary preparation for the Messiah. Since the soul of Jesus-Immanuel (as the heavenly-Adam) had been indwelt three times in the remote past by the Solar-Christos, the penetration and permeation by the Bodhisattva-Zarathustra was not an unusual or traumatic experience.

According to esoteric investigation, this particular indwelling was a combination of "ensoulment" and "enspiritment"; that is, the penetration and permeation of both the astral body *and* the ego-bearer. As stated by Rudolf Steiner:

> From the twelfth year onwards, therefore, Zarathustra was able to continue his development in the astral body and Ego-vehicle of the Nathan Jesus. (Lecture 6 given in 1910 and published in *The Gospel of Matthew*)

Though in this instance, the etheric and physical bodies of Jesus-Immanuel were not *directly* infused, the Bodhisattva-Zarathustra could still *indirectly* influence and guide them by arousing the necessary astral impulses which in turn stimulated the etheric body which, thereupon, activated physical motion and behaviour.

While the mutual sharing of the same bodily vehicles was selflessly undertaken by both Jesus-individualities, it was also an enormous personal benefit for each of them. In the case of Jesus-Immanuel, with the early indwelling of the Bodhisattva-Zarathustra, his own virginal vehicles were infused with the worldly-wisdom, life-experience, cultural refinement and multi-talented expertise of one of the foremost human initiates in history. As for the Bodhisattva-Zarathustra, he had the sanctioned and unconditional use of unique bodily vehicles that were immaculately free from any incarnational stain of Luciferic corruption and limitation.

It must be clearly understood that this indwelling process did not result in a kind of unhealthy personality split or bipolar disorder. The virginal-ego of Jesus-Immanuel was not independently resistant to the guidance and direction of the indwelling Bodhisattva-Zarathustra; but rather had the innate cosmic capacity to selflessly and seamlessly unite with another ego-individuality. In the process, the faint child-like sense of self possessed by Jesus-Immanuel was simply raised up and expanded by the more powerful ego-awareness of the Bodhisattva-Zarathustra. For a time, then, Jesus-Immanuel completely identified with the ego-self of his benevolent indweller. If he were to express this in words, it would be: "I am one with the greater-self of the Bodhisattva in me. My thoughts are one with the thoughts of the Bodhisattva; my feelings are one with his; and my will is in complete agreement with his own." In an esoteric sense, then, Jesus-Immanuel assumed the wisdom, power and authority of the Bodhisattva-Zarathustra; he does not lose his own sense of self in the process.

In an indwelling such as this, it is important to keep in mind that the bodily-vehicles belong to the "person," the ego-identity of Jesus-Immanuel, not to the Bodhisattva-Zarathustra. Jesus-Immanuel remains the same person throughout the indwelling; he is merely transformed, not annihilated. The Bodhisattva-Zarathustra is only a temporary "occupier." Neither does he become the person of Jesus-Immanuel; he is only there to assist him in a supportive capacity to help prepare for his future role as Messiah.

With the indwelling influence and assistance of the Bodhisattva-Zarathustra that began in his twelfth year, Jesus-Immanuel, together with his own pristine nature, rapidly acquired the mantle of high adeptship; he became an "instant initiate." From this moment in history, until his baptism at the age of thirty in the Jordan River, he is esoterically referred to as "Jesus of Nazareth" or the "Nazarene-Master." Again as a reminder, Jesus of Nazareth is *one* person: he is Jesus-Immanuel suffused with the forces of the Bodhisattva-Zarathustra. Jesus of Nazareth is not two persons; nor is he the person of the Bodhisattva-Zarathustra.

The Complex Preparation of the World Saviour

No doubt to anyone familiar with the conventional understanding of Jesus of Nazareth, all the foregoing esoteric detail must seem needlessly complex and confusing. The uncomplicated belief in the "simple man of Nazareth" seems to get lost in a deluge of technicalities. But on logical reflection, it shouldn't come as a complete surprise that the central figure in all of human evolution—the Saviour of the World—required extensive, exacting, meticulous and extraordinary preparation. Think of the expensive and detailed preparation in today's world for the diplomatic visitation of an important political figure, such as the queen of England or the president of the United States. Shouldn't the arrival of the World Saviour require even greater preparation—physical *and* supernatural?

The inescapable truth is that behind the most ordinary events of physical life profound supersensible forces and beings are at work. While many seekers strive for simple solutions and explanations to life's difficult questions, the fact remains that the details of life (particularly world-altering events) are always exceedingly deep and complex. As clearly expressed by Rudolf Steiner:

> Events of great sublimity take place at the beginning of our era. When, as so often happens, people say that the truth should be simple, this is due to indolence and a dislike of having to wrestle with many concepts; but the greatest truth can be apprehended only when the spiritual faculties are exerted to their utmost capacity. If considerable efforts are needed to describe a machine, it is surely unreasonable to demand that the greatest truths should be the simplest! Truth is inevitably complicated,

and the most strenuous efforts must be made if it is desired to acquire some understanding of the truths relating to the Events of Palestine. Nobody should lend himself to the objection that the facts are unduly complicated; they are complicated because here we have to do with the greatest of all happenings in the evolution of the Earth. (Lecture given in 1909; published in *The Gospel of St. Luke*)

The Adult Life of Jesus of Nazareth

At a certain point in historical time, then, there were no longer two extraordinary Jesus-children living in Nazareth, only one. From the ages of twelve to thirty, there only existed the one extraordinary person of Jesus of Nazareth. In a very real sense, Jesus of Nazareth was a brilliant fusion of the two best human natures that the world had to offer: the high-initiate, bodhisattva-nature of Zarathustra and the angel-like, virginal-nature of the heavenly-Adam—united together in one person, the individuality of Jesus-Immanuel. Not only that, but into the astral vehicles of this already exceptional human being there radiated the powerful superphysical forces of a third illustrious human nature, that of Gautama Buddha. Lord Gautama's involvement in the developmental life of Jesus of Nazareth clearly demonstrates the fact that even though he no longer incarnates in the physical world since attaining the level of buddhahood (around 600 BC), he still continues to greatly assist struggling humanity from the higher planes of existence.

According to esoteric research, shortly after the age of twelve, the young Jesus of Nazareth became part of a large blended family due to the two parental deaths that were mentioned earlier. At first his new step-brothers and step-sisters held him in high regard, recognizing the immense intellectual gifts and talents that he now demonstrated (due to the indwelling influence of the Bodhisattva-Zarathustra). They naturally expected that their exceptional step-brother would bring the family wealth and prestige when he reached adulthood and took his place in the world.

Unfortunately for them, they were sorely disappointed when the young Nazarene-Master embarked on a series of journeys throughout the Middle East, Asia and Europe. The step-siblings were not aware that these pilgrimage-journeys were under the sponsorship and arrangement of notable mystic masters (including the Persian Magi) who wanted to provide the young Jesus of Nazareth with a comprehensive training in the various ancient esoteric traditions of East and West. To Jesus' step-brothers and step-sisters, he was critically regarded as an irresponsible adventurer who contributed nothing to the family's material welfare. Jesus' step-mother Mary, however, recognized and understood the importance of his secretive journeys to foreign lands. As described in *The Aquarian Gospel of Jesus the Christ*:

> Then Jesus went his way [home from Assyria] and after many days crossed the Jordan to his native land. At once he sought his home in Nazareth. His mother's heart was filled with joy … but Jesus' brothers were not pleased … they called him indolent, ambitious, vain; a worthless fortune hunter; searcher of the world for fame, who after many years returns to his mother's home with neither gold, nor any wealth. And Jesus called aside his mother and her sister, Miriam, and told them of his journey to the East. He told them of the lessons he had learned, and the works that he had done. To others, he told not the story of his life. (Levi H. Dowling)

Much of the heart-felt joy experienced by Jesus' step-mother was the gradual intuitive experience of her own deceased son, the Zarathustra-Jesus, brightly shining through the words and actions of her mysterious step-son. Likewise, the soul of Jesus-Immanuel (the heavenly-Adam) was wondrously filled with the joy of perceiving *his* own deceased mother (the heavenly-Eve) shining through the person of his adoring step-mother.

While it is not necessary here to repeat the profound details of Jesus' many travels between the ages of twelve and thirty (the so-called "lost years") that have been meticulously chronicled in *The Aquarian Gospel of Jesus the Christ*, an accurate summation from *Mystic Christianity or the Inner Teachings of the Master* (1935) is provided instead:

> The occult legends inform us that He [Jesus of Nazareth] aroused great interest among the people of each land visited by Him, and that He also aroused the most bitter opposition among the priests, for He always opposed formalism and priestcraft, and sought to lead the people back to the Spirit of Truth, and away from the ceremonies and forms which had always served to dim and becloud the Light of the Spirit. He taught always the Fatherhood of God and the Brotherhood of Man. (Yogi Ramacharaka)

Though the akashic research provided by Rudolf Steiner does not mention much of Jesus' foreign travels (except for a significant supersensible experience at a decadent, pagan worship site) there is clear acknowledgement in a lecture given in 1913 that these journeys took place:

> When in his sixteenth, seventeenth and eighteenth years, Jesus of Nazareth began to journey about the country, he came to know the centres of heathen rites ... These journeyings continued throughout his twentieth, twenty-second, twenty-fourth years ... Working in different families, at various branches of his craft, he travelled through Palestine, and also through neighbouring heathen districts, led thither by his karma. (Published in *The Fifth*

Gospel, 2007)

The different akashic transcriptions provided in *The Aquarian Gospel of Jesus the Christ* and in *The Fifth Gospel* informatively complement each other, since Steiner's description emphasizes the inner soul experiences of Jesus of Nazareth during these years, rather than the external details of his travels that are well described by Dowling. Moreover, Steiner provides valuable specifics concerning Jesus' interaction with the Essene community in Nazareth that are not mentioned by Dowling.

According to Steiner's research, the more Jesus of Nazareth learned of the world's religious beliefs and sacred mysteries, the more anguished and sorrowful his soul became. The closer he approached thirty years of age, the peak of his powers as a highly-developed initiate, the clearer he realized that the ancient fountain of esoteric wisdom had dried up. Humanity had become almost entirely cut-off from the supernatural world and, therefore, no longer had open access to life-sustaining supersensible forces and beings. Material darkness was extinguishing the radiant light of the spirit, and inner darkness had correspondingly crept into his own sensitive soul. The anguish in his own heart echoed the world-wide anguish burning in the depths of spirit-starved human souls which desperately cried out to God for help, for a saviour, for a messiah.

At the depth of this dark night of the soul, just prior to his Baptism in the Jordan, the Bodhisattva-Zarathustra abruptly vacated the supersensitized vehicles of Jesus-Immanuel. There was no further perfection that the bodhisattva could induce by continuing to permeate the selfless soul of Jesus-Immanuel. His sudden departure, however, predictably left Jesus-Immanuel disordered, weakened and confused. Once again, to outer perception, all hope of raising-up a world-saviour appeared desperately lost. But as Jesus-Immanuel instinctually followed the inspired voice of John the Baptist and stepped into the waters of the Jordan, his compassionate soul inwardly cried aloud to God for humanitarian salvation. And as occurred three times before in the superphysical realms during ancient times, his anguished plea touched the heart of God, was divinely heard and cosmically answered—through the benign intervention of the Solar-Christos.

CHAPTER 3

THE MYSTERY OF REDEMPTION AND RESURRECTION: THE HYPOSTATIC UNION OF GOD AND MAN

3.1 The Esoteric Epiphany: The Baptism in the Jordan and the Birth of Christ-Jesus

Epiphany: The Exoteric and Esoteric Understandings

IN WESTERN CHRISTIANITY, Epiphany is a feast day, traditionally celebrated on January 6, that commemorates the "appearance" or "manifestation" (in Greek: epiphaneia) of Christ-Jesus. This is principally (but not exclusively) understood to be the appearance of the Christ-child to the three Magi.

In Eastern Orthodox Christianity, however, Epiphany (also called "Theophany") celebrates the appearance or manifestation of Christ-Jesus as the "Son of God," which occurred during the baptism in the Jordan River. Furthermore, the birth or "incarnation of Christ-Jesus" is also traditionally celebrated on January 6.

This variation of conventional Epiphanic celebrations appears somewhat arbitrary, disconnected and conflicting. For example, if the birth of Christ-Jesus is universally celebrated on December 25, why is the incarnation also celebrated on January 6? Moreover, what has the Messiah's birth got to do with his baptism?

These questions are best resolved by esoteric Christianity. As understood through supersensible investigation, it was during the baptism in the Jordan River that Jesus-Immanuel (the incarnated heavenly-Adam) was transformed into Christ-Jesus—the "Promised Messiah" and "Saviour of the World." Conventional Christianity, both East and West, makes no distinction between the newborn child-Jesus and the adult baptized Jesus. God's pronouncement at the Baptism that Jesus was his "beloved Son" is held to be merely a confirmation of what was already true at the moment of his miraculous conception—that he was the incarnation of the Son of God and the Promised Messiah.

According to esoteric Christianity, however, when Jesus-Immanuel was born in Bethlehem, he was certainly an extraordinary virgin-soul, but not the Promised Messiah. From the age of twelve to the age of thirty, through the indwelling presence of the Bodhisattva-Zarathustra, he became the high-initiate, Jesus of Nazareth. But it was only when baptized by John, that Jesus-Immanuel became the Promised Messiah, Christ-Jesus.

When the recently-vacated and disoriented Jesus-Immanuel was baptized according to John's usual method, he was forcibly and deliberately held under the water to the point of drowning. This had the near-death effect of temporarily ejecting the etheric, astral and ego-bearing vehicles from his physical body. In this sudden out-of-body condition, the anguished soul of Jesus-Immanuel sacrificially placed himself entirely in the hands of God for the salvation of humanity. As had similarly occurred in the supersensible realm on three, separate ancient instances, his prayer was answered by the downpouring infusion of the Solar-Christos, the regent of the sun. But whereas previously the Solar-Christos merely "ensouled" the superphysical vehicles of the heavenly-Adam, at the baptism in the Jordan the Solar-Christos extended his celestial power deep into the physical body as well. In an esoteric sense, then, he actually "incarnated" in the supersensitized vehicles of Jesus-Immanuel. Through this indwelling union with the Solar-Christos, Jesus-Immanuel became Christ-Jesus, the Promised Messiah. To esoteric Christianity, then, the baptism in the Jordan is in truth the incarnational birth of Christ-Jesus.

The Regent of the Sun Descends to the Earth

In order to indwell the bodily vehicles of Jesus-Immanuel at the baptismal event, the Solar-Christos had to depart the superphysical realm of the sun—at least, in part. As a highly-advanced celestial initiate, the lowest vehicle of expression for the Solar-Christos had risen to the level of life-spirit (see Figure 7). Additionally, as an archangel, he also retained the knowledge and capacity to manifest denser vehicles of expression down to the level of an astral form. As a solar being, however, any manifestation of these denser vehicles would naturally be superplanetary in power and majesty.

In order to descend to the earth, then, the Solar-Christos had to fashion for himself a superplanetary vehicle of spirit-self and a superplanetary soul vehicle or ego-bearer. Not surprisingly, these two vehicles were established over hundreds of years as the Solar-Christos gradually prepared the Hebrew people for his physical indwelling (see Figure 10 below). Fashioning these vehicles was analogous to the superphysical process accomplished by an ordinary incarnating human being who is preparing for physical birth.

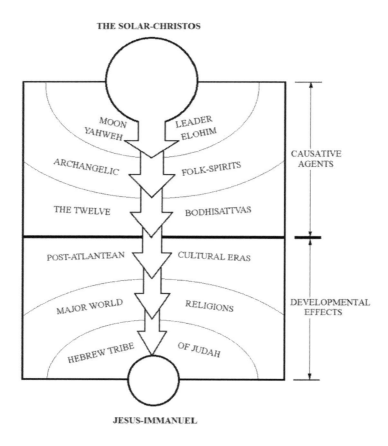

Figure 10: The Historical Stages of Incarnation Preparation by the Solar-Christos

According to esoteric research, throughout the gradual descent of the Solar-Christos to earth, his higher vehicles—down to the level of spirit-body—continued to remain in the supersensible periphery of the sun. While his superplanetary life-spirit was the highest vehicle that descended to the earth, it did not indwell the bodily vehicles of Jesus-Immanuel, but instead remained in the supersensible periphery of the earth. Similarly, though the superplanetary spirit-self of the Solar-Christos was conjoined with the bodily vehicles of Jesus-Immanuel, it remained external to them. It was only the ego-bearer of the Solar-Christos that entered into Jesus-Immanuel at the baptism. And of course this powerful superplanetary vehicle could not fully penetrate and indwell the bodily vehicles of Jesus-Immanuel without them being completely shattered. For the physical health and safety of the host vehicles, the greater part of the superplanetary substance and forces of the Solar-Christos had to remain peripherally, manifesting as an immense and glorious supersensible aura that enveloped Jesus-Immanuel.

Gradually, over the course of three and a half years—from the baptism to the ascension—the powerful superplanetary forces of the Solar-Christos entered more and more deeply into the entire physical constitution of Jesus-Immanuel, helping to transform, redeem and resurrect it.

Through Christ-Jesus the "Word Became Flesh"

At an even deeper level of esoteric understanding, the baptism of Jesus-Immanuel is much more than just another historical instance of a lawful indwelling of one being by another. Since the highest germinal-vehicle of the Solar-Christos reaches up to the universal love-principle of the Logos-Word, by uniting himself with the Sun-Being, Jesus-Immanuel[15] became directly connected to the macrocosmic being of the Logos-Word. Reciprocally, the Logos-Word was thereby directly connected to a physical human being on earth. At the baptism, then, the Word "became flesh" through the intermediary indwelling of the Solar-Christos which conjoined the bodily vehicles of Jesus with the universal principle-nature of the cosmos. In a very real esoteric sense, then, Christ-Jesus truly became the "incarnation of the Word" (see Figure 11 below).

THE PERSONS, PRINCIPLES, AND VEHICLES OF EXPRESSION	THE GREAT HIERARCHY OF BEING	THE UNION OF GOD AND MAN
GOD THE FATHER	THE TRIUNE GOD	
GOD THE SON		
GOD THE MOTHER		
UNIVERSAL WILL	THE LOGOS WORD	
UNIVERSAL LOVE		
UNIVERSAL WISDOM		
COSMIC WISDOM	SERAPHIM	
COSMIC LOVE	CHERUBIM	CHRISTOS
COSMIC WILL	THRONES	
SPIRIT-BODY	DOMINIONS	THE SOLAR-
LIFE-SPIRIT	VIRTUES	
SPIRIT-SELF	POWERS	
EGO-BEARER	PRINCIPALITIES	
ASTRAL BODY	ARCHANGELS	
ETHERIC BODY	ANGELS	JESUS-IMMANUEL
PHYSICAL BODY	HUMANS	

Figure 11: The Hypostatic Union of God and Man

As Christ-Jesus (that is, through the indwelling influence of the Christ-being), Jesus experienced in clear, day-consciousness the oneness with Universal Life—with the Living Word—that he had only instinctively and unconsciously retained in the supersensible realms as the heavenly-Adam. Moreover, through this conscious union, the thoughts, feelings and actions of Christ-Jesus could be directly influenced and empowered by the macrocosmic impulses of the Logos-Word. Naturally these macrocosmic forces worked more powerfully and penetratingly into the physical constitution of the man Jesus than even the superplanetary forces of the Christ-being.

Christ-Jesus as the "Son of God"

Since the universal love-principle is the highest macrocosmic reflection of God the Son, impulses of divine love flow directly into the heart of the Word at this empyrean level of consciousness. At his highest level of attainment, the Christ-being has germinally unfolded the universal love-principle and thereby has united himself with the Word. In consequence, impulses of divine love from the Son directly flow into his own vehicles of expression.

When Christ united his lower vehicles with Jesus at the baptism, a direct connection was established between the human physical body and the divine nature of the Son (see Figure 11). For the first time in human history, impulses of divine love could directly well-up from within the purified soul—penetrating to the very depths of physical existence—thereby fundamentally spiritualizing fallen human nature.

Previously, divine forces could only affect human nature indirectly, and from without (that is, through the external actions of less-advanced celestial beings). Unfortunately, the increasingly darkening effects of Luciferic and Ahrimanic interference on the souls and bodies of all mankind could not be halted and reversed through external means without seriously compromising human free-will. True redemption could only begin *within* the physical constitution of a willing human participant who had "hypostatically" united himself to God. That individual was Christ-Jesus.

The baptismal moment of union between Man (Christ-Jesus) and God (the Son) is biblically indicated by the proclamation: "This is my beloved Son, with whom I am well pleased" (Matt 3:17); or, as translated by esoteric Christianity: "This is my Son, imbued with my love, in whom I manifest myself" (Rudolf Steiner: *The Gospel of St. John and Its Relation to the other Gospels*; 1982). Hereafter, Christ-Jesus is accurately understood as "the Son of God"—that is, as being hypostatically united with the Eternal-Son through the intermediation of the Logos-Word.

The "Hypostatic Union" of Human and Divine – The Fusion of One Person in God

Esoteric Christianity is in agreement with the infallibly declared truth of the Catholic faith that: "The Divine and the human natures are united hypostatically in Christ; that is, joined to each other in one Person." How this occurred, however, is understood quite differently between the two viewpoints.

Simply stated, in Western theology the understanding is that the Person of the Son singly and without intermediation united himself with human nature by a miraculous physical conception at the Annunciation. In esoteric Christianity, however, the deeper understanding is that the divine person of the Son, together with the human person of Jesus, reciprocally united in a condition of hypostatic "oneness," through the intermediation of the Solar-Christos and the Logos-Word, at the baptism in the Jordan. In a more pictorial sense, at the baptism, the Son reached down through the Word and through Christ to unite with Jesus; while Jesus reached up through Christ and the Word to unite with the Son (see Figure 12 below).

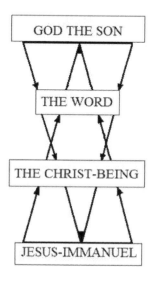

Figure 12: The Reciprocal Union of Persons

It would initially appear that to esoteric understanding there are four persons united in Christ-Jesus: (1) the human person of Jesus, (2) the celestial person of Christ, (3) the macrocosmic person of the Word, and (4) the divine person of the Son. But this would be quite incorrect; there is only one person—the divine person of the Son. To best understand how this occurs, a basic familiarity with the experience of "spiritual oneness" (also termed "mystical marriage") is necessary.[16]

In the case of Jesus, the indwelling by Christ was not experienced as a bipolar split in personality, or a loss of identity, or sense of self. Rather, the undeveloped consciousness of Jesus was raised and expanded by the indwelling, celestial consciousness of Christ; such that his own sense of self became "Christ-like" in power, wisdom and love. In this state of mystical oneness, Jesus was able to truthfully declare that "Christ and I are one." Moreover, since Christ himself, at the highest levels of his own attainment, experiences a mystical oneness with the Word, Jesus (through the indwelling of Christ) could similarly experience a small measure of this universal consciousness. During moments of macrocosmic elation, he was also able to truthfully declare that "the Word and I are one."

Furthermore, since the Word (at the highest universal levels) faithfully reflects the spiritual light of the Son, Jesus was able to glimpse the glory of the Son sparkling down through the embryonic Word-nature of Christ. At those uplifting moments, Jesus was able to experience that "the Son and I are one." He was the first human being to truthfully and knowingly declare: "I am the Son of God." In this state of spiritual oneness, as a created life-form, Jesus became one with his true self—the person of the Son. In the hypostatic union of Jesus, Christ, the Word and God, there is ultimately only one true person—the person of the Son.

Having realized his true God-self through the indwelling consciousness of Christ, Jesus became the first human "Son of God."[17] This attainment, however, did not mark the fulfillment of human redemption; but rather, just the beginning. Through the spiritual oneness with the person of the Son and the realization of inner God-consciousness, the arduous task of undoing the death-dealing consequences of the Fall could now begin within the human constitution of Christ-Jesus.

3.2 Directing the Power of God: The Temptations in the Wilderness

Beginning the Process of Human Redemption

Immediately following the hypostatic union that occurred during the baptism, whereby Christ-Jesus became the Son of God, it was crucially important for him to decide how best to begin the process of human redemption.

With the blinding realization that, through the indwelling Christ, he was the Promised Messiah whose mission was the salvation of mankind (and the world), Jesus intuitively sought out a secluded area of the surrounding countryside—away from the distractions of Nature and society—in order to be alone with God. There was no more bleak and desolate place to be alone than the Judaean Desert, also known as the "Wilderness of Judah." In that "god-forsaken" landscape, the Promised Messiah was best able to listen to the "still, small voice" of God that rose up within his own nature.[18] Unfortunately, Christ-Jesus was not entirely alone in the Wilderness—Lucifer and Ahriman were supersensibly "lying in wait" to thwart the redemptive mission of the Promised Messiah.

With the hypostatic union, the superplanetary forces of Christ, the macrocosmic forces of the Word, and the divine forces of the Son were freely made available to the will of Christ-Jesus. In other words, powerful supernatural forces could be used by Christ-Jesus for the redemption of mankind—but "how best to use them?"—that was the pressing question in the Wilderness. Since Luciferic and Ahrimanic intrusion into human affairs had resulted in seriously fractured and dysfunctional social relationships that fettered mankind to the earth, could redemption be accomplished by supernaturally changing human society? In dealing with this question, the Messiah separately considered the three primary spheres of human society: economic, religious and political.

The First Temptation in the Wilderness: The Miraculous Economic Solution

In the consideration of Christ-Jesus to use his supernatural ability to "turn stones into bread," this was much more than just a miraculous method to relieve his own hunger in the Wilderness. It was a consideration to end world hunger and poverty by using his miraculous powers to establish a fair and equitable world economy; that is, to alchemically create gold (to "use stone") to care and feed (to "create bread") for the world's poor and hungry.[19] Such a course of action would indeed have wrested oppressive economic control from the grip of Ahriman, but it would also have prevented human beings from ending world hunger and poverty themselves, through their own free moral development.

The Messiah's scripturally-recorded rejection of this social course of redemption on the grounds that "Man shall not live by bread alone, but by every word that proceeds from the mouth of God" (Matt 4:4), also indicates that he understood that simply satisfying mankind's material requirements would not satisfy the more important spiritual needs that true redemption required.

For these reasons, Christ-Jesus rejected such a supernatural option to remedy the economic ills of fallen humanity. Biblically, it is understood that "the devil" presented Christ-Jesus with this social option; esoterically speaking, it was Ahriman (Satan) himself who cleverly suggested this initial "temptation" to Christ-Jesus.

The Second Temptation in the Wilderness: The Miraculous Religious Solution

In order to address the spiritual deficiencies of fallen humanity, the Messiah also considered using his miraculous powers to establish an exalted world religion. With public displays of his supernatural powers, such as levitation ("throwing himself from the pinnacle of the temple"), he could easily convince all mankind that he was the Son of God. He could transform the Temple in Jerusalem to a glory greater than that of Solomon, and establish a resplendent worldwide Jewish faith with himself as the perpetual high priest.

Unfortunately, such a course of action would not enable human souls to unite with God within themselves. They would be entirely dependent on an external, priestly Messiah for spiritual guidance and direction; thereby losing the free-will capacity to spiritually develop on their own. Once again, Christ-Jesus rejected a second temptation in the wilderness to redeem fallen humanity through miraculous social means.

Since this supernatural, religious solution would involve extravagant, supernatural displays of pomp and ceremony—thereby greatly appealing to human vanity, pride and excess—it is easy to conclude that Lucifer was the principal instigator of this particular temptation.[20]

The Third Temptation in the Wilderness: The Miraculous Political Solution

The third major test in the Wilderness, of the Messiah's moral strength and courage, involved the political sphere of human society. In this instance, the temptation was to use his supernatural power as the Son of God to forever end human warfare and civil strife. Using his miraculous abilities, he could easily assume the throne of King David, and establish himself as the divinely-appointed king of the Jews. Further employing his supernatural powers, he could assemble a vast army and defeat every enemy of Israel, making it the foremost nation on earth. As the undisputed head of worldwide governance, he could put an end to war as one of the brutal consequences of the Fall.

Once again, to enact such a social scenario would necessitate the perpetual negation of human free-will. Essentially, mankind would become the passive, servile subjects of a benevolent dictator; which would hardly be a true redemptive solution. Thankfully, Christ-Jesus rejected this course of action as well.

Since this temptation was, at its centre, a desire for personal world domination, no doubt Lucifer *and* Ahriman (who are both consumed with megalomaniacal intentions) were joint instigators of this scenario.

3.3   The True Plan of Redemption: The Road to Calvary

True Redemption as an Individual Process

Having heroically engaged his highest moral wisdom and strength to reject the three major temptations to use his supernatural power to redemptively assist mankind by outwardly changing human society, it became abundantly clear to Christ-Jesus that true redemption could only be an individual process of body and soul.[21] Any global application of supernatural force, in any of the three social spheres of human activity (economic, religious or political), would seriously interfere with the development of individual free-will, thereby resulting in a paralyzing condition of "psychic enslavement," rather than true redemption.

In order to preserve human free-will so that mankind could continue to become truly independent sons and daughters of God, the Messiah realized that he could not socially impose redemption on unwilling human beings. Since each person had to freely choose the path of redemption, the Son of God clearly understood that he must forge that path himself in order to become the guide and "way shower"—not the benevolent dictator. By the free, internal redemption of the individual, human society would naturally be redeemed as well.

To forge the path of redemption for all mankind, the Messiah concluded that he must live "as a man among men"; that he could not exist socially aloof and apart as the divinely-appointed "global chief economist, universal high priest and supreme world leader." By choosing to live as an ordinary member of society, he could use his advanced wisdom to set an example of how to properly live: how to think, feel and act without Luciferic or Ahrimanic interference. By setting a visible example in his own life, it would leave others free to follow or not; which would, thereby, not compromise their own free-will capacity.

By living an ordinary life, any outward display of supernatural power would be reserved for special circumstances, mainly to do with healing, education or protection. Moreover, such instances would be carefully chosen to avoid the inclination of those involved becoming dependent on the Messiah for supernatural solutions to their everyday problems.

The Problem of Death

A further serious consequence of Luciferic and Ahrimanic interference, which could not be redeemed by any supernatural change of human society was, of course, death.

While the Messiah could certainly use his supernatural power to perpetuate his own bodily existence, and thereby avoid death for himself, all other human beings would continue to die.

The problem was that corruption of the human astral and etheric bodies, through the actions of Lucifer and Ahriman, had resulted in an increasing densification and materialization of the physical body. Consequently, the materials and forces of the physical body became increasingly subject to the earthly forces of gravity, magnetism and electricity; as well as certain subterranean (chemical and nuclear) forces of destruction.

The unfortunate result, then, was that since ancient Lemurian times, the human physical form increasingly fell prey to sickness, impairment, deterioration, damage and decay. In order to continue to progress, the human soul needed to regularly abandon disrepairable physical bodies and to rebuild new ones; that is to say—it needed to repeatedly die.[22] Prior to the Lemurian Fall, the human form was transparent, and it existed in a rarified condition above the surface of the earth. Powerful life forces continually rejuvenated, metamorphosed and replicated it—such that it was essentially immortal.

If the physical form had continued to densify and to materially harden, in time the soul would have needed to abandon it altogether as an ineffective vehicle of expression, which would have brought an abrupt end to human evolution on earth. This dire consequence had to be prevented by the progressive beings who guide human destiny; otherwise there would have been a damaging "ripple-effect" throughout the cosmos.

How Was Death to be Overcome and Eliminated from Human Evolution?

In order to halt the downward decline of the human physical body, and to raise it back up to its former condition of immortality, it was of course necessary to undo thousands of years of damage effected by Luciferic and Ahrimanic intrusion. Since this damage was caused by powerful regressive celestial-beings, and unprevented by equally powerful progressive celestial-beings, it was obviously beyond any human capacity to rectify. The powerful celestial-being who, out of divine love for humanity, sacrificially chose to restore the physical human form, and thereby eliminate the need for death, was of course the sun-being, Christ.

Christ, then, purposely united with Jesus at the Baptism in order to overcome physical death so mankind could continue its important evolutionary destiny on earth. With his moral victory over the three temptations in the Wilderness, it was thereafter clear to Christ-Jesus that, to begin human redemption, he needed firstly to direct his prodigious supernatural powers internally, not externally, in order to completely heal and fully restore his own astral, etheric and physical bodies.

Even though Jesus, as the heavenly-Adam, was benignly protected from Luciferic and Ahrimanic intrusion in the superphysical realm; and Christ, as the regent of the sun, was also unaffected by their regressive effects, in order for the Messiah to incarnate and "live among men," it was still necessary to inhabit astral, etheric and physical bodies that had been densified and materialized by the Fall. By doing so, Christ-Jesus (as expressed biblically) "took on the sins of the world so as to save mankind." Occupying these densified forms meant that they were also subject to mortal corruption and in need of constant revitalization and repair.

Moreover, even though these vehicles of expression had been vibrationally raised to a higher level of development through the prior indwelling of the Bodhisattva-Zarathustra, they were still subject to the shattering effects of powerful supernatural forces instreaming from Christ, the Word and the Son. In order to fully experience and transform his own human life as "the Way, the Truth and the Life;" that is, as the one real path to redemption, the Messiah understood in the Wilderness that he must also die. Only by experiencing death himself, and overcoming it through divine assistance, could this also become a free-will possibility for others. In his own words:

> "I lay down my life, that I may take it again. No one takes it from me, but I lay it down of my own accord. I have power to lay it down, and I have power to take it again; this charge I have received from my Father." (John 10:17, 18)

At the conclusion of his moral testing in the Wilderness, Christ-Jesus had clear foreknowledge that his life as a man among men would end abruptly and brutally in a premature death. A life dedicated to courageously speaking the truth and always doing what was morally upright and good, would predictably arouse the murderous intent of corrupt and evil-minded civic and religious authorities. Prior to beginning his mission on earth, then, the Promised Messiah resolutely understood that the path he had chosen for mankind's redemption would lead him inevitably to Calvary—to a horrific death by crucifixion.

3.4   Becoming "the Way, the Truth and the Life"

Morally Transforming the Human Astral Body

The moral testing of the temptations in the Wilderness began the Messiah's supernatural work of renewing and restoring the darkened and densified astral body. This transformative work was to continue for the next three and a half years through the daily moral choices that were required in living amongst his fellow man. Key to establishing a redemptive "way" of living—a new code of moral conduct that would permanently heal and rectify the weakened astral body—was the superhealing power of divine love. Of all the superplanetary and macrocosmic power available to Christ-Jesus, none was more efficacious than the impulses of divine love streaming into his soul and body from the Son. This was a love that was new to humanity; an all-embracing love that transcended the boundaries of gender, family, tribe, nation, race—even species. This was a love issuing from the very heart of God that embraced all of creation.

The new way of life exemplified and established by Christ-Jesus, then, grew out of the seed of divine love that was planted in his soul by the Son. Soon after the moral testing in the Wilderness, as he began the daily events of his life teaching and healing throughout the lands of Israel, the Messiah gathered together a few loyal disciples and a large crowd of interested followers to outline his new code of moral conduct—the "way of love." These new soul-transformative moral principles, that have become the ethical foundation of "true Christian life," are together known as the Sermon on the Mount.

The Sermon on the Mount: Overcoming Sin and Evil

The densification and darkening of the "fallen" astral vehicle eventually began to seriously impair mankind's relationship with the superphysical realm. Though this corruption of the astral body (together with the etheric and physical bodies) was initiated by regressive Luciferic and Ahrimanic beings, mankind was not simply a passive spectator to the process; but was instead an active—though naïve—participant. Lemurian humanity, soon after receiving the spark of self-conscious awareness and the accompanying gift of an independent will, was "seduced" into misdirecting this free-will capacity in ways that were contrary to the natural, God-given laws of harmony and health. This resulted in a gradual vibratory debasement of astral substance that would later affect etheric and physical substance as well. This misuse of free-will is termed, in Western theology, "sin."

Sin, then, has the negative effect of darkening and estranging the human soul (astral body) from the heavenly realm (that is, from God). "Evil" is here understood as the deliberate and knowing application of free-will to sin; that is, to intentionally "turn away" from God. By the time of the Messiah's incarnation, the majority of mankind—through sin and evil—had entirely lost the once innate clairvoyant experience of celestial beings and supernatural events. Even after death, when the soul was separated from the body, perception of the superphysical realm grew increasingly dark and gloomy. In a very real sense, then, mankind could no longer "enter heaven"—before or after death. The Messiah's Sermon on the Mount was formulated to change all that.

The Sermon on the Mount: "The Way Back to Heaven"

The overarching moral directive of the Sermon on the Mount was "Repent: for the kingdom of heaven is at hand" (Matt 4:17). In other words, "Turn away from your old destructive behaviour (from sin and evil), adopt the new moral principles of love, and the gates of heaven will be reopened for you, even during your lifetime." During this sermon, the Messiah presented moral admonitions that were radically different from those before, such as:

> "You have heard that it was said, 'An eye for an eye and a tooth for a tooth.' But I say to you, Do not resist one who is evil. But if any one strikes you on the right cheek,

turn to him the other also." (Matt 5:38, 39)

"You have heard that it was said, 'You shall love your neighbor and hate your enemy.' But I say to you, Love your enemies and pray for those who persecute you, so that you may be sons of your Father who is in heaven; for he makes his sun rise on the evil and on the good, and sends rain on the just and on the unjust." (Matt 5:43–45)

The Messiah also used the Sermon on the Mount to establish a new relationship with God and mankind, as one between a loving Father and his wayward children; and not one between a vengeful deity and his cursed creation. Moreover, Christ-Jesus also established how we should pray to our Father-God with the now-famous, "Lord's Prayer."

Out of the moral impulses of divine love, the Messiah also raised up the ancient moral laws of Moses, the Ten Commandments, to a higher code of conduct:

"Think not that I have come to abolish the law and the prophets; I have come not to abolish them but to fulfill them." (Matt 5:17)

The Law of Moses, then, was not erased or supplanted but rather suffused with the new "law of grace":

"You shall love the Lord your God with all your heart, and with all your soul, and with all your mind. This is the great and first commandment. And a second is like it, You shall love your neighbor as yourself. On these two commandments depend all the law and the prophets." (Matt 22:37–40)

Clearly, when one is filled with divine love, then the commandments of Moses will be freely enacted: one will not murder, or steal, or commit adultery, or blaspheme God, or bear false witness or covet your neighbour's possessions.

Be Perfect, as Your Father in Heaven is Perfect

Since the Sermon on the Mount was concerned with moral conduct and behaviour, the Messiah emphasized the necessity of putting his new moral principles into action; otherwise there was no redeeming effect for the individual. This was made abundantly clear in scripture, where he stated:

> "Not every one who says to me, 'Lord, Lord,' shall enter the kingdom of heaven, but he who does the will of my Father who is in heaven." (Matt 7:21)

> "Every one then who hears these words of mine and does them will be like a wise man who built his house upon the rock." (Matt 7:24)

The redemptive ladder to heaven could only be climbed by each individual, with Christ-Jesus as the sure guide. The Messiah was not a "scapegoat" [23] upon which lazy individuals could heap their sins and, thereby, redeem their soul and re-access heaven. As the way-shower back to God, Christ-Jesus in all his actions set the ideal example in his own life for all mankind to follow. He continually demonstrated the all-embracing love of God in his actions towards others. He compassionately healed the sick in body and soul; he was kind and compassionate to social outcasts, such as prostitutes and tax collectors; he treated men and women, Jew and Samaritan, family and foreigners, rich and poor, with equal dignity and respect.

By demonstrating the way back to heaven (God) in his own life, Christ-Jesus didn't just present moral teachings *about* the way; he *became* "the Way." Moreover, since the way to heaven was essentially to unite oneself with God, and Christ-Jesus was already hypostatically united with the Son, he could truthfully declare: "I am the way ... to the Father" (John 14:6).

Proclaiming "the Truth"

In his redemptive mission to reopen the gates of heaven and lead fallen humanity back to God, it was also necessary that Christ-Jesus redirect mankind's attention away from falsehood and back to the truth. Since the darkening effect of sin and evil had increasingly blinded human souls from perceiving the light of God in the superphysical realm around them, error and falsehood concerning the true facts of the physical world increased as well. The deception that the physical world was the only reality, and that the superphysical realm (including God) did not exist, increasingly took hold in the human soul. This perceptual "lie" was largely due to the corrupting influence of Ahrimanic beings; hence, Christ-Jesus referred to "the devil" (Ahriman) as "a liar and the father of lies" (John 8:44).

In redirecting human attention back to the superphysical realm and to God, after his moral victory in the Wilderness Christ-Jesus took every opportunity as an itinerant teacher to "proclaim the gospel (good news) of heaven"—to re-open mankind's eyes to the divine truth. To the uneducated multitudes, he often cloaked profound truth in allegorical form: "I will open my mouth in parables, I will utter what has been hidden since the foundation of the world" (Matt 13:35). To his initiated disciples, however, he spoke plainly and opened up "the secrets of the kingdom of heaven" (Matt 13:11).

Some of the "heavenly truth" that Christ-Jesus publically proclaimed had previously been known, but kept secret, within the confines of the ancient Mysteries. Some sacred truth was direct revelation from the Son that had never been known in the history of the world. Such was the Messiah's revealed truth concerning the divine Trinity; that the one God was a perfect unity of three divine persons: the Father, the Son and the Holy Spirit. While many ancient religions worshipped deific triads—such as Isis, Horus and Osirus in Egypt; and Brahma, Vishnu and Shiva in India—these bore little resemblance to what was revealed by Christ-Jesus. Moreover, the revelation that "God is love," that the very nature of God is divine love, was a truth that only the Son could reveal. Such sacred truths were beyond the capacity of human reasoning to logically deduce.

The Transfiguration of the Etheric Body by Divine Truth

As the new moral precepts of love established by Christ-Jesus worked to transform his astral vehicle, the revelation of sacred knowledge—the "light of divine truth"—did much to transform his etheric body. The light of divine truth has a corresponding affinity with the light ether of the physical world. Not long after the death of John the Baptist and following the miracle of the loaves and the fishes, the repeated proclamation of divine truth had so powerfully transformed the etheric body of Christ-Jesus, that for a brief period of time his physical body was "transfigured": it became semi-transparent, radiated a blinding white light and levitated above the earth. As described in *The Aquarian Gospel of Jesus the Christ*:

> Then Jesus, taking Peter, James and John, went forth unto a mountain top to pray. And as he prayed a brilliant light appeared; his form became as radiant as a precious stone; his face shone like the sun; his garments seemed as white as snow; the son of man became the son of God. He was transfigured that the men of earth might see the possibilities of man ... And [the three disciples] awoke, and saw the glory of the Lord; and more, they saw the glory of the heavenly world, for they beheld [Moses and Elijah] ... The three disciples were amazed, and suddenly

the ethers were surcharged with song, and forms as light as air moved all about the mountain top. And then from the glory of the upper world they heard a voice that said, 'This is the son of man, my chosen one to manifest the Christ to men. Let the earth hear him.' (Levi H. Dowling)

The sublime truths of existence that were revealed and proclaimed by the Messiah, then, were much more than just abstract ideas; they were vivifying knowledge that conformed to reality. The divine truth that radiated into his being from the Son was infused with life-giving, deeply transformative power. Through the realization and daily manifestation of this "living knowledge," Christ-Jesus was one with the truth. Moreover, since the highest truth is the reality of God and Christ-Jesus was already hypostatically united with the Son, he could authoritatively declare: "I am ... the truth" (John 14:6).

Declaring: "I am the Life"

The etheric body is also esoterically termed, the "life-body," since it is responsible for the life activities of the physical body; such as growth, adaptation, metabolism, movement and reproduction. As the transfiguration demonstrated, the penetration and transformation of the Messiah's etheric body had a direct impact on his physical body. By consistently and devotedly applying the moral impulses and sublime truths of divine love in his daily physical life, the forces of the Son increasingly became "the life" of the Messiah's physical body. All life in the universe, however, including physical life, derives from the One Life, God. By being hypostatically united to the Son, Christ-Jesus could also knowingly declare: "I am ... the life" (John 14:6). It was only the powerful life-forces of the Son that were able to penetrate the densest materialization of the fallen physical vehicle of Christ-Jesus and raise it back up to a heavenly condition.

3.5 The Crucifixion-Mystery: Christ-Jesus Enters the Earth

The Mineralization of the Human Body

With the increasingly densifying effects of sin and evil, the once diaphanous human form that drifted about in the steamy atmosphere of Lemuria gradually '"fell to the earth"; that is, it became increasingly subject to terrestrial matter and energy—particularly earth gravity and mineral substance. Over time, the external affinity to earthly material grew so strong that the human form began to incorporate dense mineral substance into itself; thereby becoming perceptibly visible and much heavier (more subject to gravity).

This Lemurian "fall into visibility" has been allegorically described in the Bible where ancestral humanity (Adam and Eve), after committing the first sin of free-will disobedience (eating the fruit of the tree of knowledge of good and evil), saw their bodies for the first time:

> So when the woman saw that the tree was good for food, and that it was a delight to the eyes, and that the tree was to be desired to make one wise, she took of its fruit and ate; and she also gave some to her husband, and he ate. Then the eyes of both were opened, and they knew that they were naked. (Gen 3:6, 7)

As the physical human form eventually congealed into tangible tissue, there also developed the mechanical need for a hardened internal scaffolding to support the densified body in an upright and mobile position. At first this support took the form of thick cartilage; later it would harden into bone.[24]

The slow process of densifying (mineralizing) the physical human body, then, eventually established the human skeleton.

The Lemurian "fall into flesh" is also allegorically mentioned in the Bible in a brief episode just prior to the expulsion of ancestral humanity (Adam and Eve) from the Garden of Eden (supersensible existence): "And the LORD God made for Adam and for his wife garments of skins, and clothed them" (Gen 3:21).

The Formation of the Human Skeleton

The mineral kingdom, being entirely comprised of various chemical elements, is considered by physical science to be lifeless—completely dead. Likewise, esoteric science will often refer to the mineral kingdom as "lifeless," even though supersensible research indicates that everything in the cosmos (including atomic particles) is a manifestation of the Universal Life—the Logos-Word—and therefore has some degree of life in it. Keeping this in mind, minerals are esoterically regarded as lifeless because they are not infused with an independent etheric vehicle and, hence, do not exhibit the recognized signs of life: metabolism, reproduction and so on.

Even though bone is actually comprised of living tissue (such as marrow, endosteum and periosteum), since half of the material (by weight) forming the human skeleton is "bone mineral" or carbonated calcium apatite, the skeleton can be regarded as the most lifeless structure in the physical body. As such, it is an apt symbol for death (the skull and crossbones, for example). Moreover, even though there is a general loss of bone calcium during the aging process, there is a corresponding increase in the hardening and calcification of the soft tissues of the body. Simply stated, increased mineralization of the physical body eventually leads to death. That is to say, incorporating too much lifeless material within the physical body eventually results in a completely lifeless body.

It would logically appear, then, that the mineralizing process that led to the formation of the human skeleton was antithetical to progressive human development. But surprisingly, this conclusion isn't entirely true. In order to understand this apparent contradiction, consider that the crystallizing, calcification process in the bones has a corresponding etheric and astral rarefaction that stimulates a dull form of knowing; hence the popular expression, "I feel it in my bones." Moreover, since dense matter is naturally resistant to superphysical forces, the undeveloped human soul has been able to stimulate a coarse sense of self by opposing this material resistance. The mineralized skeleton, then, has also contributed to the primitive early development of ego-awareness in humanity.[25]

Brain Mineralization Necessary for Intellectual Thinking

Furthermore, the crystallizing process as it occurs in the human brain is a necessary requirement for intellectual thinking. As explained by Rudolf Steiner in a lecture given on 28 October 1923:

In the centre of the human head within the structure of the brain there is an organ shaped like a pyramid, the pineal gland. This pineal gland, situated in the vicinity of the corpus quadrigemina and the optic thalamus secretes out of itself the so-called brain sand, minute lemon-yellow stones which lie in little heaps at one end of the pineal gland, and which are in fact the mineral element in the human head. If they do not lie there, if man does not bear this brain-sand, this mineral element, within him, he becomes an idiot or a cretin. In the case of normal people the pineal gland is comparatively large. In cretins pineal glands have been found which are actually no larger than hemp seeds; these cannot secrete the brain-sand.

It is actually in this mineral deposit that the spirit-man is situated; and this already indicates that what is living cannot harbour the spirit, but that the human spirit needs the nonliving as its centre-point, that this is above all things necessary to it as independent living spirit. (Published in *Man as Symphony of the Creative Word*; 1991)

Interestingly, the small calcifications within the pineal gland known as "brain sand" (or corpora arenacea) are hydroxylapatite crystals—the modified form of which is known as "bone mineral"—the primary material of the skeleton.

The Word Became Bone

From the foregoing, we get some indication of why the progressive beings who oversee and guide human evolution permitted the "fall into material existence." It was through the densification and mineralization of the physical body that human beings were able to develop an earthly ego and earthly intellection.[26] While this "detour into matter" can thereby serve as a temporary developmental stage in human evolution, mankind was not destined to remain an earthly being; but was to freely unfold a spiritualized self together with spiritualized cognition.

Like mold and mildew in a house, however, the problem with taking dense mineral matter into the physical body is that once it gets inside it's extremely difficult to get rid of it. While a small degree of mineralization was useful in the past, at the time of Christ-Jesus the process had not only increased but was actually accelerating. If nothing was done to halt and reverse the death-dealing process, the physical body would soon turn to stone. Human forms would quite literally become grotesque statues in the Ahrimanic graveyard of the earth. Whereupon the true destiny of humanity would come to a tragic and sorrowful end.

In order to fully redeem mankind and forever put an end to the process of death, the Messiah clearly understood that only the most powerful of supernatural forces could overcome the fierce resistance of dense matter in the physical form, and thereby eliminate the deadly effects of excessive mineralization. Only the Son-force of divine love was powerful enough to completely penetrate dense matter; not even the superplanetary forces of Christ or the macrocosmic forces of the Word were sufficient.

In the three and a half years from the Baptism to the Crucifixion, the superplanetary ego-bearing soul of Christ (and the macrocosmic forces of the Word) had penetrated deep into the physical body of Jesus. At the point of his death on the cross, the supernatural forces of the Redeemer had reached the depth of the mineralized skeleton. As the Word "became flesh" at the Baptism, the Word "became bone" at the Crucifixion. Christ-Jesus fully understood, prior to his death, that to completely "raise up" the fallen physical form it was necessary to "roll away the stone"; that is, to spiritualize the mineralized skeleton—and only divine forces could accomplish that task. His only recourse was to put his entire life in the hands of God.

The Sacrifice of Christ-Jesus on Mount Calvary

Even though Jesus (as the heavenly-Adam) and Christ (as the sun-being) had never experienced human death before, what transpired at the Crucifixion was basically the same overall process of expiration as that experienced by ordinary humanity—except for three significant differences.

The first difference was that Christ-Jesus remained fully conscious and entirely self-aware throughout the entire process; unlike the loss of consciousness that typically occurs for most souls shortly after death.

The second noteworthy difference was that the entire after-death process was furiously accelerated; what typically takes years or even centuries to work through was experienced by Christ-Jesus in less than three days (from Good Friday to Resurrection Sunday).

The third crucial difference was that the superplanetary forces of Christ, the macrocosmic forces of the Word, and the divine forces of the Son were infused into every detail of this particular death process. Not surprisingly, then, this radically transformed the entire process, and provided mankind with an enduring example of how best to die. For paradoxically, it is only by properly dying that death itself can be overcome.

As Christ-Jesus approached the final moment of his death on the cross, "crying with a loud voice, [he] said, 'Father into thy hands I commit my spirit.' And having said this he breathed his last" (Luke 23:46). With these concise and often overlooked last words, the crucified Redeemer demonstrated the true meaning of self-sacrifice as a crucial first step to overcome death—since self-sacrifice determines the correct way to exit the corporeal body and "cross over to the other side" (that is, to enter the superphysical realm).

What Christ-Jesus profoundly indicated with his dying breath was that to overcome death he had to begin by "dying to himself." As related in the Bible:

> And Jesus answered them, 'The hour has come for the Son of man to be glorified. Truly, truly, I say to you, unless a grain of wheat falls into the earth and dies, it remains alone; but if it dies, it bears much fruit. He who loves his life loses it, and he who hates his life in this world will keep it for eternal life. If any one serves me, he

must follow me; and where I am, there shall my servant be also; if any one serves me, the Father will honor him.' (John 12:23–26)

In other words, in order to consciously re-enter heaven (the supernatural realm) and to live eternally (without death), he had to offer his entire life to God; he had to "commit his entire spirit into the hands of the Father." This did not mean that it was necessary to deliberately destroy his physical body; but rather, at the threshold of the soul separating from the body, when the Messiah freely gave all that he had—his entire self-existence—back to God, then God responded by preserving and spiritualizing this free gift of self-existence; which would in due course raise him up to eternal life.

The Nature of True Sacrifice: The "Mystic Death"

To freely give up his entire self-existence to God was the ultimate sacrifice that Christ-Jesus could make in order to overcome death. But what exactly does this sacrifice involve? In numerous ancient cultures, ritual sacrifice was regarded as a means of pleasing or pacifying a wrathful or vengeful deity. In order to be efficacious, the sacrificial offering (oblation) —whether object, plant, animal or human—had to be valuable in some way, and it had to be completely destroyed (or killed).

In the case of ancient Hebrew culture, Yahweh-Elohim encouraged the practice of plant and animal sacrifice, not as an appeasement to his anger, but as a lesson in self-giving. A gift to another has more meaning when it is highly prized to the gift-giver, when it is entirely given away (nothing is held back or conditional), and when there is no thought of reward for the gift-giver. By ritually giving the best animal of the herd or the best fruits of the harvest, and then having that animal killed or foodstuff destroyed, the ancient Hebrew worshipper was giving something back to God as thanksgiving for all that God had given him. True sacrificial self-giving would, in turn, evoke unsolicited spiritual and material blessings from God.

As Christ-Jesus had established a higher standard of moral conduct by infusing the Law of Moses with divine love, so too did he establish, by his death on the cross, a higher standard of self-sacrifice by infusing it with divine love. The greatest gift that any human being can make to God is, of course, the gift of oneself—the free, unconditional gift of one's entire self-existence without thought of recompense or reward. "Committing his spirit into the hands of the Father" at the threshold of death meant that Christ-Jesus unreservedly offered up to God all that he had as a human being: his body, his soul, his thoughts, his feelings, his dreams, his abilities, his memories, his earthly possessions, and his ties to family and friends. Moreover, since the man Jesus was hypostatically united to Christ, what was also sacrificially offered up to God was the life of Christ as a superhuman being. And since Jesus and Christ were both hypostatically united to the Word, the macrocosmic life of the Word was also offered up to God. Even at the divine level, since Jesus, Christ and the Word were together hypostatically united to the Son, the person of the Son correspondingly gave himself in love to the Father-Mother God. Such was the perfect sacrifice on the cross.

By sacrificially giving his *entire* hypostatically-united life to God, the crucified Redeemer was in fact echoing the nature of divine love itself, as well as demonstrating the moral principle, "You, therefore, must be perfect, as your heavenly Father is perfect" (Matt 5:48). Since the divine nature is forever pouring forth its life for the sake of all creation with no advantage for itself (since it is already perfect), in order to unite oneself to God and to echo that perfection, each person must sacrificially do likewise.

"Dying to oneself," as Christ-Jesus demonstrated on the

cross, does not mean that one's self-existence as a created being is totally annihilated.[27] Instead, by sacrificially shedding all attraction to worldly things, the weight of the earthly ego falls away, thereby enabling the soul to ascend and spiritually unite with the true self in God. As somewhat explained by St. Paul in the Letter to the Ephesians (Chapters 4 and 5):

> Put off your old nature which belongs to your former manner of life and is corrupt through deceitful lusts, and be renewed in the spirit of your minds, and put on the new nature, created after the likeness of God in true righteousness and holiness ... Therefore be imitators of God, as beloved children. And walk in love, as Christ loved us and gave himself up for us, a fragrant offering and sacrifice to God.

As understood by esoteric Christianity, then, the sacrifice on Calvary was not a case of the Father-God ritually killing the Son-God as atonement for the sins of mankind (as professed by conventional Christianity); but instead was Christ-Jesus, the Son of God, offering up his entire life to God for divine assistance to overcome death.

The Mystic Death as a True Blood Sacrifice

As Christ-Jesus perfectly exemplified on the cross, the sacrificial act of placing one's entire self-existence in the hands of God—of "dying to oneself"—does not result in a total annihilation of self. Instead, true self-sacrifice has the profound spiritualizing effect of transmuting the lower self (earthly ego) into the higher self (heavenly ego). Not surprisingly, this spiritualizing process has an elevating effect on the physical body as well.

It is esoterically understood that the ego-soul has a particular affinity with the circulatory system of the body.

More precisely, the ego-soul finds singular expression through the warmth ether generated in red blood. Unfortunately, any corruption of the ego-soul will cause a corresponding degradation of the blood. As mankind became more and more attached to the physical, material world through Luciferic and Ahrimanic interference, the human ego-soul became increasingly earthbound. So too, blood circulation within the body became increasingly driven by the carnal passions and desires of the worldly ego-soul. As with the rest of the physical body, the blood system became increasingly densified and mineralized because of the Fall.

For the human ego-soul, then, the debasement of the blood was a downward spiral: the more earthbound the ego-soul became, the more corrupted the blood became; and the more corrupted the blood became, the more earthbound the ego-soul became. There seemed to be no end to this vicious cycle of degeneration—that is, until the mystic death of Christ-Jesus.

With the mystic death, the perfect "sacrifice of self" to God by Christ-Jesus miraculously removed most all of the residual corrupting effects still remaining in his blood. On the cross, then, the blood of Christ-Jesus was substantially purified of death-dealing mineralization and contamination. In the Gospel of John, this profound blood purification event on the cross was indicated when "one of the soldiers pierced [Christ-Jesus'] side with a spear, and at once there came out blood and water" (John 19:34).

Through the sacrifice on the cross, the purified blood of the Redeemer not only became the perfectly transmuted medium for the superplanetary ego-soul of Christ, but also the macrocosmic ego-hood forces of the Word and the divine person-hood forces of the Son. As drops of this supercharged blood fell to the earth, a numinous detonation was ignited in the etheric envelope of the earth. The entire planetary ether was suffused and irradiated with the distillated blood of the Redeemer. From that moment on, the entire etheric envelope of the earth began to glow with supersensible light.

Unfortunately, even though the blood of the Redeemer had been miraculously purified of all the contaminating effects of human self-centeredness—of human egoism—by the sacrifice on the cross, it was still not fully redeemed. There still existed a root cause to the corruption of the blood that lay deep in the body, an evil blot of primeval blood-lust that still needed to be exorcised.

What Happened to Christ-Jesus after Death?

After heroically bearing the agonizing suffering on the cross, when the moment of death mercifully occurred for Christ-Jesus, the gospel accounts record some profound events that are little understood outside of esoteric Christianity. As described in the Book of Matthew:

> [T]here was darkness over all the land … and the earth shook, and the rocks were split … [and] the curtain of the temple was torn in two, from top to bottom." (Matt 27:51)

Further details are provided in the Book of John:

> [W]hen [the Roman soldiers] came to Jesus and saw that he was already dead, they did not break his legs … For these things took place that the scripture might be fulfilled, "Not a bone of him shall be broken." (John 19:33, 36)

In order to understand the deep significance of the perceptible events surrounding the mystic death of Christ-Jesus (what Rudolf Steiner termed the "Mystery of Golgotha"), it is necessary to esoterically investigate what took place supersensibly during and after the death on the cross.

As one approaches the moment of death, what typically happens is that the etheric vehicle (together with the astral vehicle and the ego-bearing soul) begins to slowly lift out of the physical body. When this occurs, the biological functions of life begin to shut down, usually accompanied by a corresponding loss of consciousness. However, prior to slipping into the slumber of death, since the etheric vehicle is the repository of all earthly memory, a fleeting review of one's entire life (from the end to the beginning) flashes before one's inner eye.[28]

In the case of the crucified Redeemer, since the etheric and astral vehicles were permeated with the superplanetary forces of Christ, there was no loss of consciousness or self-awareness before or after death. It was immediately after consciously experiencing the instantaneous flash of his entire life in memory that Christ-Jesus freely offered up his own life as a sacrificial gift of love to God.

A similar, consciously experienced, death-like entry into the supernatural realm, known as the "temple sleep," was once performed by initiates in the ancient Mysteries. However, unlike the out-of-body experiences of the ancient initiates that were trance-induced and conducted in secret, the soul of Christ-Jesus did not artificially exit the physical body; nor was he safely guided through the superphysical realm by hypnotic-like instruction from a temple hierophant. At the Crucifixion, the separation of body and soul was fatal and not artificial, being the result of sever mortal injury. Moreover, the sacrificial death of Christ-Jesus took place in public; not in the protective confines of the Mystery temple. And most significantly, it was the infallible, divine guidance of the hypostatically united Eternal Son that safely ferried Christ-Jesus to "the other side," not the fallible guidance of a temple priest.

While the initiates of the ancient pagan Mysteries were, for a time, able to consciously experience much of what occurs in death while still alive, they certainly did not have the power to overcome death. In fact, by the time of Christ-Jesus, the supernatural realm had grown exceedingly dark and foreboding, even for the Mystery initiates.

By turning his attention upward to the light of God during the final moments of death, the focus of the Saviour's concentration was intuitively on the superphysical point in the head where the etheric vehicle is anchored to the physical (in the central area of the forehead). Clairvoyantly, this point is perceived as a small, radiant burst of light—an inner "mystic star." As the etheric vehicle of Christ-Jesus gradually exited the physical form, so too the mystic star slowly rose up out of the body.

Crossing the Great Abyss

Supersensibly perceived, the actual point of death is when the etheric body, astral body and ego-bearing soul together sever all connection with, and permanently exit, the physical body. Once the etheric vehicle has sufficiently withdrawn, what generally occurs is a loss of consciousness; what is esoterically termed, the "soul-slumber." As described by Yogi Ramacharaka in *The Life Beyond Death* (2010):

> The soul leaving the physical body (in the 'Astral body') is plunged into a deep sleep or state of coma resembling the condition of the unborn child for several months before birth. It is being prepared for re-birth on the Astral Plane … This period of soul-slumber is like the existence of the babe in the mother's womb—it sleeps that it may awaken into life and strength.
>
> Not only is the soul slumber a time of rest and

recuperation for a world-weary soul, but it also protects the unprepared soul from consciously experiencing some of the shattering events that occur relatively soon after death.

If full clairvoyant consciousness is present, as was the case with Christ-Jesus, immediately upon exiting the physical body there ominously appears before the discarnate soul a yawning chasm of nothingness that separates the sensory world left behind from the supersensible world yet beyond. This terrifying drop into seeming oblivion is esoterically termed, the "Great Abyss."

Various ancient cultures were knowledgeable about the Great Abyss, and incorporated their understanding in mythological imagery. The ancient Greeks, for example, referred to this fearful boundary between the world of the living and the world of the dead (Hades) as the river Styx. They also believed that newly-departed souls needed to cross this perilous boundary in order to properly live in the afterworld. Also, in ancient Hindu mythology, what separated the earth from the realm of the dead (Naraka) was called the river Vaitarani. Only sinful souls were forced to cross this difficult and terrifying river. In Japanese Buddhist tradition, the dead needed to cross the river Sanzu to reach the afterlife. It was further believed that good souls could use a special bridge to cross the frightening Sanzu, while evil souls had to wade through deep, serpent-infested waters.

To modern-day esoteric understanding, the Great Abyss is simply the large sphere of etheric force and substance that surrounds and penetrates the earth; what can correctly be termed, the "planetary etheric vehicle." Nevertheless, encountering this etheric region in an out-of-body condition can be a terrifying experience for the unprepared. Etheric substance is clairvoyantly characterized by extreme emptiness. It has a disturbing quality of being "emptier than space," a sort of negative space. As such, this vacuum of etheric emptiness has a relentless, centripetal sucking action.

When this planetary region of etheric emptiness is encountered after death, or through initiatory development, it is a daunting confrontation—like standing at the precipice of a bottomless pit that is irresistibly drawing the soul in. Moreover, while the sphere of planetary ether that extends above the surface of the earth exudes warmth and light, the levels that extend into the subterranean regions of the earth are comprised of corrupted and debased etheric substance. To the esoteric investigator, electricity is light ether that has been corrupted by Luciferic activity; magnetism is chemical (sound) ether that has been corrupted by Ahrimanic activity; and nuclear energy is life ether that has been corrupted by asuric[29] activity.

Not only does the Great Abyss draw the soul into it, then, but the subterranean ethers also have a strong tendency to pull the deceased's etheric body downwards. As the various mythological stories indicate, an exemplary soul will predictably pass through (or "cross") the planetary etheric void in their journey after death, while an evil soul will be drawn in and become tethered to the subterranean earth. Typically, the excarnate etheric body is sloughed off from the astral vehicle after several days, and then dispersed into the planetary and superplanetary ethers. In contrast, an etheric body hardened by immorality or drawn to the earth by strong passion (such as despair, revenge, lust or hatred) will not easily disintegrate, but may instead haunt or roam the earth as a ghostly "spectre" for many years.

Despite never having encountered the Great Abyss before, Christ-Jesus had no difficulty facing the void and passing through it. Similar to his physical levitations on water, crossing the Great Abyss was easily accomplished through the superplanetary forces of the indwelling Christ-ego hypostatically united to the Word and the Son. Moreover, by resolutely focusing on the golden light of the mystic star, attention was "directed to the Father" (that is, trained on his highest, spiritual nature), which provided an etheric sphere of protection around him. By floating in this "bubble zone," Christ-Jesus was securely ferried to "the other side."

The Phantom of the Physical Body

Precisely as the ancient mythological stories described, crossing the Great Abyss after death did not lead the soul of Christ-Jesus into heaven but, rather, into hell—the dark underworld. This, of course, was due to mankind's fall into materiality and the gravitational effects of mineralization on the physical body. Even though it is superficially understood that Christ-Jesus shed his physical body on the cross after death, esoterically understood, that is not entirely accurate. What is actually discarded with the death of every human being, then and now, is the physical corpse—the lifeless chemical body. But this cadaver of elements and minerals is not the actual physical body. The actual physical body is an invisible form which determines the overall shape and arrangement of the various chemical components.

Little is known or mentioned of this invisible human form outside of Rosicrucian circles.[30] In *The Secret Doctrine of the Rosicrucians* it is referred to as the "garment of Elemental Substance," and described in the following way:

> Elemental Substance, in the sense in which the term is used by the Rosicrucians in this connection, is a very subtle, tenuous form of substance—a form of substance which may be regarded as the 'ancestor' of the most subtle form of matter known to science today. It lies far back of the plane of the electrons, ions, or corpuscles of which matter (as commonly known) is composed ... [T]he garment[] of Elemental Matter, is the *pattern* upon which the ordinary physical body is built. It is the 'ghost' of the physical body, and persists after the disintegration

of the latter. The *intelligence* or *consciousness* manifesting in this garment of substance is quite simple and elementary, and performs merely the office of providing and sustaining a *pattern* or *form* upon which the ordinary physical body is built.

From the foregoing information, it is understood that the transparent physical body that survives for a time after death is composed of rarefied, primordial matter that underlies chemical substance at an elemental level of existence. The Rosicrucian initiate, Rudolf Steiner, has more accurately termed the elemental human form, the "phantom," rather than the "ghost," since ghosts or spectres are understood to be etheric, rather than physical, phenomena. Steiner's own clairvoyant research has further confirmed that the physical phantom body was first established during mankind's primeval past; more specifically, during the Ancient Saturn Period of earth evolution. As described in a lecture given on 10 October 1911:

> The observation of the physical human body, in itself, belongs to the most difficult clairvoyant problems, the hardest of all! ... This Phantom is the Form-shape which as a spiritual texture works up the physical substances and forces so that they fill out the Form which we encounter as the man on the physical plane ... We know that the foundation, the germ, of this Phantom of the physical body was laid down by the Thrones during the Saturn period ... In fact, the Phantom, which cannot be seen with the physical eye, was what was first there of the physical body of man. It is a transparent body of force. (Published in *From Jesus to Christ*)

It was actually the phantom of the physical body that was corrupted by Luciferic and Ahrimanic interference, and which resulted in its deadly attraction to dense mineral matter. As further described by Rudolf Steiner:

But into the human organisation, in so far as it consists of physical body, etheric body, and astral body, the Luciferic influence penetrated, and the consequence was the disorganisation of the Phantom of the physical body ... Death was indeed the result of the disorganisation of the Phantom of the physical body ... If no Luciferic influence had come in, the destructive and reconstructive forces in the physical body would have remained in balance ... At the beginning of human evolution it was intended that the Phantom should remain untouched by the material elements that man takes for his nutrition from the animal, plant, and mineral kingdoms ... The human Phantom, according to its intended development through the Saturn, Sun, and Moon periods, should not have been attracted to the ashy constituents but only to the dissolving salt constituents. (From lectures given on 11 and 12 October 1911, and published in *From Jesus to Christ*)

Even though Jesus (as the heavenly-Adam) had been shielded from Luciferic and Ahrimanic interference since Lemurian times, and who therefore possessed an unblemished physical phantom himself, when he incarnated in Bethlehem for the first time he assumed a fallen physical form as inheritance from his parents. This form, however, was the best that the Hebrew people could generate after centuries of careful preparation by Yahweh-Elohim. As such, it was already highly rarified with a far-diminished attraction to dense, mineralized matter. It was of course necessary for Christ-Jesus to occupy such a wounded phantom, otherwise his physical body would have been entirely invisible to others, and he would thereby have gained little first-hand experience with the desperate plight of humanity. In more biblical terms, though Jesus himself was "without original sin," out of compassion for humanity, he sacrificially "took on the sins of the world" (that is, a similarly damaged phantom) in order to assist mankind.

The Mineralized Phantom and Earth Gravity

Throughout his life, however, Jesus' virginal ego-soul—together with the indwelling influences of Christ and the Bodhisattva-Zarathustra—assiduously laboured to purify and de-mineralize the inherited phantom body. Even though at the time of death his phantom body possessed little attraction to the remaining chemical components, it still harboured a deep-rooted and primeval seed of corruption within it, a persistent "thorn in the body." Deep within the heart of every human phantom, including the purified phantom of Christ-Jesus, was imbedded a cold, hard cinder of debased materiality that didn't belong. It was this primeval black density that was ultimately responsible for the skeletal hardening of the body and the debasement of blood circulation.[31] The human phantom, then, would never be fully redeemed as long as it remained. Unfortunately, Christ-Jesus fully understood that this persistent stain caused by original sin could not be removed during life, but only after death. And, it could only be removed at its source—deep within the earth.

When Christ-Jesus discarded the lifeless corpse of chemical matter upon the cross, he continued to occupy an imperfect physical phantom for a short while after death.[32] Unfortunately, even though his phantom was highly-refined and de-mineralized, the last-remaining "spot" of evil corruption caused by sin still strongly subjected the discarnate physical form to earthly gravity. As a result, rather than immediately ascending to the upper astral world (heaven) soon after death, the Saviour's phantom was instead drawn downward into the lower astral world (hell) by powerful gravitational attraction (see Figure 12 on page 142).

Since matter is essentially condensed etheric substance, it still retains the inward, centripetal force of attraction possessed by its parent material. Atomic particles are simply small, compressing eddies or vortexes of matter. Similar to the way a whirlpool will draw objects into it, particles of dense matter will draw other physical substance towards it. Large accretions of matter, such as a planet, will have a collective force of physical attraction, which is commonly referred to as "gravity."[33]

The gravitational pull of a planet such as earth is observed to be toward the centre of the sphere. What typically occurs after death, then, is that the physical phantom body is irresistibly drawn toward the centre of the earth.[34] Once the phantom has been stripped of the corpse of chemical matter, it easily passes through subterranean material. Since the etheric, astral and ego-bearing soul vehicles continue to occupy the phantom body for a time after death (until they too are discarded) they are also drawn towards the centre of the earth. In the case of regular humanity today, the descent of the phantom into the earth's interior is not consciously experienced; but unconsciously occurs during the initial soul slumber. In ancient times, however, this descent was semi-consciously experienced because of the atavistic clairvoyance still retained by humanity.

Entering the Subterranean Astral Plane of the Earth—The Gateway to the Underworld

If consciously passing through the planetary etheric sphere after death (that is, "crossing the Great Abyss") isn't shattering enough, entering the subterranean astral sphere of the earth is downright terrorizing for an unprepared soul.[35] Once again, the fact that most departed souls fall into a deep soul slumber during this inexorable descent, is clearly a great blessing provided by wise guardian beings.

As with the experience of crossing the Great Abyss after death, the journey into the underworld was also known and experienced by ancient cultures and imaginatively portrayed in their mythological stories. In Egyptian mythology, for example, the dead journeyed to Duat, the realm under the earth that was connected to Nun, the primordial waters of the Abyss. Duat was where the soul was weighed and judged, which determined the rewards and punishments experienced in the afterlife. In Mayan mythology, the underworld was called Xibalba, which meant "place of fright." All souls went to Xibalba after death, except those who died a violent death—only they went straight to heaven. In Aztec mythology, the souls of the dead descended through eight dangerous layers of the underworld until they reached the ninth and lowest level, known as Mictlan.

In ancient Greek mythology, the underworld was known as "the realm of the shades" or Hades (after the god of the underworld). Below the underworld was an even gloomier pit of torment and suffering called Tartarus, the dark abode of Chronus and the other Titans. The Orphic Mysteries regarded Tartarus as the primordial condition from which the cosmos was created. Moreover, the founder of the Orphic Mysteries, Orpheus, was believed to have descended to the underworld during life, and who managed to escape. The Orphic initiates attempted to re-experience his supernatural journey during the temple sleep.

For those with conscious clairvoyance, after descending through the etheric sphere of the earth, entering the subterranean astral realm was literally experienced as a horrific puncture through the surface of the earth. The soul entered a destructive underground region characterized by fiery magmatic turbulence, violent volcanic upheaval, and grinding crustal earthquakes. When Christ-Jesus entered this

Ahrimanic realm in full consciousness, he was still surrounded by a spherical force-field of divine protection and guided by the mystic star. In contrast to crossing the Luciferic realm of the etheric Abyss (which was experienced as a free-floating descent) entering into the subterranean lower astral was experienced as a soul-wrenching, plummeting free-fall into compressive dark-matter.

When the superplanetary soul-ego of Christ-Jesus crossed into the subterranean astral underworld, shortly after death on the cross, fissures in the earth literally cracked open and powerful earth tremors were felt in and around Jerusalem—exactly as described in Matthew's Gospel:

> [T]here was darkness over all the land ... and the earth shook, and the rocks were split ... [and] the curtain of the temple was torn in two, from top to bottom. (27:51)

Not only was the 60-foot-high curtain (the "veil") covering the inner sanctuary (the "Holy of Holies") of the Jerusalem temple split down the middle at that time, but also on a planetary level, the gateway to the astral underworld was split asunder by the spiritual light issuing from the Crucified-One.

The Journey to the Centre of the Earth

As Christ-Jesus plummeted ever deeper into the earth, he knew he was descending into hell. Knowledge of this after-death descent is still indicated today in the revised Catholic translation of the Apostles' Creed, which states: "[He] was crucified, died and was buried; he descended into hell; on the third day he rose again from the dead." Since Christ-Jesus had never experienced such crushing material oppression and such utter spiritual darkness, his noble soul silently cried aloud within itself, "My God, my God; why have you forsaken me."

As the relentless force of gravity drew him further downward, it was clear to his clairvoyant perception that the subterranean substances and energies were becoming increasingly more primeval and debased. While he was descending spatially through the earth, it also seemed as though he was travelling back in time—back to the primordial beginning of the cosmos. Unfortunately, this gravitational pull into denser and denser primeval matter was not the same as travelling back through the akashic records to the beginning of the cosmos.

The actual conditions, circumstances and events at the dawn of time have long since disappeared, except as a memory-like impression in the akashic records—the universal mind-material of the Logos-Word (what has also been termed, "the book of Nature" or "the book of God's remembrance"). Any primordial matter or energy still in existence from those ancient times would be an unnatural anomaly, a degenerate hold-over, and would therefore persist contrary to progressive evolution. Fortunately, the most elementary of primordial matter and energy is no longer in existence; but unfortunately, there is obsolete matter and energy from the beginning of our solar system (the Ancient Saturn Period) that have continued to survive in a super-densified, highly-degenerate form.

Such is the subterranean material within the earth. The progressive beings who guide our planetary evolution have deliberately and safely contained this "slag of the system" within the confines of the earth. To be gravitationally pulled deeper and deeper into increasingly older and more degenerate matter was therefore not a journey into the past, but a descent into evil. The gravitational pull toward the centre of the earth was an evil impulse to move away from the light of God, and to go backward to a more primeval existence in material darkness.

Sorath—The Evil Lord of Hell

The retention and corruption of the primeval matter and energy that is imprisoned within the earth did not just happen on its own. As with the debasement of etheric and astral substance and force by Luciferic, Ahrimanic and asuric beings, the corruption of subterranean matter and energy can be largely attributed to one particular, powerful evil being—a being known esoterically as "Sorath."

Not a great deal is esoterically known of this mysterious evil entity, primarily because he does not naturally belong to our own solar system.[36] As a primeval being himself, Sorath has grown exceedingly powerful over vast stretches of time as a result of his continued opposition to the light of God. Due to his resolutely backward evil direction, he eventually detached himself entirely from his own evolutionary life-wave; but (for some evil reason of his own) managed to insinuate himself into our planetary evolution during the Ancient Saturn Period. From the very first moment he slipped into our system, he was noticed and his evil influence contained by equally powerful progressive celestial beings. The result is that he is currently imprisoned within the supernatural confines of the earth's interior, with little hope of escape.

It was certainly not the intention of progressive celestial beings that mankind should fall under the gravitational spell of Sorath. The main reason why he was imprisoned within the earth, and not elsewhere, was not that he had particular malevolent designs on humanity; but rather he had particular sinister designs on the sun—he wished to vaingloriously rule the entire solar system from a blackened, degenerate base in the sun. Unfortunately for mankind, it just happened that the earth was the closest planet Sorath's maleficent powers could take him before being constrained by the progressive sun-beings. The fact that Sorath arrogantly intends to somehow assume evil control of the sun is why he is esoterically referred to as the "sun-demon." Moreover, because of this overweening evil ambition he has declared himself the arch-enemy of Christ. Regarding Sorath, the prophetic Book of Revelation written by St. John the Evangelist refers to him as the two-horned beast with a dragon's voice that rises out of the earth during the end times and whose number is 666 (Rev 13:11–18).

Christ, then, as the regent of the sun, was well aware of Sorath's existence prior to entering the earth's interior after death. He knew that to fully redeem the human phantom body and thereby free humanity from the gravitational grip of hell, he would have to confront Sorath—not as before (from the powerful sphere of the sun)—but rather in Sorath's own evil domain. Using the pictorial language of mythology, Christ-Jesus knew that he needed to be "swallowed up in the belly of the beast"; that is, he needed to "crawl under the scaled skin and enter the black heart of the dragon."[37]

No doubt, from Sorath's perspective, the descent of Christ-Jesus into his infernal dungeon was an evil opportunity to destroy his avowed arch-enemy, and to plan his own terrestrial escape. Unfortunately for Sorath, the hypostatically-united forces of Christ, the Word and the Son—which infused the phantom body of Jesus—proved far too powerful against his own evil, gravitational grip. Instead of Christ-Jesus being engulfed and suffocated by material evil, his descent into hell pierced the earth's debased interior with a laser-like shaft of blazing divine light, which thereby opened the subterranean gates of hell to the instreaming forces of heaven.

Though the forces of evil saw victory in the Messiah's heart being pierced on the cross with a Roman spear, little did they guess that through this sacrificial death an opposing lance of heavenly white light would pierce the very heart of darkness in the earth; and thereby achieve lasting victory over evil and death.

At the Centre of the Earth—The Evil Heart of the Beast

When the torturous free-fall into hell had stopped, it was horribly clear to Christ-Jesus that he had reached the very centre of evil—the heart of Sorath's power. To clairvoyant perception, here was primeval matter of the most debased nature—feverish, flesh-coloured substance that was continually seething and writhing with elemental vitalism.[38] Though Christ-Jesus was enveloped in this evil matter, his vehicles were still encapsulated by a transparent sphere of divine protection. While the abrupt stoppage at the planetary core was only momentary in time, it seemed excruciatingly forever in the mind of Christ-Jesus as he silently prayed, "My God, help me."

Suddenly, the undulating, viscerous core "turned in on itself," and with a horrible heaving and convulsive internal disgorgement, it miraculously turned "inside out." Through the hypostatic presence of divine light in Christ-Jesus, the corrupted primeval matter was no longer gravitationally pulling inwardly away from the light of God, but had slowly begun to radiate outwardly toward the light of God. In other words, the power of divine love in Christ-Jesus had arrested the backward, evil contraction of corrupt matter at the earth's core and reversed its direction. In this way, the evil nature of the earth's core had slowly begun to be transmuted or "redeemed."

What this momentous event signified for the future of earth evolution was that over time the planet's core will exert less and less gravitational force on physical matter, including the human phantom. Moreover, due to the spark of divine light kindled at the core through Christ-Jesus, the earth had begun to radiate supersensible light outwardly. Through the sacrificial action of the sun-being Christ (in hypostatic union with Jesus, the Word and the Son), the earth was now slowly becoming a planetary sun-source which will, in time, re-unite with the radiant solar-centre of our system.

3.6 Rising from the Tomb: The Glorious Resurrection of Christ-Jesus

The De-mineralization and Redemption of the Human Phantom

Even though the evil nature of the degenerate matter at the earth's core had begun to be transmuted and redeemed by the power of divine love radiating from Christ-Jesus, it will still take long ages before it is vibrationally raised to the level of the sun. Nevertheless, the earth's core no longer has the same inexorable gravitational pull on the human phantom as it had prior to the death of Christ-Jesus. In the case of the Redeemer's own phantom body, once the transmutation of the earth's core had commenced, then the dark "thorn in the body" disappeared. All residual attraction of the Redeemer's phantom to dense mineralized matter and all gravitational influence upon it correspondingly ended. In more biblical terms, the stain of original sin on the body, that resulted in death, was entirely washed away by the Saviour's descent into hell.

In essence, the hidden thorn in the phantom body was an evil seed of corrupt matter, of the same nature as the earth's degraded core, which had been covertly implanted by Sorath.[39] Once the physical, etheric and astral bodies of mankind had fallen to a particular level of debasement through Luciferic and Ahrimanic influence, the souls of the dead were forced to pass through Sorath's dark subterranean domain on their way to rebirth. During this semi-conscious sojourn in hell, Sorath was able to plant this evil seed of primeval matter in the discarnate phantom body.[40] This black thorn in the body forced the soul after each death to return again and again to the subterranean recesses of hell. By doing so, Sorath had been able to recurringly feed and strengthen his implanted seed of evil destruction.

Once again, through instinctual clairvoyance, certain ancient cultures knew of Sorath's infernally implanted seed and clothed this knowledge in mythological form. In ancient Greek mythology (in connection with the Eleusinian Mysteries), the goddess Persephone (Kore) was forcibly abducted by Hades and taken to the underworld. Due to the loud protestations of Demeter, her mother, Hades was forced by Zeus to release her. The lord of the underworld complied, but tricked Persephone into eating four pomegranate seeds before leaving. Since consuming any food or drink in the underworld binds the soul there, Persephone was required to return to hell for four months out of every year.

With the removal of the last "spot" of Sorathic corruption, the phantom of Christ-Jesus was entirely purified and "spotless"—the first, fully-restored phantom since the Lemurian Fall.

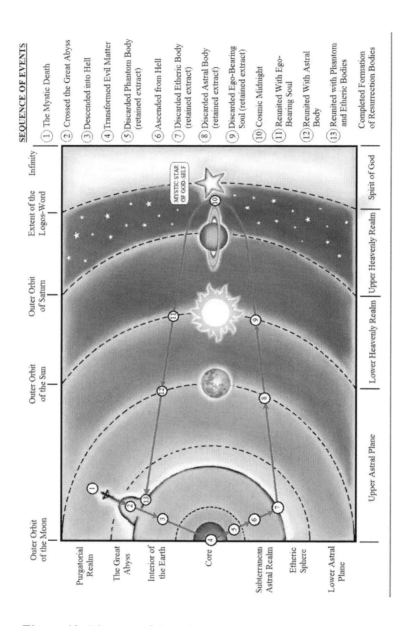

Figure 12: Diagram of the After-Death Events of Christ-Jesus
(From Good Friday until Paschal Sunday)

The Dawn of a New Earth and a New Heaven

At the very centre of the earth's core, in the very heart of Sorath's evil materialization, the hypostatic presence of Christ-Jesus generated a heavenly nucleus of pure white light. The mystic star that had accompanied his descent and which provided the enveloping, divine protection pierced through the heart of Sorathic matter. This microcosmic star-seed will, in time, transmute the entire interior of the earth, as well as each dark-seed of evil implanted by Sorath in the human phantom. At that moment, the earth was born anew as a nascent sun, and the superplanetary ego-soul of Christ-Jesus became the new planetary ego-soul (the planetary-spirit) of the earth.[41]

With the victory of divine love at the centre of material corruption in the earth, Christ-Jesus knew the reign of death and evil were over, and in his soul he softly uttered, "Praise God; it is finished." Moreover, when the writhing, viscerous core-material regurgitated itself "inside out," the entire cosmos—at its most elemental level—also turned itself inside out. Henceforth, all universal matter—at its core—was infused with a spark of divine love. Matter itself now possessed the inner capacity, an innate moral force, to resist evil manipulation. The victory of Christ-Jesus over material evil signalled the dawn of a new day of cosmic creation; it was (to echo anthroposophical terminology) a "cosmic turning point of time."[42] Or, as expressed in paragraph 349 of the *Catechism of the Catholic Church*:

> The *eighth day*. But for us a new day has dawned: the day of Christ's Resurrection. The seventh day completes the first creation. The eighth day begins the new creation. Thus, the work of creation culminates in the greater work of redemption. The first creation finds its meaning and its summit in the new creation in Christ, the splendor of which surpasses that of the first creation.

143

The Ascent to the Surface and the Discarded Phantom

All that transpired from the mystic death on the cross, to crossing the Great Abyss, to descending to the earth's core—was accomplished by Christ-Jesus in less than a day of earth-time. More exactly, it only took nine hours, from his death at 3 p.m. until 12:00 midnight on Good Friday. Time, of course, in the superphysical realm does not conform to physical constraints. A moment of earth-time (the life-memory flash, for example) can be experienced as a lengthy superphysical event, while a brief period of superphysical time may last for thousands of years of earth-time.

The viscerous eversion at the earth's core that turned debased matter "inside out," acted as propulsion on Christ-Jesus, launching him upward toward the light. With the same speed that he had descended into the earth, he began to ascend out of the earth. As he was propelled upward toward the light, his soul felt like a submerged man rising to the water's surface, anxiously gasping for life-giving air.

As he sped upwards, exhilarating joy expanded his soul, further increasing his ascent. Soon after exiting the earth's inner core (not the earth's surface), as typically occurs after death, Christ-Jesus discarded his phantom body. After having just fully redeemed the human phantom, immediately discarding this highly-prized accomplishment would appear to be a senseless and wasteful occurrence. But appearances aren't always the full reality. Normally when the phantom is discarded deep within the earth after death, an extract or distilled essence is retained by the departed soul as the germinal substance to later construct a new phantom for rebirth.[43] The outworn and discarded phantom is left to be rapidly and violently fragmented by the destructive forces surrounding the earth's core.

In the case of Christ-Jesus, however, the fully-redeemed phantom was still enveloped in divine protection. Instead of fragmenting the phantom into small pieces, the dissipating and explosive forces near the earth's core multiplied and replicated innumerable exact copies of the Redeemer's phantom. Discarding the fully-redeemed phantom of Christ-Jesus, then, was not a terrible loss for humanity, but was instead a huge gain. Since the newly-purified elemental substance of the Redeemer's phantom was only minimally affected by gravity, the countless phantom replicas slowly rose up out of the tomb of the earth and dispersed themselves throughout the etheric envelope of the planet.

Once the phantom of Christ-Jesus had been discarded, the etheric and astral bodies were no longer weighed done by earth gravity and thereby were accelerated in their rise to the surface. As Christ-Jesus continued to rapidly ascend, the interior of the earth became increasingly filled with radiant light, and his soul became increasingly filled with exhilarating joy. As had similarly occurred with his initial descent into the earth's interior, when Christ-Jesus broke through the Ahrimanic sub-crustal zone of the planet, earth tremors were felt in various places on the surface, including in and around Jerusalem.

The Etherization of the Crucified Corpse

Rather astoundingly, according to the clairvoyant investigations of Rudolf Steiner, after-shocks in Jerusalem at that time actually opened up, and then closed, a small fissure in the floor of the stone sepulchre where the corpse of Christ-Jesus had been entombed. As was the Jewish burial custom at that time, the corpse of Christ-Jesus was embalmed with costly spices (a mixture of aloes and myrrh) and then wrapped with linen cloth. Since the phantom body had been purified of all strong attraction to dense matter during life and since it had vacated the chemical body at death, the elements and minerals of the crucified corpse were only loosely held together by molecular cohesion. Prolonged contact in the tomb with the highly aromatic spices caused a powerful chemical reaction to occur whereby the entire corpse, in two days, was completely volatilized—it "vanished into space."

The only perceptible material remaining was a fine, highly etherized powder—similar to the shimmering, etherized dust on a butterfly's wings.[44] Since the divine forces of Christ-Jesus had also completely penetrated the powerful mineralizing forces of his skeleton during the hours of his crucifixion, even his bones volatilized into super-fine dust. In order to de-mineralize the entire skeleton, it was important that it remain intact; hence the esoteric meaning of the gospel passage:

> [W]hen [the Roman soldiers] came to Jesus and saw that he was already dead, they did not break his legs ... For these things took place that the scripture might be fulfilled, "Not a bone of him shall be broken." (John 19:33, 36)

When the earth-tremors of the Redeemer's ascent to the surface opened up a small fissure in the floor of the stone tomb, the shaking motion of the earth sifted much of etherized powder into the fissure, before it was immediately closed up. All that remained where the corpse had been were the linen burial cloths, still in a wrapped position. As described by Rudolf Steiner:

> Then it was only necessary that those people mentioned in the [Gospel] narrative should come to the body with their strange preparation of spices and bring about a chemical union between these special substances and the body of Jesus of Nazareth ... Very little was needed then to cause this body to become dust; ... but that which had been placed in the grave disintegrated and became dust.

And according to the latest occult investigations, it is confirmed that there was an earthquake. It was astonishing to me to discover, after I had found from occult investigation that an earthquake had taken place, that this is indicated in the Matthew Gospel. The earth divided and the dust of the corpse fell in, and became united with the entire substance of the earth. In consequence of the violent shaking of the earth, the clothes were placed as they were said to have been found, according to the description in the John Gospel. It is wonderfully described in the Gospel of St. John. (From a lecture given on 9 January 1912 entitled, "Esoteric Studies: Cosmic Ego and Human Ego")

The lustrous, iridescent powder of the corpse of Christ-Jesus that seeped into the earth had a similar action to that of butterfly substance. Whereas the etherized matter of butterflies radiates a "spirit-light" into the cosmos, the etherized matter of the Redeemer's corpse radiated a spirit-light into the earth's dark interior. Since all material, forces, and events pertaining to the life of Christ-Jesus are hypostatically-infused with the divine power of the Son, they are all "stamped with eternity"; they all have a quality of lasting permanence. To clairvoyant perception, then, the coruscating powder of Christ-Jesus' corpse did not dissipate into cosmic space, but instead continues to irradiate the earth's mineralized interior.

The Ascent into Space and Discarding the Redeemed Etheric Body

The divine "stamp of eternity" was also placed on the etheric body of the Redeemer. Typically after death, the etheric body is unconsciously discarded by the soul after about three or four days. After its extrication, the etheric body expands outwardly in all directions, growing to immense size and proportion, as it gradually diffuses and dissipates into the planetary and superplanetary ethers. Such was not the case, of course, with the etheric body of Christ-Jesus.

As he jettisoned through the surface of the earth on his ascent from hell, Christ-Jesus did in fact discard his etheric body within the etheric envelope of the earth. His purified and redeemed etheric body did not begin to dissipate, however, but instead retained the form and shape it possessed during life. Moreover, somewhat similar to the subterranean replication of the redeemed phantom body, the centrifugal forces of etheric expansion did not fragment or disintegrate his etheric body, but instead multiplied it into innumerable exact replicas. Furthermore, these countless copies were dispersed throughout the etheric envelope of the earth.

When Christ-Jesus broke through the crustal surface of the planet on his accelerated ascent, he didn't stop there in order to appear on earth. Though he retained a distillated extract of the extricated etheric body, he continued to rapidly ascend in the sky. Discarding the phantom body and the etheric body was like dropping the first- and second-stage launching devices on a shuttle-mission into outer space. Few things can compare to the exhilaration of the victorious Redeemer as he joyously sped upwards and outwards into the all-embracing cosmos.

Once the etheric body has been shed and a germinal extract retained, the deceased soul typically undergoes a purifying, purgatorial process that often lasts for about a third of its past life on earth. During this time, the deceased is still in a state of soul slumber, and the events of the previous life are re-experienced as intensely vivid dreams. These hyper-intensified astral dreams proceed in a reverse direction, from death back to birth, with the wise result that the deceased soul better understands the cause and effect relationships of its actions. In this way the soul learns from its successes and its failures to better prepare for the next incarnation. This retrospective purification takes place within the astral realm that extends from the earth to the orbit of the moon; the realm referred to in Catholicism as "Purgatory," and in Eastern teaching as "Kamaloka."

Discarding the Redeemed Astral Body

Since Christ-Jesus led an exemplary life on earth, there was no need to linger in the Purgatorial realm, and so his blazing ascent into the heavens continued unabated. Nevertheless, as typically occurs at this transition stage, Christ-Jesus still relinquished his astral body upon exiting the outer orbit of the moon. A germinal extract of the redeemed astral body was, of course, retained by his higher self.

Ordinarily by discarding the astral body, the soul is able to enter more fully into the upper astral plane that spatially exists between the moon and the sun. Upon entering this plane, the soul is usually semi-aroused from its dream-filled slumber and begins to slowly perceive its astral surroundings. Unless one has developed clairvoyant senses prior to death, however, these perceptions are in the form of internal visions, rather than objective sensory experience. Even though upper-astral awareness is subjectively experienced, these inner visions are not delusional or arbitrary, but correspond to objective reality; they faithfully reflect the beings and events of the upper astral realm.

Once again, however, the after-death events of Christ-Jesus continued to be "extra-ordinary." Not only was Christ-Jesus fully-conscious and completely self-aware throughout this entire time, but as with his redeemed phantom and etheric bodies, his discarded astral body did not regularly dissolve into the superplanetary ocean of astrality. Rather than centrifugally dissipating into the cosmos, his purified astral body retained the size and form that it had on earth, and instead spun off innumerable replicas of itself into the astral space bordering the upper orbit of the moon.

Moving further out into supersensible space through the orbital spheres of Venus and Mercury, the astral regions became brighter and brighter as Christ-Jesus journeyed toward the sun. The sun was not a destination, however, but simply another "drop-off zone" where Christ-Jesus discarded his redeemed ego-bearing soul (please refer to Figure 4, if needed) in order to enter the heavenly planes that lie farther out in cosmic space. Somewhat surprisingly, though the realm of the sun was the natural abode of the indwelling Christ-being, there was no strong impulse (on his *ascent* after death) for the Redeemer to remain there, but rather to continue the celebratory "joy-ride" into the star-filled heavens.

Discarding the Redeemed Ego-bearing Soul

Even though the redeemed bodily vehicles did not expand to immense proportions as they dissipated into cosmic space (as typically occurs), the consciousness of Christ-Jesus was nevertheless increasingly elevated to superplanetary levels of awareness as he journeyed outwardly into cosmic space. Similar to the replications of the redeemed phantom, etheric and astral bodies, the discarded ego-bearing soul of Christ-Jesus did not dissipate into astral space, but was instead multiplied into countless replicas by the strong centrifugal forces of the sun. Moreover, since the ego-bearing soul is comprised of three soul vehicles: sentient soul, intellectual soul and consciousness soul, there were actually three different kinds of soul-replications that were spun off.

As the Redeemer sped past the sphere of the sun, his lower "transport-vehicles" had been reduced down to the three sheaths of his higher self. The phantom body, etheric body, astral body and ego-bearing soul continued only as germinal extracts. Once past the sun, the cosmos spread out before the onrushing Redeemer as an all-embracing, life-filled ocean of pulsating, vibrant sound. The *microcosmic* mystic star that had safely led Christ-Jesus through the frightening interior of the earth was hereafter a *macrocosmic* star-point whose pure white light joyfully drew him farther and farther out into the great, wide universe. This was the divine light of God that comforted, instructed, protected and victoriously raised him up from the hell of the earth's interior into the heavenly realms of the cosmos.

As the Redeemer continued to blaze out into the universe, past the orbital spheres of Mars and Jupiter, the sound-filled spatial expanse became increasingly darker. But unlike the dark interior of the earth, the cosmic darkness was warm and welcoming. As with the externalization of the mystic star, as Christ-Jesus approached the far reaches of the solar system, the microcosmic voice that had instructed him through the earth's terrorizing interior had outwardly transformed into a macrocosmic voice. He felt comforted and illuminated by the enveloping effusion of cosmic words and cosmic ideas which radiated the eternal love of God. After discarding his dense bodily vehicles, the Redeemer felt an increasing sense of pure "being" that infused cosmic space, and which was filled with the love of God.

As he focused on the distant, divine star-point, he was also filled with the realization that God was infinitely small as well as infinitely great; that in the great wide expanse of the universe, only the infinite point of God's white light was ultimately real; all else was dark nothingness. As with the experience of descending into the earth's dark interior, as Christ-Jesus travelled outwardly in space, he felt as though he was also travelling backwards in time, back to the inception of the solar system. Moreover, as he ascended upward in consciousness, it felt as though he was also penetrating deeper into the cosmos. At the outer reaches of the planetary system, as Christ-Jesus approached the orbital circumference of Saturn, it was like converging to a mysterious "point of reversal" where "in" was also "out," "forward" was also "backward" and "up" was also "down."[45]

The Victorious Return to Earth

Suddenly, the outward trajectory into cosmic space was reversed as Christ-Jesus was spun around and hurled back towards the earth. It felt as though he had entered a kind of "cosmic switching station" that controlled the supersensible "traffic" of planetary life and activity. As he sped back towards the earth, the Redeemer noticed that he was no longer discarding material from himself, but was instead attracting universal force and substance to himself. The distilled extracts of his discarded vehicles had begun to germinate and grow.

Typically when a soul is returning from heaven to earth on the way to rebirth, it once again falls into a condition of deep unconsciousness, esoterically termed the "second soul slumber." In the words of Yogi Ramacharaka:

> [T]he soul, falling into the second soul slumber, is caught up by the currents of the Karmic attraction, and is carried on toward re-birth in an environment, and with ties, in accordance with the sum of its character and desires. (*The Life Beyond Death*; 2010)

As further described by Rudolf Steiner:

> In the Saturn sphere full content is bestowed upon [the soul] as the expression of the Cosmic Word out of which everything was created ... Beyond Saturn a spiritual sleep begins, whereas during the previous stages one was

spiritually awake [in a dream-like condition] ... During this period we again travel through all the spheres, but with a dimmed consciousness ... We now contract, quickly or slowly according to our karma, and during this process of contraction we come once more under the influence of the forces emanating from the Sun system. (From a lecture given on 3 November 1912, and published in *Life Between Death and Rebirth*; 1978)

Though Christ-Jesus made no pause in the realm of the sun when he ascended from the earth soon after his death, on his return journey from cosmic midnight he did abide there for a brief time. While momentarily resting in the golden radiance of the sun, the indwelling spirit of Christ in Jesus temporarily re-connected with the higher vehicles of his solar nature that had remained behind in the superphysical sun when he had incarnated on earth at the Baptism. As his own "I AM" consciousness transcendently unfolded and he bathed in the divine light of his real self, he understood that he had a free-will choice to remain with the sun or return to the earth. As the Solar-Christos, he fully understood that he could disengage from the vehicles of Jesus-Immanuel and withdraw his own superplanetary vehicles (his ego-soul, spirit-self and life-spirit) back to the sun. From the sphere of the sun, he could remain the planetary-spirit of the earth and guide human redemption from a distance. Without hesitation, he knew that the will of divine love, his own will, was to return to the earth. By remaining united to it, he could continue to assist mankind's redemption from within the earth, and from within the human soul.

Resurrecting the Discarded Vehicles of Christ-Jesus

On his freely-chosen return journey to the earth after death, the victorious Redeemer did not succumb to soul slumber, but remained fully-conscious and self-aware. While the typical soul is dreamily unconscious during its cosmic descent, the new vehicles for re-birth are fashioned according to the germinal extracts that were retained, and assisted in this assembly by wise celestial beings. Christ-Jesus, however, before exiting the sphere of the sun consciously re-united with his original ego-bearing soul (not one of the spun-off replicas) that had been discarded there earlier. The fresh and pristine universal substance that was attracted to the germinating soul extract combined with the discarded ego-bearing soul to create a powerful new vehicle in human evolution—a *resurrected* ego-bearing soul. While Christ-Jesus (in hypostatic union with the Son) had greatly purified his inherited fallen vehicles during life, it was only after undergoing the entire process of death that divine forces could further transform his "redeemed" vehicles into "resurrected" vehicles.

As Christ-Jesus quickly descended to the earth, gloriously clothed in his newly-resurrected soul vehicles, he re-entered the orbital sphere of the moon and re-united with his original astral body that had been previously discarded. As with the resurrection of the ego-bearing soul in the realm of the sun, the original astral body preserved in the domain of the moon was completely transformed by the germinating extract, which attracted new and pristine astral force and substance from the cosmos. The result was a fully redeemed and resurrected astral body—the first one in human history.

It would normally take many years for a reincarnating soul to construct a new ego-bearing soul and a new astral body for rebirth. In the case of Christ-Jesus, however, the basic formulation was done in a matter of hours, though the completion process continued for several days afterward.[46]

Clothed in his resurrected soul and his resurrected astral body, Christ-Jesus further descended to the earth prepared to similarly unite with his discarded etheric and phantom bodies.

Normally, once a new etheric body has been prepared, the reincarnating soul would be united with the physical embryo supplied by the parents. But since Christ-Jesus had fully redeemed his fallen vehicles and thereby overcame death, there was no need for him to physically incarnate, ever again. Rather than incarnating within an embryonic physical body supplied by heredity, Christ-Jesus instead re-united with his original physical phantom that had been recently vacated after his death on the cross. Instead of relying on genetic reproduction and rebirth as the means to obtain a new physical body, Christ-Jesus was able to revitalize and renew his discarded phantom body and thereby generate a resurrected physical body that was immortal—no longer subject to illness, debilitation and death.

As commonly known in esotericism, after death the discarded etheric body possesses a residual affinity with the physical corpse, due to mutual interpenetration during life. As a result, the etheric body will typically be drawn to the burial site of the corpse, where it can be clairvoyantly observed to be hovering over the grave, slowly dissipating into etheric space. Similarly with Christ-Jesus; even though his corpse had volatilized into super-fine powder and seeped into a temporary fissure in the floor of his tomb, the original phantom and etheric bodies were still attracted to the rarified cadaverous substance, and hovered about the inside of the tomb. So when Christ-Jesus returned to the earth shortly before dawn on Paschal Sunday morning to re-unite with his discarded bodies, he found them in the stone sepulchre where his corpse had been placed.[47]

As with the resurrection of his ego-bearing soul and astral body, the Saviour's original etheric body and phantom form were completely transformed by their germinating extracts. New and revitalized etheric and elemental substance fashioned a resurrected etheric body and a resurrected physical phantom—vehicles that were unique in the history of the world. Once the unification and resurrection process was complete, Christ-Jesus stood upright within the tomb, victoriously raised up from death by the divine forces of God, and clothed in radiant garments of glistening white. To this his soul cried out: "My God, my God, how you have glorified me!"

As the first rays of dawn appeared in the east, the tomb of Christ-Jesus was ablaze with light. As the Redeemer had once called out to the entombed disciple whom he loved, "Lazarus, arise and come forth," a voice that shook the very earth called out, "Christ-Jesus, arise and come forth!" Whereupon a mighty celestial being rolled away the huge stone covering the entrance to the tomb. The victorious Saviour stepped into the dawning light and exclaimed, "I AM risen! All hail the new day of the Lord!"

CHAPTER 4

THE MYSTERY OF THE RISEN SAVIOUR: THE NEW REGENT OF THE EARTH

4.1 The Esoteric Significance of the Resurrection

The Difference Between Redemption and Resurrection

IN ESOTERIC CHRISTIANITY, it is important to be clear about the difference between the "redemption" of Christ-Jesus and the "resurrection" of Christ-Jesus. In the case of "redemption," which occurred during life and shortly after death, Christ-Jesus restored his inherited vehicles of expression (the phantom form, etheric body, astral body) to their original, immortal condition prior to the Lemurian Fall. These vehicles had been permanently damaged by Luciferic, Ahrimanic, asuric and Sorathic interference, such that they became increasingly subject to the forces of destruction and death. Though the virginal ego-bearing soul of Jesus-Immanuel was not corrupted by original sin, it was still partially contaminated by the intimate interpenetration and interaction with the inherited, three lower bodies.

By leading an exemplary life in conformity with divine love, Christ-Jesus was able to greatly purify his vehicles from all the "effects" of inherited corruption. Moreover, shortly after death he was able to additionally remove the "cause" of evil inclination in human nature, the "seed of material debasement" implanted in the phantom form by Sorath, the sun-demon. After his descent into hell, Christ-Jesus temporarily discarded his redeemed vehicles, but retained a distillated extract of each. Instead of deteriorating and disintegrating, as usually occurs after death, these vehicles continued to exist as they had during life. Moreover, this continued existence engendered a process of replication that spun-off innumerable exact copies into superphysical space. For the benefit of humanity, the various replications of the Saviour's redeemed vehicles have been available for use by devoted Christians in the centuries that followed the Crucifixion.

In the case of "resurrection," which occurred immediately upon returning to earth from cosmic midnight, Christ-Jesus re-united with his *original* discarded vehicles, thereby infusing them with the seed-extracts that had been activated in the higher heavenly realm. Normally, the germinating extracts would fashion completely new vehicles in accordance with the reincarnating soul's karma; but with Christ-Jesus, they worked to completely transform the discarded vehicles into something entirely new as well—resurrected vehicles. The resurrected vehicles of Christ-Jesus, then, are superior to his redeemed vehicles, which resembled the immortal vehicles that humanity possessed before the Fall. It was of course necessary for Christ-Jesus to re-unite with his former vehicles on earth since it would not be in accordance with progressive evolution for him to physically re-embody in a human embryo once again. The resurrection vehicles have not been replicated (like the redeemed vehicles), but belong exclusively to the Risen Saviour.

How do Resurrection Bodies Differ From Redeemed Bodies?

The vehicles that humanity possessed before the Lemurian fall into sin, sickness, evil and death were inherently innocent, immortal, invisible and ethereal. Despite their rarified condition, these vehicles were still primitive and animal-like in form and function. For example, since Lemurian humanity had only recently received the spark of self-awareness, the various vehicles of expression had not yet been adapted to the demands of a fully developed ego-being; demands such as a brain organ that permitted intellectual thought, and a nervous system that conveyed external sensory perceptions.

Even though the various vehicles of body and soul had fallen into corruption by the time of Christ-Jesus, they had still been much refined in form and function (no longer animal-like in appearance but distinctly human), and were better adapted to the requirements of a developed ego-being on earth. Nevertheless, by eliminating the corrupting effects of densification and over-mineralization, the redeemed vehicles would be restored to immortality, but also to a state of invisibility and to a weightless, ephemeral condition whereby they would have very little contact with the physical earth. Redeemed vehicles would once again be invisibly levitating above the surface of the earth with little capacity for intellectual thought or external sense perception. This would, of course, diminish human ego-awareness and thereby reverse progressive evolutionary development.

To truly assist fallen humanity, then, Christ-Jesus had to do more than just redeem and restore the corrupted vehicles of body and soul to their edenic, paradisal condition. He also needed to resurrect them; that is, he needed to transform the purified vehicles so as not to lose all the positive advantages of true ego-awareness. Hence the necessity to undergo death. For it was only by discarding each vehicle after death, extracting their life-essences, ascending to God with these extracts at cosmic midnight to infuse them with the forces of divine love, returning to earth, and then re-uniting the discarded vehicles with the activated seed-extracts, that Christ-Jesus could fully transform the vehicles of redemption into vehicles of resurrection.

In a very real sense, the Saviour's resurrection vehicles united heaven and earth. The resurrection vehicles were very different from the pristine, uncorrupted human vehicles in Lemurian paradise that existed entirely in a tenuous, "heavenly" condition. Likewise, the resurrection vehicles were very different from the densified, corrupted vehicles in Graeco-Roman times that were entirely confined to the physical, material world. Instead, the Risen Saviour was able to materialize and de-materialize his resurrection vehicles at will; thereby alternating between visibility and invisibility. By being able to voluntarily pass from earth to heaven and heaven to earth, Christ-Jesus became the first "dweller in two worlds."

The "Materialization" of the Resurrected Phantom

There are a number of biblical instances that describe the ability of the Risen Saviour to materialize and de-materialize his form at will. In one familiar example, known as the "supper at Emmaus," the Risen Saviour met with two disciples (Zachus and Cleophas) who were walking home to Emmaus on Paschal Sunday. The disciples did not recognize Christ-Jesus and invited the "stranger" for supper.

> So he went in to stay with them. When he was at table with them, he took the bread and blessed, and broke it, and gave it to them. And their eyes were opened and they recognized him; and he vanished out of their sight. (Luke 24:29–31)

After the Risen Saviour disappeared at dinner, the two disciples returned to Jerusalem to inform the eleven apostles about their experience. As they were relating their story:

Jesus himself stood among them, and said to them, "Peace to you." But they were startled and frightened, and supposed that they saw a spirit. And he said to them, "Why are you troubled, and why do questionings rise in your hearts? See my hands and my feet, that it is I myself; handle me, and see; for a spirit has not flesh and bones as you see that I have." And when he had said this, he showed them his hands and his feet. And while they still disbelieved for joy, and wondered, he said to them, "Have you anything here to eat?" They gave him a piece of broiled fish, and he took it and ate before them ... "And behold, I send the promise of my Father upon you; but stay in the city, until you are clothed with power from on high." Then he led them out as far as Bethany, and lifting up his hands he blessed them. While he blessed them, he parted from them, and was carried up into heaven. (Luke 24:36–51)

From the foregoing Gospel details, it is clear that the resurrected form of Christ-Jesus was not simply an etheric or astral appearance. It was not the ghost or spectre of Christ-Jesus that appeared to the apostles and disciples; but a "materialization," a bodily densification that was sufficiently substantial for others to see, touch and hear; and to actually ingest solid food.

What is here described as the "materialization" of the Saviour's resurrection body may appear at first to contradict statements made by Rudolf Steiner which declared that Christ-Jesus was clothed in a "densified" etheric body after the resurrection; statements such as the following from a lecture given on 9 January 1912 entitled, "Cosmic Ego and Human Ego," and published in *Esoteric Studies* (1941):

[T]he Christ Spirit clothed Himself with an etheric body condensed, one might say, to physical visibility. So the risen Christ was enveloped in an etheric body condensed to physical visibility; and thus He went about and appeared to those to whom He could appear. He was not visible to everyone, because it was actually only a condensed etheric body which the Christ bore after the resurrection ...

And in the specially contracted ether body, from which were drawn the constituents of the new ether body with which the Christ clothed Himself, [the crucifixion] wound-marks were made visible—were peculiarly thickened spots ... so that even Thomas could feel that he was dealing with a reality ...

[W]e have to do with an etheric body, condensed to visibility by the Christ force; and that then also the Emmaus scene could occur. We find it described in the Gospel, not as an ordinary receiving of nourishment, but a dissolution of the food directly by the etheric body, through the Christ forces, without the cooperation of the physical body.

Though Steiner did not explicitly mention the phantom body of Christ-Jesus in the preceding statements, it is nevertheless understood that the Risen Saviour was also clothed in a resurrected phantom body as well as a resurrected etheric body when he appeared to his followers.[48] Like the etheric body, the resurrected phantom body would also be invisible to physical sight under ordinary conditions. When Christ-Jesus intentionally condensed the lower part of his etheric body, as Steiner has described, part of his physical phantom body correspondingly "materialized"; that is, it densified to visible sight by temporarily attracting rarefied mineral matter to itself. Through a similar effort of will, the Risen Saviour could likewise attenuate his condensed lower etheric body which would correspondingly de-materialize the physical phantom and return it to its natural state of invisibility.

Unlike the corrupted phantom bodies of fallen humanity which retained a deadly attraction to dense mineral matter from incarnation to incarnation, the resurrected phantom of Christ-Jesus was able to attract or dispel rarefied (not densified) mineral matter at will. By doing so, the Saviour's phantom body could visibly descend to the earth, or invisibly ascend into heaven (the supersensible realm).

The focus that Rudolf Steiner placed on the resurrected etheric body was clearly to emphasize the fact that the Risen Saviour no longer inhabited the mineralized, corporeal physical body that he had before death. Moreover, any future expectation that Christ-Jesus would appear in his crucified body would be a serious misunderstanding of his mission, since any further dwelling in a mortal physical body would be entirely contrary to human salvation.

The fact that the Risen Saviour no longer occupied the corporeal body he possessed before death is evidenced in the Gospels of John and Mark where Mary Magdalene encounters the Risen Saviour for the first time on Paschal Sunday morning. The scriptural accounts relate that she didn't recognize the resurrected Christ-Jesus, and thought he was the cemetery gardener. As a devoted disciple who had been at the foot of the cross just days before, it is highly unlikely that she would not have recognized Christ-Jesus (even in grief), unless he looked quite different after his resurrection. Similarly, the two other disciples from Emmaus who walked, talked, and dined with the Risen Saviour later on Paschal Sunday did not recognize his resurrected appearance either.

Special Abilities of the Resurrected Vehicles

While both the redeemed vehicles (that have been replicated) and the resurrected vehicles of Christ-Jesus are immortal; that is, they are no longer subject to the forces of death and destruction, only the resurrection vehicles possess the capacity to materialize and de-materialize at will (thereby alternating between heaven and earth). Moreover, the resurrection vehicles of the Risen Saviour possess other extraordinary abilities that the redeemed vehicle copies don't have. One such ability is the gift of "bi-location"; the capacity to be present in more than one physical location at the same time. In fact, with the resurrection vehicles, Christ-Jesus can be in millions of world locations simultaneously—during the Catholic and Orthodox celebration of Holy Communion, for example. Regarding the bi-location ability of the resurrected etheric body (which of course also applies to the other resurrected vehicles), Rudolf Steiner has stated:

> [T]here is [the Saviour's] etheric body that will move about in the physical world, but is the *only* etheric body able to work in the physical world as a human physical body works. It will differ from a physical body in this respect only, that it can be in two, three, nay even in a hundred, a thousand places at the same time ... This will come about because in the course of the next millennia men will become aware of the presence of the Etheric Christ in the world. (From a lecture on 1 October 1911 entitled "The Etherization of the Blood," and published in *The Reappearance of Christ in the Etheric*; 2003)

A further extraordinary capacity of the resurrected vehicles (that is not possessed by the redeemed vehicle copies) is the gift of "immutability." Immutability of vehicles, in this case, means much more than just remaining "changeless" in form throughout the ages. While the redeemed vehicle copies certainly possess a capacity for perpetual self-repair and thereby remain changeless, the resurrection vehicles are further characterized by their overflowing capacity to unceasingly pour themselves out in loving self-sacrifice without being diminished in any way. It could also be termed the gift of "miraculous regeneration." Analogous to the miracle of the loaves and the fishes, the resurrected vehicles can continuously emanate nourishing, life-giving force and substance without becoming depleted in any way. While a thousand different individuals may be simultaneously influenced by a thousand redeemed vehicle replicas, the *single* resurrection vehicles of Christ-Jesus (through bi-location) can simultaneously pour out salvational grace to a thousand different people—without any decrease in force or substance. This regenerative capacity of the resurrected vehicles to provide life-giving sustenance simultaneously at multiple locations is once again demonstrated in the Holy Communion sacrament of the Catholic and Orthodox churches.

4.2. The Continued Indwelling of the Christ-being in Jesus

The Gnostic-Style Under-Emphasis of "the Man Jesus"

Once the inherited vehicles of Christ-Jesus had been fully redeemed and resurrected after death, the Christ-being did not vacate them, and then happily return to the sphere of the sun. Typically, a lawful indwelling is only for a short period of time, as evidenced by the indwelling of Lord Maitreya in Jesus-Pandira, and by the indwelling of the Bodhisattva-Zarathustra in Jesus-Immanuel. Moreover, in the previous three superphysical instances when Jesus-Immanuel (as the heavenly-Adam) had been indwelt by the Solar-Christos (the Christ-being), it was only for a short, temporary period of time. After the victorious resurrection over death, however, the Christ-being freely chose to continue to indwell the resurrected vehicles of Jesus-Immanuel for an extended period of time; in fact, until "the end of the age" (Matt 28:20). This of course was a sacrificial decision to continue to labour for the salvation of all mankind *internally* within the environment of the earth, not just *externally* from the realm of the sun.

The Saviour's long-term cosmic goal is not only to "raise up" the vibratory level of the earth and reunite our planet with the sun, but to actually transform the earth itself into a "sun within the sun." As well, struggling humanity is intended to be raised up to its own "high estate"; that is, to a point in the future where advanced individuals are able to formulate and inhabit their own resurrected vehicles. In biblical terms, this far-distant time is commonly known as the "Last Judgement" or the "Final Resurrection." In esoteric terms, this anticipated time is a planetary stage of earth evolution known as the future "Vulcan Period."[49]

Unfortunately today, many esoteric students of Rudolf Steiner's spiritual science have a Gnostic-style tendency to exclusively emphasize the activities of the resurrected Christ-being and completely ignore "the man Jesus"; that is, Jesus-Immanuel. It's crucially important for esoteric Christians to acknowledge that even though the resurrection vehicles would not have been formed without the superplanetary involvement of the Christ-being, these vehicles still belong to Jesus-Immanuel. Furthermore, in order for the Christ-being to lawfully indwell these resurrected vehicles well into the future, it was still necessary to have the complete free-will consent of Jesus-Immanuel.

Contributing to this erroneous under-emphasis of Jesus-Immanuel is the mistaken notion that the Christ-being inhabited ego-less human vehicles at the baptism. When, for example, Rudolf Steiner states that "the ego" vacated the physical, etheric and astral bodies of Jesus prior to the baptism,[50] the ego that is referred to is the indwelling ego of the Bodhisattva-Zarathustra. The human being who possessed those bodily-vehicles still remained; Jesus-Immanuel did not vacate his own vehicles. Since Jesus-Immanuel (as the heavenly-Adam) was supernaturally shielded from the Lemurian fall into materiality, he still retained an immaculate, "virginal ego" upon incarnating in Bethlehem.[51] However, through the highly-advanced, indwelling influence of the Bodhisattva-Zarathustra for 18 years (from age 12 to age 30), the innocent ego of Jesus-Immanuel was profoundly transformed and developed. While his own tender ego-soul was certainly eclipsed by the powerful superplanetary ego-soul of the Christ-being at the baptism, it is not entirely accurate to think that the threefold bodily vehicles of Jesus had no occupying human ego.

No doubt, the persistent emphasis that Rudolf Steiner placed on the Christ-being in his prolific writings was to counter the growing materialistic intellectualism of the late-nineteenth and early-twentieth centuries that was entirely focused on "the simple man of Nazareth."[52] Moreover, it is certainly correct (and spiritually uplifting) to interpret the life of Christ-Jesus from the viewpoint of the Christ-being, as long as the *indwelt* Jesus-being is not forgotten or ignored. Likewise, it is just as correct to interpret the life of Christ-Jesus from the viewpoint of the Jesus-being, as long as the *indwelling* Christ-being is not forgotten or ignored.

For example, from the viewpoint of the Christ-being, his superplanetary ego-soul partially indwells and interpenetrates the physical body, etheric body, astral body and nascent ego-bearing soul of Jesus-Immanuel. Through this indwelling, he is able to lead, inspire and direct the thoughts, feelings and actions of Jesus in order to accomplish the work of human salvation. From the point of view of Jesus-Immanuel, however, he has willingly invited the indwelling influence of the superplanetary ego-soul of the Christ-being into his body and soul. At every moment, he endeavours to unite his personal free-will with the superior wisdom and direction of the indwelling Christ-being. By doing so, he cooperates and provides the necessary vehicles for the Christ-being to accomplish the work of human salvation.

The Gnostic-Style Over-Emphasis of the Christ-being

As well as a Gnostic-style under-emphasis of Jesus, there is also an unfortunate Gnostic-style tendency among some Christian esotericists to over-emphasize the role and importance of the Christ-being in human salvation. To be sure, the inherited fallen vehicles of Jesus would not have been redeemed and resurrected without the indwelling activity of Christ. But it is also vitally important to keep in mind that Christ, like all created beings in the universe, is entirely dependent on God for his life and existence. Somewhat ironically, the higher a being ascends in power, wisdom, love and majesty, the clearer is the realization that everything in creation is a gift from God. The indwelling Christ was, of course, firmly aware of this fact and repeatedly reminded his followers of his complete dependence on God with such statements as the following:

> Jesus said to them, "Truly, truly, I say to you, the Son can do nothing of his own accord, but only what he sees the Father doing; for whatever he does, that the Son does likewise." (John 5:19)

> "I can do nothing on my own authority; as I hear, I judge; and my judgment is just, because I seek not my own will but the will of him who sent me." (John 5:30)

> "[E]ven though you do not believe me, believe the works, that you may know and understand that the Father is in me and I am in the Father." (John 10:38)

"For I have come down from heaven, not to do my own will, but the will of him who sent me; and this is the will of him who sent me, that I should lose nothing of all that he has given me, but raise it up at the last day. For this is the will of my Father, that every one who sees the Son and believes in him should have eternal life; and I will raise him up at the last day." (John 6:38–40)

And as he was setting out on his journey, a man ran up and knelt before him, and asked him, "Good Teacher, what must I do to inherit eternal life?" And Jesus said to him, "Why do you call me good? No one is good but God alone." (Mk 10:17–18)

From the foregoing words of Christ himself, speaking through Jesus, it is clear that no matter how eternally grateful we are to Christ for his enduring self-sacrificing love for humanity, those impulses of universal love originate in God. As Jesus was willingly directed by Christ, so was Christ hypostatically guided by the divine impulses of the Son flowing down through the Logos-Word. Christ himself made it abundantly clear, then, that he doesn't act on his own for human salvation; but in union with God.

Understanding the Resurrected Relationship of Christ and Jesus

It is also important to keep in mind that until the end of the age, until the future Vulcan Period, the Christ-being and the Jesus-being are united—the superplanetary ego-soul of the Solar-Christos continues to indwell the resurrected bodies and the human ego-soul of Jesus. So, for example, whenever references are made in esoteric Christianity to Christ becoming the new planetary-spirit of earth, it must be understood that it is Christ united to Jesus—Christ-

Jesus—who is the new regent of the earth. Likewise, whenever references are made in esoteric Christianity concerning the "Second Coming" of Christ in the etheric, it must be understood that the superplanetary ego-soul of Christ does not appear apart or disconnected from the resurrection vehicles of Jesus; it is Christ-Jesus who appears.

Furthermore, in certain situations in the past when the Christ-being acted independently, after the resurrection that was no longer the case. For instance, prior to the resurrection it would be accurate to say that the Christ-being alone was at the centre of the twelve bodhisattvas; that the twelve great teachers of mankind received inspiration from the Christ-being on the plane of life-spirit in the realm of the sun.[53] After the resurrection, however, it is Christ-Jesus—the Christ-being indwellingly united to the Jesus-being—who is the central thirteenth member of the circle of bodhisattvas. Moreover, the bodhisattvas now contact Christ-Jesus in the superphysical aura of the earth, no longer in the superphysical aura of the sun.

It is admittedly difficult at first to visualize the resurrected relationship of Jesus, the human being, and Christ, the superplanetary sun-being. Perhaps a simple analogy in this instance will help. Imagine a royal gardener standing in a lush palace courtyard, who bends down to tend a struggling plant situated in a small, barren plot of ground. He puts on a glove that was lying on the infertile soil and proceeds to nurture, cultivate and water the poor plant. The gardener compassionately vows that he will not remove the glove or leave the barren ground until the plant is healthy and as tall as he is.

In this simple analogy, Christ, of course, is the royal gardener and the lush palace courtyard is our planetary system. The small plot of barren ground is the earth, and the struggling plant represents mankind. The glove that the Christ-gardener puts on his hand is the human constitution, the "covering" of Jesus. Analogously, as the royal gardener stands in the luxuriant courtyard, the spirit-man of Christ stands in the realm of the sun. For Christ to send down his superplanetary ego-soul to the earth is analogous to the gardener reaching down and contacting the small plot of dry ground. Similarly, the spirit-man of Christ has always remained within the sun;[54] the earthly incarnation of Christ at the Baptism was simply an act of extending part of his nature (reaching down with his "superplanetary arm") to the earth, and then sheathing his ego-soul (his "superplanetary hand") within the human constitution (the "earthly glove") of Jesus. With his ego-soul indwelling Jesus, Christ similarly nurtures and quenches the spiritual hunger and thirst of struggling humanity with his superplanetary spirit-self and life-spirit that he has "poured out" into the earth (see Figure 13 below).

The resurrected union of Christ and Jesus until the end of the age has also resulted in some very unique characteristics of the new planetary regent of the earth. Normally, the regent of a planet is a progressive spirit of form, an elohim-being, who guides the destiny of a planet from the realm of the sun. Only regressive spirits of form are normally active within the periphery of the planet. The moon, however, is an exception to this normal course of planetary activity, since Yahweh-Elohim, a progressive spirit of form, works primarily in the periphery of the moon and not from the sun.

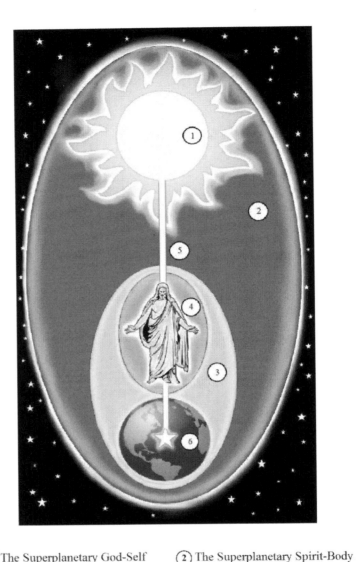

① The Superplanetary God-Self   ② The Superplanetary Spirit-Body

③ The Superplanetary Life-Spirit   ④ The Superplanetary Spirit-Self

⑤ The Hypostatic Spirit-Connection   ⑥ The Planetary God-Self

Figure 13: The Superplanetary Vehicles of Christ-Jesus as Regent
of the Earth

In the case of planet earth after the resurrection, it is not a progressive spirit of form who guides planet earth, but the Christ-being, who normally operates at the level of a spirit of motion. Moreover, the Christ-being progressively operates from the periphery of the earth as well as from the sun. Even more confusingly, due to the resurrected union of Christ and Jesus, it is equally correct to say that the human-being Jesus, guided and directed by the indwelling Christ, is now the regent of the earth. Esoterically speaking, then, it is a whole lot easier and less confusing to say that "Christ-Jesus"—Christ and Jesus united—is the new regent of the earth.

4.3 The Ascension of Christ-Jesus into the Heavenly Shambhala

The Life and Activities of Christ-Jesus after the Resurrection

The biblical records don't provide much information about the activities of Christ-Jesus following his glorious resurrection from the tomb. The Gospels describe a few materialized appearances to his closest disciples in Jerusalem, and the Acts of the Apostles further add that he made numerous appearances to the apostles for forty days in order to teach them deeper mysteries of heaven:

> To them he presented himself alive after his passion by many proofs, appearing to them during forty days, and speaking of the kingdom of God. (Acts 1:3)

The Aquarian Gospel of Jesus the Christ, however, provides much more detailed information that was transcribed from the akashic records by Levi H. Dowling (1844–1911).

These records relate that the Risen Saviour made materialized appearances to a gathering of wise men at the

palace of Prince Ravanna in India; to the Magian priests in
Persia; to the Jewish priests and authorities in the Jerusalem
temple; to Grecian priests at the oracle in Delphi; to two
disciples in Rome and a thousand other witnesses there; and
to Egyptian priests in the temple of Heliopolis. With all these
appearances, the Risen Saviour delivered a message similar to
the following:

> And Jesus said, My brothers of the Silent Brotherhood,
> peace, peace on earth; goodwill to men! The problem of
> the ages has been solved; a son of man has risen from the
> dead; has shown that human flesh can be transmuted into
> flesh divine. Before the eyes of men this flesh in which I
> come to you was changed with the speed of light from
> human flesh. And so I am the message that I bring to
> you. To you I come, the first of all the race to be
> transmuted to the image of the AM. What I have done, all
> men will do; and what I am, all men will be. But Jesus said
> no more. In one short breath he told the story of his
> mission to the sons of men, and then he disappeared.
> (Chapter 176:26–31)

The Ascension into Invisibility and Reasons for It

After forty days of making numerous materialized
appearances to initiates and disciples throughout the world,
the Risen Saviour decided to stop materializing his
resurrected vehicles and to "disappear from sight." The
earthly withdrawal of Christ-Jesus from physical sensory
visibility is termed, "the ascension." The biblical accounts
present scant information regarding the ascension, while
Christian esotericism furnishes a wealth of interesting detail.
In the Acts of the Apostles, only the following information is
given:

[As the apostles] were looking on, [Christ-Jesus] was lifted up, and a cloud took him out of their sight. And while they were gazing into heaven as he went, behold, two men stood by them in white robes, and said, "Men of Galilee, why do you stand looking into heaven? This Jesus, who was taken up from you into heaven, will come in the same way as you saw him go into heaven." (Acts 1:9–11)

The Gospel of Mark adds the following:

So then the Lord Jesus, after he had spoken to them, was taken up into heaven, and sat down at the right hand of God. (Mk 16:19)

To begin with, two questions naturally arise concerning the ascension: (1) "Why did Christ-Jesus do this?" and (2) "Where did he go?" Even though the Risen Saviour can materialize his resurrected vehicles at any time entirely at will, for the past two thousand years he has chosen to do this only on very rare occasions. Why is that?

Though there are a number of necessary reasons for the ascension, the foremost one was determined well before the resurrection. As Christ-Jesus fully realized from the temptations in the Wilderness, if he remained *physically* present and visible on earth for all time, then humanity would undoubtedly become entirely dependent on him for their material, social and spiritual well-being. This would stifle the progressive development of free-will and thereby smother positive self-advancement (ego-evolution).

By vanquishing sin, sickness, evil and death through the redemption and resurrection of his own fallen vehicles (which re-established the broken heavenly connection to God) Christ-Jesus became the "way-shower," the victorious guide to salvation. In order for others to similarly attain salvation, it must be a fully-conscious, voluntary process of active participation. While each person is responsible for their own salvation, Christ-Jesus has compassionately vowed to guide and assist all mankind in this rescue-mission until the end of the age.

A second important reason for the ascension of Christ-Jesus was that by withdrawing from physical visibility, those who seek his advice and assistance are thereby directed away from the earthly and pointed in the direction of the heavenly. Christian followers are thus motivated to develop their own superphysical senses in order to contact the Risen Saviour.

By withdrawing from regular physical visibility, a further important reason for the ascension was to provide Christ-Jesus with a protective "cloak of invisibility." By not being localized in physical space and time, adversarial powers would have no earthly focus for any malicious assaults directed at the Risen Saviour.

Even after his ascension from sight, however, Christ-Jesus has on rare occasions chosen to materialize in his resurrection form. The first such biblically-recorded appearance was to a fanatical Pharisee named Saul of Tarsus, who was persecuting and executing Christians during the time of the apostles. This early materialized appearance of the Risen Saviour had such a powerful effect on Saul that he fell to the ground and was blinded for three days. As a result, Saul was converted to Christianity and became St. Paul, the great "apostle to the gentiles."

The Ascension "Up Into the Clouds of Heaven"

Unfortunately, the biblical pronouncement that Christ-Jesus "ascended into heaven and is seated at the right hand of God" is interpreted by most Protestant denominations to mean that the Risen Saviour physically left the earth, went away to a distant heaven to be with God, and will not return to the earth until the "Second Coming," which heralds the

"Final Judgement" and the end of the world.

Fortunately, the Catholic and Orthodox faiths don't share this interpretation, and have always held that Christ-Jesus is not far-away in heaven, but is spiritually present in his mystical body the Church; infusing his resurrected life in the seven sacraments of baptism, confirmation, Holy Communion, confession, holy orders, marriage and the anointing of the sick.

From the clairvoyant information of esoteric Christianity, it is further understood that when Christ-Jesus ascended "up into the clouds," he took up supersensible residence in the etheric envelope surrounding of the earth. This was not simply an ethereal return to the pre-fallen, edenic state in Lemurian times that was experienced by primordial mankind. Similar to the interpenetration of the human etheric body by the astral and soul vehicles, the etheric envelope of the earth is interpenetrated by the substance and forces of the astral and soul worlds. The upper region of the etheric envelope is consequently highly organized, differentiated and inhabited by a wealth of elemental creatures and highly advanced beings. Since Lemurian times, then, the basic paradisal realm once inhabited by primordial mankind has not remained stagnant, but has extensively evolved and transformed.

The Fabled Land of Shambhala

In Buddhist, Tibetan and Theosophical literature, this planetary etheric realm is known as "Shambhala." Interestingly, Shambhala began as an ancient geographical location, as an island situated in a vast prehistoric sea in eastern Asia—in the area of what is now the Gobi Desert. After the last great flood, the island of Shambhala was occupied by a colony of Atlantean survivors under the leadership of an archangelic bodhisattva known in the East as

"Manu." Prehistoric, post-Atlantean cultures, such as the ancient Indian and the ancient Persian, were established by initiate-emissaries sent out from Shambhala.

As post-Atlantean civilizations sank deeper and deeper into earthly materialism (termed the "Age of Darkness" or "Kali Yuga"), the sacred centre of Shambhala was correspondingly uplifted into the invisible protection of the etheric realm. Throughout the Age of Darkness, the invisible centre of Shambhala expanded throughout the etheric envelope of the earth, eventually emerging as the magical kingdom or "Fairy-land of Shambhala." During Kali Yuga, Shambhala has been the "heavenly" abode of the bodhisattvas and has only been accessible to the most highly advanced initiates.

According to *The Theosophical Glossary* (H. P. Blavatsky; 2010), Shambhala is:

> [A] very mysterious locality on account of its future associations. A town or village mentioned in the *Purânas,* whence, it is prophesied, the Kalki Avatar will appear. The "Kalki" is Vishnu, *the Messiah on the White Horse* of the Brahmins; Maitreya Buddha of the Buddhists, Sosiosh of the Parsis, and Jesus of the Christians (See *Revelations*). All these "messengers" are to appear "before the destruction of the world," says the one; before the end of Kali Yuga say the others. It is in S'ambhala that the future Messiah will be born. Some Orientalists make modern Murâdâbâd in Rohilkhand (N.W.P.) identical with S'ambhala, while Occultism places it in the Himalayas.

As intimated in the Theosophical quotation above, Shambhala is associated with the Messiah, Christ-Jesus, who was believed to appear near the end of Kali Yuga. This esoteric notion has been confirmed by the clairvoyant research of Rudolf Steiner. In a lecture given on 9 March

1910 entitled, "Correspondences Between the Microcosm and the Macrocosm" (and published in *The Christ Impulse and the Development of the Ego-Consciousness*; 2010), the following information was presented:

> Man's physical environment will present a totally different aspect in the course of the next 2,500 years, through the addition of an etheric realm, which indeed is already here now, but which he will learn to perceive. This etheric sphere is even now spread out before the eyes of those who have carried their esoteric training as far as 'Illumination' ... Hence the traditions, which have preserved recollections of the old clairvoyance, tell us of an unknown Fairy-Land which has now disappeared from sight ... It is that Land from whence at certain times the Initiates—and at all times the Bodhisattvas—drew fresh forces ... Only to the highest Initiates is it accessible. But it is always stated that some day this Land will return to earth. That is true; it will return to earth! And the guide thereto will be He Whom men will see, when, through the vision of the Event of Damascus, they reach the Land of Shamballa ... The old forces can no longer lead man thither ... But the Christ-Event, which will be vouchsafed to man in this [twentieth] century through his newly-awakened faculties, will bring back the Fairy-Land of Shamballa, which through the whole of Kali-Yuga could only be known to the Initiates.

In esoteric answer to the question, "Where did Christ-Jesus go when he ascended into heaven?"—the Risen Saviour was vibrationally "raised up" into the heavenly "cloud-land" that encircles the earth—the planetary etheric region known as Shambhala. The term, "heavenly," is used here in a broad, general way to mean "superphysical." The true heavenly planes of the celestial world are of course much higher in vibration than the etheric and astral planes surrounding the earth. Within this planetary etheric region, Christ-Jesus sits at the centre of the twelve bodhisattvas and, as regent of the earth, directs the course of world evolution from the new heart-capital of Shambhala—the "New Jerusalem."

As the centre of civilization has migrated westward in post-Atlantean times: from India, to Persia, to Egypt, to Greece and Rome, and to Euro-America—so has the heart-centre of Shambhala shifted from Mongolian Asia, to the Tibetan Himalayas, to northern India (Himachal Pradesh), to the Middle East (Israel). This translocation of the etheric Shambhala centre throughout time accounts for the difficulty that secular investigators have in finding or authenticating Shambhala.

With the ascension of Christ-Jesus into Shambhala, the heart-centre was repositioned to the etheric space above the city of Jerusalem, biblically known as the "New Jerusalem." As the new "Lord of Shambhala," Christ-Jesus supersedes Amitabha, the "buddha of comprehensive love." For many centuries, Amitabha directed the western region of Shambhala, referred to in Buddhist writings as the "Pure Land" of Sukhavati, and he continues to assist Christ-Jesus in this capacity.

4.4 The Etheric Appearance of the Risen Saviour

The Process of Planetary Etherization

For the two thousand years since the ascension, the superplanetary forces of Christ-Jesus, united with the macrocosmic forces of the Word and the divine forces of the Son, have slowly and subtly raised the overall vibrational level of the earth. As a result, the age of spiritual darkness known as Kali Yuga has come to an end,[55] and human life and activity has become vibrationally "etherized." Unfortunately, due to the continuing and pervasive stranglehold of materialistic thinking in human minds, this initial etherization has not been entirely progressive. Rather than being immediately raised up to an increased awareness of the etheric realm of Shambhala (as intended), humanity has instead become enmeshed in the technological application of sub-earthly etheric forces; particularly electro-magnetic energy and nuclear energy. The obsessive proliferation of wireless technologies, such as radio, television, cell phones and computers is ample testament to this regressive etherization. While these etheric technologies can certainly be used for the betterment of mankind, they should not hypnotically distract human attention away from the etheric realm of Shambhala and the Risen Saviour.

Therefore, Christ-Jesus as lord of Shambhala and regent of the earth continues to labour for the *progressive* etherization of the planet. Increasingly, then, beginning in the early twentieth century, individual human beings will become spontaneously aware of a paradisal, "heavenly" realm mysteriously surrounding them. Moreover, particularly in moments of personal distress, Christ-Jesus will appear to them in his resurrected form, as he did to St. Paul on the road to Damascus. Christ-Jesus will increasingly descend out of the "cloud-land" of Shambhala, and individually appear as the Risen Saviour to many throughout the world. These visible appearances of the Risen Saviour are collectively termed, in esoteric Christianity, the "second coming of Christ-Jesus."

This esoteric understanding of the second coming of Christ-Jesus is of course much different than the conventional Christian conception. Conventionally, the Second Coming or "Parousia" of Christ-Jesus is a one-time, world-wide, future appearance that signals the end of the world and the final judgement of every human being, dead and alive. While esoteric Christianity also attests to a future process whereby humanity will be separated according to the personal acceptance or rejection of Christ-Jesus as the Risen Saviour, this distant occurrence is distinguished from the resurrected appearances that began in the early twentieth century.

Together with occasional *visible* materializations of his resurrected form, the Risen Saviour will also become increasingly perceptible to humanity in his *invisible* resurrected form. Concurrent with the overall planetary etherization of the earth, for the past two thousand years Christ-Jesus has also tirelessly worked in the subconscious regions of human nature to develop cognizant clairvoyant perception, beginning with etheric sight. As a result, ordinary individuals, not just trained initiates, will increasingly display a natural clairvoyant capacity for etheric perception.

The Etheric Shadow-Land of "Agharti"

Unfortunately, clairvoyant ability, like science and technology, is a "double-edged sword"; that is, it can be used for good or evil purposes. Somewhat predictably, together with the etheric growth and expansion of the radiant land of Shambhala, there has perniciously spread an etheric shadow-land referred to in Buddhist literature as "Agharti." As with Shambhala, all sorts of wild conjectures surround Agharti, proliferated by materialistic-minded charlatans and investigators. Fanciful conjectures such as: Agharti is a system of underground caves in Tibet; or Agharti is a city at the core of the earth; or Agharti is the inhabited space inside a hollow earth. According to reliable esoteric investigation, Agharti is a dark, subterranean etheric realm inhabited by black magicians and degenerate human beings opposed to Christ-Jesus.

The black heart-centre of Agharti has also migrated throughout post-Atlantean times; but instead of progressively moving from east to west, it has regressively moved from west to east: from prehistoric Mexico, to pagan Europe, to ancient Rome, to old Sicily, to modern Israel.[56] As the pure-heart of Shambhala is now situated in the etheric region above Jerusalem, the black-heart of Agharti is now situated in the subterranean region below Jerusalem. In the Apocalypse of St. John, the Jerusalem-centre of Agharti is referred to as:

> Babylon ... the great city which has dominion over the kings of the earth ... Fallen, fallen is Babylon the great! It has become a dwelling place of demons, a haunt of every foul spirit, a haunt of every foul and hateful bird; for all nations have drunk the wine of her impure passion, and the kings of the earth have committed fornication with her, and the merchants of the earth have grown rich with the wealth of her wantonness ... for thy merchants were the great men of the earth, and all nations were deceived by thy sorcery. And in her was found the blood of prophets and of saints, and of all who have been slain on earth. (Apoc 17, 18)

The Subterranean Etheric Realms of Agharti, Ahriman and Sorath

The subterranean etheric realm of Agharti should not be esoterically equated with the subterranean etheric realm of Ahriman. Agharti lies just below the surface of the earth and is inhabited primarily by evil human beings and fallen angels. The subterranean realm of Ahriman, on the other hand, lies at a deeper level of the earth's interior and is inhabited mainly by demonic fire-spirits (archangels). The Ahrimanic realm, therefore, is much more powerfully destructive than Agharti. The black magicians and fallen angels of sub-surface Agharti merely employ the corrupted subterranean ethers for their evil designs; but it is actually the deeper Ahrimanic beings that instigate the debasement and degradation of the light and chemical ethers.

At an even deeper and more malevolent level of subterranean iniquity is the infernal realm of Sorath at the earth's core. The evil inhabitants of this realm are depraved ego-beings (archai), known as "asuras," who instigate the corruption of life ether into nuclear energy. As the twelve bodhisattvas are centred around Christ-Jesus in Shambhala, so do twelve mighty demons surround Sorath in the infernal regions below Agharti. Together with fallen-Lucifer and Ahriman, there is Asmodeus (the demon of revenge), Merigum (the demon of turbulence), Apollyon (the demon of fury), Astaroth (the demon of defamation), Mammon (the demon of temptation), Moloch (the devourer of infants), Nisroch (the demon of hatred, despair and fatality), Lilith (the demon of debauchery and abortion), Adramelek (the demon of murder) and Belial (the demon of anarchy).

From his odious subterranean imprisonment, Sorath and his twelve diabolical co-conspirators direct the black magicians and fallen angels of sub-surface Babylon to war against the New Jerusalem in the etheric realm above them. Since Sorath has been effectively contained within the bowels of the planet by powerful celestial beings, he is unable to escape from the earth. The most that he can do is to "rise up out of the abyss"; that is, he can extend his evil influence up through the corrupted ethers of Agharti and the undifferentiated etheric substance enveloping the earth. Unfortunately for Sorath (but fortunately for humanity), his infernal etheric influence can only extend as far as the corrupted brain tissue of black magicians and evil-minded individuals.

As Christ-Jesus continues to raise the planetary vibration of the earth, even the dark interior of the earth will gradually become more sun-like. In time, Sorath and his fellow demons—assuming they will continue their evil intentions—will have no dark place to hide, and no dense matter to corrupt. As "toothless tigers," they will be increasingly enveloped in light and love, with no evil weapons to harm themselves or to harm others. Though not even God will arrest the free-will capacity to do evil, the forces of divine love can and will continue to spiritualize the matter and energy of the universe—which will effectively and benevolently surround and contain any evil.

The New Star-Centre of Planet Earth

The core of the earth has never been the exclusive domain of Sorath, and comprised only of debased primeval matter and energy. There have always been higher-vibrational realms associated with the centre of the earth; but these realms have had little to no contact with the corrupted aspect of the core. The group-souls of terrestrial plants, for example, reside in a heavenly plane of existence that is connected to the earth's core. Perhaps even more surprisingly, celestial beings of the First Hierarchy: thrones, cherubim and seraphim, radiate their mighty forces outwardly from the macrocosmic centre of the earth. Unfortunately, prior to the subterranean descent of Christ-Jesus, even the powerful celestial beings of the First Hierarchy were unable to penetrate and transmute the debased and corrupted core.

When Christ-Jesus descended to the centre of the earth after death, his hypostatic union with the divine Son—"the mystic star of his God-Self"—seared a small, spiritual opening in the debased matter of the earth's core. This established a direct link with the higher planes of heavenly existence, thereby permitting the gradual influx of macrocosmic forces from the advanced beings of the First Hierarchy. By establishing this inter-dimensional portal, Christ-Jesus connected heaven and earth in a way that was not previously possible.

The gradual inflow of macrocosmic forces into the earth's corrupted core is also working to transform the earth from planet to star, and to re-unite the earth with the sun in the far-distant future. As to the future fate of Sorath, hopefully he will turn away from evil and turn back toward God. If not, he will most certainly "fall out" of our particular evolution, as he has previously fallen out of other evolutionary life-waves in the primeval past.

The Seasonal Ascent and Descent of Christ-Jesus as Regent of the Earth

As planetary regent, and from his seat of authority in the etheric New Jerusalem, Christ-Jesus has united the individual life-rhythms of his own existence with the planetary life-rhythms of the entire earth. Analogous to waking and sleeping in human experience, the superphysical planetary vehicles and elemental beings of the earth rhythmically contract inwardly and expand outwardly over the course of a year. During the winter months, the elemental life-forces of the earth are most contracted inwardly toward the planetary centre; whereas in the summer months, the elemental life-forces of the earth are most expanded outwardly into the cosmic periphery. As a result, the earth as a planetary organism is most "awake" during the winter months (even though plant and animal life is dormant and hibernational at this time); and most "asleep" during the summer months (even though plant and animal life is most physically active at this time).

On the subject of the seasonal cycles of the year, as the alternating process of planetary "inbreathing" and "outbreathing," Rudolf Steiner stated the following in a lecture given on 1 October 1923 entitled, "Michaelmas-Soul":

We are nowadays little inclined to observe this in-and out-breathing of the earth. Human respiration is more a physical process; the breathing of the earth is a spiritual process—the passing out of the elemental earth-beings into cosmic space and their re-immersion in the earth. Yet it is a fact that just as we participate, in the tenor of our inner life, in what goes on in our circulation, so, as true human beings, we take part in the cycle of the seasons ... We shall learn to sense the course of the year as we do the expressions of a living, soul-endowed being ... In this way the human being evolves: he transforms himself in the course of the seasons by experiencing this alternation of nature-consciousness [in spring-summer] and self-consciousness [in autumn-winter]. (Published in *Michaelmas and the Soul-Forces of Man*; 1946)

The ascended Christ-Jesus, then, does not statically remain within the spiritual centre of Shambhala throughout the year; but instead journeys inwardly toward the centre of the earth in wintertime and outwardly into the wide expanse of the cosmos in summertime. Each year, he reaches the very centre of the earth at midnight on Christmas Eve. In other words, Christ-Jesus did not just descend into the infernal depths of the earth only once after his crucifixion, but he sacrificially does this annually for the ongoing salvation of humanity. Moreover, each year that he descends to the earth's primeval core, the spiritual light of the planetary star-centre that he established there grows brighter and stronger, thereby steadily weakening Sorath's evil influence.

In the centuries following his ascension into heavenly Shambhala, Christ-Jesus (through his exoteric Church) has instituted the four primary Christian festivals as celebrations of his annual, planetary ascent and descent: Christmas (at the winter solstice), Easter (at the spring equinox), St. John's Eve (at the summer solstice) and Michaelmas (at the autumn equinox).

4.5 Pentecost and the Descent of the "Holy" Spirit-Self of Christ-Jesus

The Esoteric Understanding of the Pentecostal Holy Spirit

Fifty days after his resurrection (or ten days after his ascension), Christ-Jesus sent down the Holy Spirit upon his step-mother, the apostles and 108 dedicated disciples, who had gathered together in Jerusalem according to his instructions. As biblically described, the descent of the Holy Spirit:

> [C]ame from heaven like the rush of a mighty wind, and it filled all the house where they were sitting. And there appeared to them tongues as of fire, distributed and resting on each one of them. (Acts 2:2, 3)

According to conventional Christianity, the Third Person of the Trinity—the Holy Spirit of God—directly descended upon the gathering, thereby filling each individual with the wisdom, courage and language skills necessary to spread the gospel message, and to begin the world-wide establishment of the new Christian church. This understanding is basically shared by esoteric Christianity, but with further detail concerning the Holy Spirit.

To esoteric understanding, it was the superplanetary spirit-self of Christ-Jesus that individually descended upon the first Christians at Pentecost. Recall that the superplanetary spirit-self of the Christ-being was too powerful to indwell the prepared vehicles of Jesus at the Baptism. Instead, the spirit-self of Christ externally enveloped the other vehicles of Jesus. In fact, according to esoteric Christianity, it was this same spirit-self of Christ that descended from heaven "like a dove" (Matt 3:16) at the baptism in the Jordan, and which was likewise referred to as the "Holy Spirit."

Equating the spirit-self of Christ with the divine person of the Holy Spirit is not entirely incorrect. Even in undeveloped human beings, the nascent vehicle of the spirit-self is a Trinitarian reflection of the Holy Mother-Spirit, as the life-spirit is a Trinitarian reflection of the Eternal Son, and the spirit-body is a Trinitarian reflection of the Heavenly Father. The divine forces of the Holy Spirit of God do indeed flow into the spirit-self vehicles of all created beings.

The esoteric significance of Pentecost, however, is that the superplanetary spirit-self of Christ-Jesus was also "raised up" as a "resurrected" vehicle, and therefore has the capacity of bi-location and miraculous regeneration. The multiple outpourings of the Saviour's spirit-self at Pentecost, and with it the divine forces of the Holy Spirit, was a clear demonstration by Christ-Jesus that though he is supersensibly invisible, he is not absent or far distant from humanity. The multiple bi-locations of his spirit-self are truly manifestations of "the Comforter, the Counsellor and the divine Teacher" that Christ-Jesus promised to send to his disciples after the ascension. As expressed in the gospel of St. John:

> Nevertheless I tell you the truth: it is to your advantage that I go away, for if I do not go away, the Counselor will not come to you; but if I go, I will send him to you. And when he comes, he will convince the world concerning sin and righteousness and judgment: concerning sin, because they do not believe in me; concerning righteousness, because I go to the Father, and you will see me no more; concerning judgment, because the ruler of this world is judged. "I have yet many things to say to you, but you cannot bear them now. When the [Holy] Spirit of truth comes, he will guide you into all the truth." (John 16:7–13)

The Descent of the Saviour's "Holy" Spirit-Self and the

Birth of the Christian Church

When the resurrected spirit-self of Christ-Jesus individually descended upon the Christian faithful at Pentecost, it was of the nature of an "oversoulment"; that is, it did not indwell the body and soul vehicles of those present, but instead externally enveloped each of their heads as a spiritual halo (refer to Figure 9, if necessary). It is crucially important to esoterically understand that these Pentecostal oversoulments were not multiple *copies* of the spirit-self of Christ-Jesus, but rather multiple *bi-locations* of the one spirit-self of Christ-Jesus. In other words, the descent of the Holy Spirit at Pentecost was manifold, bi-located appearances of the Risen Saviour in the vehicle of his resurrected, superplanetary spirit-self.

Since each individual oversoulment was in fact Christ-Jesus himself, this shared outpouring of the one resurrected spirit-self served to mystically unite all the disciples gathered at Pentecost. This mystical union is understood by esoteric Christianity and mainstream Christianity to be the "birth of the Christian Church."[57]

In its fundamental nature, then, the Christian Church is not simply a material building, temple or institution; but rather a living assembly of faithful disciples united into one mystical body by the "holy" spirit-self of Christ-Jesus. Christ-Jesus is the single "head" of the Church, and the various oversouled members comprise the unified "body" of the Church. Moreover, the mystical union of Christ-Jesus and his body the Church is infused with divine love, wisdom and power. This intimate union has been allegorically described as the loving union of a bride-groom (Christ-Jesus) and a bride (his Church). In the words of the *Catechism of the Catholic Church*:

> The unity of Christ and the Church, head and members of one Body, also implies the distinction of the two

within a personal relationship. This aspect is often expressed by the image of bridegroom and bride. (Paragraph 796)

What the soul is to the human body, the Holy Spirit is to the Body of Christ, which is the Church. To this Spirit of Christ, as an invisible principle, is to be ascribed the fact that all the parts of the body are joined one with the other and with their exalted head; for the whole Spirit of Christ is in the head, the whole Spirit is in the body, and the whole Spirit is in each of the members. The Holy Spirit makes the Church "the temple of the living God." (Paragraph 797)

Within most current denominations of Christianity, the ritual or sacrament of baptism functions as a ceremonial method of "calling down" the holy spirit-self of Christ-Jesus, in order to incorporate the baptized candidate as a "living cell" in the mystical body of the Church.

The intimate social relationship of Christ-Jesus and his people, the Church, is unique in human history. Though there were other instances of "communal unification" in the past, these were quite different from the ecclesiastical unity of the Risen Saviour. In the distant Lemurian past, for example, when mankind was still in an animal-like stage of development without the gift of self-awareness, individual human life-forms were similarly conjoined by a common "group-soul." But though our Lemurian human ancestors were united by a more advanced being, they possessed no individualized ego or capacity for free-will. At that time the group-soul completely dictated the behaviour of each human life-form, similar to the instinctual control exerted by the group-souls of today's animals.

Moreover, in later post-Atlantean times, individual human beings were conjoined into clans, tribes, cultural groups and nation-states by "folk-souls." These folk-souls were

191

archangelic-like beings who worked at a subconscious level to develop the etheric bodies of a select group of human beings. As with the ancestral group-souls, the various folk-souls worked at an instinctual level of consciousness below ego-awareness and did not actively promote free-will development.

The unique relationship of Christ-Jesus and his people the Church, however, is intended to elevate individual human ego-awareness to the advanced level of the spirit-self consciousness of Christ-Jesus. As well, this communal unification in no way infringes on personal free-will; but, instead, actively promotes true spiritual freedom. Christ-Jesus, then, is more than just the group-soul or the folk-soul of the Church; he is currently the holy spirit-self of the Church.

In time, as mankind continues to advance, Christ-Jesus will also "send down" his superplanetary life-spirit and his superplanetary spirit-body upon his people the Church, further elevating them to his own high estate "at the right hand of the Father."

CHAPTER 5

THE MYSTERY OF SALVATION: WALKING IN THE FOOTSTEPS OF CHRIST-JESUS

5.1   Integrating the Redeemed Vehicles of Christ-Jesus

Replicas of the Redeemed Vehicles as Important Salvational Resources

BY REDEEMING AND resurrecting his body and soul vehicles, Christ-Jesus forged a path to salvation, not only for himself, but for all those who choose to follow. Though there are unique details in every human life, the overall path to salvation is fundamentally the same for everyone; it is a path that echoes the one established by Christ-Jesus. Moreover, salvation from sin, sickness, evil and death is never forced on anyone; each person must freely choose to be saved, and must tread the path to salvation by their own efforts. The pilgrim on the path, however, is not left alone and abandoned without help or comfort. As Saviour, Christ-Jesus has provided struggling humanity with numerous guides, supports and resources along the path, to help ensure success. One such valuable resource is the extended use of the various replicas of his redeemed vehicles.

Recall that after his mystic death, Christ-Jesus discarded each of his body and soul vehicles as he victoriously journeyed outwardly into the heavenly realm of the celestial world. While this process of vehicular shedding typically occurs after death, for most human beings it takes hundreds, even thousands of years to complete. With Christ-Jesus, however, the process was furiously accelerated, such that it was completed in less than a day and a half. Moreover, unlike typically discarded vehicles, those of Christ-Jesus did not dissipate into superphysical space. Not only did each of the discarded vehicles miraculously endure, but multiple exact copies of each vehicle were immediately replicated as well—multiple copies of his redeemed physical phantom, his redeemed etheric body, his redeemed astral body and his redeemed ego-bearing soul vehicles.[58]

These miraculous vehicular replications didn't just float about superphysical space vacuously and without purpose or usefulness, but were instead beneficially attracted to numerous worthy disciples of Christ-Jesus during the centuries that followed the birth of his Church. Once attracted to a worthy Christian disciple, the redeemed replica would mystically integrate with the disciple's own vehicles to provide uplifting and transformative guidance and help.

According to Rudolf Steiner's clairvoyant research, from the fourth to the twelfth century, replicas of the Saviour's redeemed etheric body were mystically integrated into numerous Christian disciples, such as St. Augustine of Hippo (354–430) and John Scotus Erigena (c.815–c.877). From the twelfth to the fifteenth century, however, it was mostly the replicas of the Saviour's redeemed astral body that were mystically integrated into Christian disciples, such as St. Francis of Assisi (c.1181–1226) and St. Elizabeth of Hungary

(1207–1231). During this time, replicas of the Saviour's redeemed soul vehicles were also woven into the soul fabric of other Christian disciples. St. Thomas Aquinas and many other Scholastic philosophers, for example, had a replica of the Saviour's redeemed intellectual soul woven into their own intellectual soul vehicles.

By the sixteenth century, Christian discipleship had sufficiently advanced to begin attracting replicas of the Saviour's redeemed consciousness soul. Since the consciousness soul is the primary soul vehicle of self-awareness, integrated replicas characteristically convey the egoity, the selfhood, of Christ-Jesus. In rare instances prior to the sixteenth century, replicated ego-bearing vehicles of Christ-Jesus were also integrated into the souls of medieval mystics such as Johannes Tauler (c.1300–1361) and Meister Eckhart (c.1260–c.1327), as well as the fourteenth-century founder of Rosicrucianism, Christian Rosenkreutz.

Once human self-awareness becomes sufficiently "Christed"; that is, once a Christian disciple consistently identifies with the self-consciousness (the "I Am") of Christ-Jesus, and thereby experiences his own true self as the selfhood of God (the Son), then the forces of the spiritualized ego can sufficiently penetrate the substance of the physical body to such a degree that an attraction is established with a replicated phantom of the Risen Saviour. In other words, replicas of the Saviour's redeemed phantom body can also be integrated into the human physical body; but only after extensive spiritual development is achieved.

Only the highest Christian initiates, then, have begun to integrate the replicated phantom body of Christ-Jesus. Nevertheless, by doing so, the lengthy, multi-incarnational process of forming one's own resurrection vehicles is greatly accelerated.

The Positive and Negative Effects of Replica Integration

By attracting and integrating the various replicas of the Risen Saviour's redeemed vehicles, Christian disciples can significantly accelerate their own rate of evolutionary development. In actual fact, through this integration the faithful disciple becomes increasingly "Christ-like" much faster, and much easier.

By integrating a replica of the Saviour's etheric body, the Christian disciple is infused with the profound life-memories of Christ-Jesus, which greatly assist in establishing accurate knowledge and clear understanding of earthly and heavenly life. By integrating a replica of the Saviour's astral body, the Christian disciple is infused with the deeply devotional feelings and sentiments of Christ-Jesus, which greatly assist in personally experiencing the internal, emotional life of the incarnated Saviour, and his loving relationship with God. By integrating a replica of the Saviour's ego-bearing soul, the Christian disciple is infused with the moral values and enlightened conscience of Christ-Jesus, which greatly assist in making decisions and forming judgements in conformity with the intentions of God. By integrating a replica of the Saviour's phantom body, the Christian disciple is infused with regenerative forces of physical harmony and vitality, which greatly assist in keeping the physical body strong, youthful and healthy.

Since the integration of the redeemed replicas often results in a rapid, Christ-like transformation in thought, in feeling, in activity and sometimes even in appearance, reasonable care must be taken by the Christian disciple to avoid developing a "Christ-Jesus delusion" (or "Christ complex"); that is, entertaining the mistaken notion that one is *actually* the Risen Saviour. This is especially so after an ego-bearing replica of Christ-Jesus has been suddenly and mystically integrated into one's own soul. In this case, the ego of the Christian disciple may become immediately and overwhelmingly infused with the sublime personhood of Christ-Jesus. If the disciple is unprepared or unfamiliar with the mystical process of vehicular integration, it is very easy to conclude that he (or she) has actually become Christ-Jesus. Tragically, in our current materialistic culture, many unknowing individuals have spent time in psychiatric facilities dealing with a Christ complex, without understanding the underlying mystical reason for the disorder.

5.2 The Supersubstantial Body and Blood of the Saviour: The Mystery of Holy Communion

The "Transubstantiation" of Bread and Wine

On the path to salvation, in addition to becoming Christ-like by mystically integrating replicas of the Saviour's *redeemed* body and soul vehicles, the devoted Christian disciple can also choose to unite sacramentally with the Saviour's *resurrected* body and soul vehicles. This miraculous process of sacramental unification is commonly known as "Holy Communion." In esoteric Christianity, it is also referred to as the "sacred mystery of the bread and wine."

The religious ritual of sharing bread and wine is very ancient in human history, as biblically indicated when the primordial priest-king, Melchizedek, "brought out bread and wine" to the Hebrew forefather, Abram (Gen 14:18). Moreover, the age-old, Jewish ritual feast known as the Passover Seder is characterized by the solemn partaking of wine and the consumption of unleavened bread ("matzoh"). On the night before his crucifixion when Christ-Jesus celebrated the Passover meal with his twelve disciples, by blessing the bread and wine (that is, by offering them up to

God the Father), he mystically united his own body to the bread and his blood to the wine. By doing so, he transformed the traditional Jewish ritual into a powerfully-new Christian sacrament.

In its highest and most efficacious form within the liturgies of the Catholic and Eastern Orthodox churches,[59] the ceremonial bread and wine are miraculously "transubstantiated" into the resurrected "body" and "blood"—the resurrected "substance" and "life-force"—of the Risen Saviour. The term "transubstantiated" means that the fundamental substances of the consecrated bread and wine have been miraculously changed, but the outward appearances remain exactly the same. In other words, to empirical observation, the transubstantiated bread and wine still look, feel, taste and smell like bread and wine, even though their essential underlying material has become the resurrected substance (body) and life-force (blood) of Christ-Jesus.

It's important for esotericists to understand that transubstantiating bread and wine in the sacrament of Holy Communion is not an occult process of "magic," whereby a priest-magician manipulates subtle forces of Nature to transform ordinary matter into supernatural substance. Rather, it is Christ-Jesus himself who acts as high-priest by "sending down" and oversouling the officiating priest with his holy spirit-self. Through the oversouled words ("This is my body ... this is my blood") and the oversouled actions of the officiating priest, the original sacrifice and mystic death on the cross is "re-presented,"[60] as Christ-Jesus lovingly offers his entire life up to God the Father. The Father-God eternally responds with a downpouring of divine love, thereby "raising up" (transubstantiating) the sacramental bread and wine into the resurrected "body" and "blood" of the Saviour.

The consecrated bread and wine, then, are not

transubstantiated into physical flesh and blood; but rather into the materialized substance and life-force of the Saviour's resurrection vehicles.[61] In its pure, invisible state, resurrected substance and life-force are manifestations of supernatural light. In Holy Communion, then, the supernatural light-substance of the Saviour is miraculously materialized in the form of ordinary bread and wine. Rather than appearing in his full resurrected glory, Christ-Jesus in Holy Communion *appears* as humble food and drink. The question naturally arises, "Why does he do this?"

Uniting with the Risen Saviour in "Holy Communion"

Part of the answer to this question is connected to the reasons for the Saviour's ascension; that is, his wise decision to not make regular, fully-materialized physical appearances in his resurrected form. By remaining invisible to ordinary sight, esoteric Christian disciples are encouraged to develop their etheric and astral senses in order to contact the Risen Saviour; and exoteric Christian followers are encouraged to develop perceptual "faith" as an intuitive method of discerning supernatural truth.

A second important reason for the Risen Saviour to sacramentally materialize in the form of bread and wine is to physically demonstrate the humble nature of divine love. Though divine love is infinitely great and powerful, it is also infinitely meek and lowly. Furthermore, though divine love requires nothing for itself, it continually gives of itself—like lowly bread and wine—to nourish and sustain all of creation.

A third, deeply-profound reason to retain the appearances of consecrated bread and wine has to do with the way these substances are received by the worthy Christian disciple. They must be consumed. As Christ-Jesus biblically explained:

"I am the living bread which came down from heaven; if

any one eats of this bread, he will live for ever; and the bread which I shall give for the life of the world is my flesh ... Truly, truly, I say to you, unless you eat the flesh of the Son of man and drink his blood, you have no life in you; he who eats my flesh and drinks my blood has eternal life, and I will raise him up at the last day. For my flesh is food indeed, and my blood is drink indeed. He who eats my flesh and drinks my blood abides in me, and I in him. As the living Father sent me, and I live because of the Father, so he who eats me will live because of me. This is the bread which came down from heaven, not such [manna] as the fathers ate and died; he who eats this bread will live for ever." (John 6:51–58)

Even ordinarily when food and drink are consumed, it is an intimate and mysterious process, whereby external matter is taken into the body, biologically transformed, and then incorporated into the fluids and tissues that maintain physical life. In a similar (though supernatural) process, when the transubstantiated bread and wine are consumed, the worthy communicant is mystically united with the entire person of the Risen Saviour—"body, blood, soul and divinity."[62] In the sacrament of Holy Communion, then, the communicant does more than simply integrate a replicated vehicle of Christ-Jesus, but actually undergoes a mystical process of mutual interpenetration and unification with the "real presence" of the Saviour. Christ-Jesus is taken into the body and soul of the communicant, and the communicant is taken into the body and soul of Christ-Jesus; thereby spiritually uniting them both in the oneness of God. In other words, during Holy Communion, a temporary degree of hypostatic union takes place between God and communicant, with Christ-Jesus acting as mediator.

Expressed in yet another way, the worthy communicant in Holy Communion is temporarily indwelt by the Risen Saviour. Since most communicants in the exoteric Church have not undertaken esoteric training to develop clairvoyant perception, the mystical union that occurs with the consumption of the supersubstantial bread and wine is experienced almost entirely subconsciously; that is, below conscious awareness. Moreover, as the ingested bread and wine is slowly dissolved within the body, the Risen Saviour is correspondingly de-materialized and returns to invisible, superphysical existence. As a result, the indwelling of Christ-Jesus and the hypostatic union with God that occurs during Holy Communion is only temporary, hence the need to regularly partake of the Blessed Sacrament.

Holy Communion as an Exoteric and Esoteric Path to Christ-Jesus

It should be obvious, then, from the foregoing information that there is a deep and pervasive *esoteric* component to Holy Communion, even though it is a practice of the exoteric Church. Moreover, for the esoteric Christian with even rudimentary clairvoyant ability, Holy Communion is a richly rewarding experience, and a profound developmental assist on the long road to salvation. This fact has been echoed by Rudolf Steiner in a lecture given on 13 October 1911 entitled, "The Exoteric Path to Christ" (published in *From Jesus to Christ*):

> For those who desired to come to Christ, the Holy Communion was a complete equivalent of the esoteric path, if they could not take that path, and thus in the Holy Communion they could find a real union with Christ. For all things have their time. Certainly, just as it is true in regard to the spiritual life that a quite new age is dawning, so is it true that the way to Christ which for centuries was the right one for many people will remain for centuries more the right one for many ... [I]n the best

sense of inner Christian development the Holy Communion has spiritualised the human soul and filled it with the Christ.

5.3 The Chalice and the Lance: The Mystery of the Holy Grail

The Sacred Chalice of the Holy Blood

In connection with the blood of Christ-Jesus, a hidden esoteric path of Christian development was also established in the early centuries following the ascension. This esoteric Christian path centres primarily around an important holy relic—the chalice which Christ-Jesus used as the communion cup at the Passover meal on the night before his death.

After the Last Supper, it is historically unclear what became of the holy chalice. According to Catholic tradition, it was first safeguarded by St. Peter, who used it to celebrate Holy Communion until his martyrdom. After that, the holy chalice was said to have been passed down to St. Peter's papal successors, until Sixtus II (in 258 AD) secretly sent it to Spain to prevent Roman emperor Valerian from acquiring it. In Spain, the holy chalice was placed under the protectorship of the Spanish monarchs, until it became the property of the cathedral in Valencia.

Though there are a number of conflicting esoteric legends regarding the history of the holy chalice, a common narrative was that after the Last Supper the sacred relic was kept by Joseph of Arimathea, who used it the following day to collect blood from the Saviour's body as it was taken down from the cross. Shortly afterward, Joseph was imprisoned. Prior to his release, the Risen Saviour appeared to Joseph, and instructed him concerning the mysteries of the holy chalice. Shortly thereafter, Joseph (together with family, friends and followers) took the sacred relic, journeyed to western Europe, and there established a secret family brotherhood to guard the holy chalice.

Some legendary accounts relate that Joseph settled in Britain, some claim France.[63] Clairvoyant research, however, confirms Catholic tradition that the holy chalice came to be secretly guarded in pre-medieval Spain. In the epic poem, "Parzival," written by Wolfram von Eschenbach (c.1170–c.1220), the exact location was said to be the "marvelous castle at Montsalvat in the Pyrenees." The guardians of the holy chalice would later (around 750 AD) become known as the "Knights of the Holy Grail." These Spanish knights were not synonymous, of course, with the Arthurian Knights of the Round Table in Britain (though some writers have mistakenly equated the two chivalric orders).

The Hidden History of the Holy Grail

So how did the sacred chalice of Christ-Jesus come to be esoterically known as the "Grail" or the "Holy Grail"? One possible explanation is that the term is derived from the Old French word, "graal" or "grael," meaning "a cup or bowl of metal, wood or earth." If one accepts that the holy chalice was secretly guarded in northern Spain during the Middle Ages, then another reasonable etymology for "Holy Grail" is from the Spanish word, "sangréal"—since "sang réal" means "royal blood"; that is, the "sacred blood" of Christ-Jesus, "king" of heaven and earth. Moreover, by separating the letters of sangréal slightly differently into "san gréal," then the word becomes "Holy Gréal" or "Holy Grail."

Even from what has been briefly said so far, it is obvious that the esoteric significance of the Holy Grail lies in the fact that it was associated with the sacrificial blood of the Saviour;

particularly since the sacred chalice was used by Christ-Jesus to miraculously transform the Passover wine into his supersubstantial blood (life-force). Even if Joseph of Arimathea didn't actually use the chalice to physically collect the Saviour's blood at the crucifixion, the essential life-substance that was transubstantiated in the chalice at Passover was the same purified blood that was shed on the cross.

As a sacred relic, the Holy Grail was believed to possess miraculous powers, particularly of healing and bodily regeneration. Once the hidden history of the Holy Grail was popularized by Chrétien de Troyes in a twelfth-century romantic poem entitled, "Perceval, the Story of the Grail," the "Quest for the Holy Grail" became a widespread, idealized endeavour throughout Europe and the Middle East. Initially, the secret guardianship of the Holy Grail involved real historical figures, actual historical events and specific geographical locations. But as time went on, the physical details of the Holy Grail became increasingly allegorical and symbolic; thereby transcending time and space.

Some of the hidden historical figures associated with the Holy Grail are Titurel, the Spanish king who originally built the protective castle at Montsalvat; Amfortas, the second son of Titurel (also known as the "Fisher King"), who inherited the royal guardianship of the Grail castle; Parzival (Parsifal, Perceval), a virtuous knight who successfully "discovered" the castle and the Grail, and who later succeeded his uncle Amfortas as the Grail king; Herzeleide, the mother of Parzival and sister of King Amfortas, who died of a broken heart; princess Sigûne, the granddaughter of Titurel and a cousin of Parzival; Schionatulander, the young knight betrothed to Sigûne who was tragically killed; Lohengrin, the son of Parzival who also became a Grail-knight with the title "Knight of the Swan"; and Klingsor, the evil Duke of Terra de Labur, who opposed the Grail-knights through black magic from his kingdom ("Chastel Merveille") in southern Italy (Calabria) and from a pagan worship-site in Sicily ("Calot Bobot").

The Grail as an Early Stream of Esoteric Christianity

As a fundamental current in the hidden stream of esoteric Christianity, it is important to keep in mind that the sacred chalice of the Holy Grail was *never* at the centre of a formal religion; of an institution of theistic worship, veneration and faith—as *was* the sacramental chalice of Holy Communion. One simple clue to this important difference was the fact that the chalice of Holy Communion was celebrated in a church, whereas the Holy Grail was safeguarded in a castle.

Furthermore, the "quest" for the Holy Grail was primarily a path of the head, of intellectual thinking; not a path of the heart, of devotional feelings. In Holy Communion, the path to the Risen Saviour was (and still is) primarily experiential and below conscious awareness. The sacred content of the chalice had to be consumed and the consecrated bread (the "host") had to be eaten in a devotional mood of faith. With the Holy Grail, however, the path to the Risen Saviour was primarily conceptual; the mysterious content that was once held in the holy relic had to be contemplated and understood in full conscious awareness.[64]

There is, therefore, no single definitive answer or solution to the "mystery" of the Holy Grail. As a Christian path to knowledge of the spirit, the primary focus of the protectors and the seekers of the Holy Grail was to spiritually comprehend the foremost Christian mystery, the "Mystery of Golgotha"; that is, the mystery of the salvational death and resurrection of Christ-Jesus. In an effort to intellectually comprehend the Mystery of Golgotha, it was often necessary for the Grail-seeker to understand and assimilate the spiritual knowledge of the past—the secret gnosis and the ancient mystery-wisdom. The old clairvoyant knowledge, however, had to be considered in a completely new way; "it had to be seen through the eyes of Christ-Jesus"; that is, it had to be grasped in waking consciousness, and it had to be understood in relation to the resurrection of the Saviour. As further explained by Rudolf Steiner in *An Outline of Esoteric Science* (1989):

> A knowledge thus arose among these new [Grail] initiates that included everything that was the subject of ancient initiation, but in the center of this knowledge there radiated the higher wisdom of the mysteries of the Christ event. Only in a small degree could such knowledge flow into general life, while the human souls of the fourth period of culture [during the Middle Ages] had to consolidate the faculties of intellect and feeling. Thus it was at that time a very "hidden knowledge" ... The "hidden knowledge" flows, although quite unnoticed at the beginning, into the mode of thinking of the men of this period ... The "hidden knowledge," which from this side takes hold of mankind now and will take hold of it more and more in the future, may be called symbolically "the wisdom of the Grail." If this symbol, as it is given in legend and myth, is understood in its deeper meaning, we shall find that it is a significant image of the nature of what has been spoken of above as the knowledge of the new initiation, with the Christ mystery at its center. The modern initiates may, therefore, also be called "initiates of the Grail."

As here indicated by Rudolf Steiner, among the legendary Grail-knights were some highly-advanced seekers ("new initiates") who had direct knowledge of Christ-Jesus and the superphysical realms.[65] Moreover, according to esoteric research, there were at least two bodhisattvas who incarnated as Grail-knights: Parzival was an embodiment of Mani, the founder of Manichaeism; and Schionatulander was an embodiment of Master Thomas (Rudolf Steiner). By the twelfth and thirteenth centuries, exalted Christian initiates no longer incarnated within the Grail stream, and so the Knighthood of the Holy Grail slowly died out. Ironically, by the time vague information about the Holy Grail became publically known, the Knighthood no longer existed and any historical details had already become romanticized, fictionalized, and the stuff of legends.

At a deeper esoteric level, however, a much more profound symbolic and allegorical process occurred with the historical demise of the Grail-Knighthood. Due to the involvement of advanced Christian initiates, powerful spiritual forces were infused into the lives, locations and events surrounding the Holy Grail. Consequently, much of the historical detail was imbued with timeless archetypical meaning and significance. The people, places and events of the Grail, then, became microcosmic and macrocosmic prototypes and symbols for superphysical knowledge. Through this transformative process, ancient mystery-wisdom was imaginatively "Christianized."

Various Mystery-Truths Clothed in the Symbolism of the Grail Story

Once the physical relic of the Grail-chalice became conceptually abstracted and transformed into a changeable symbol, then various esoteric Christian "mysteries" concerning humanity and the universe could be clothed in the imagery of the Grail. For example, if the Grail-chalice symbolized any vessel that contained the purified blood of the Saviour, then the Grail-vessel could microcosmically represent the physical or etheric heart of the Christian initiate, which held the "etherized" blood of Christ-Jesus. Or on a planetary level, the entire sphere of the earth could represent the Grail-vessel that held the redeemed blood of the dying Saviour that fell to the ground at the crucifixion.

Moreover, if the Grail-chalice is visualized as being a silver receptacle, and the Grail-blood is associated with the radiating, life-giving forces of the Solar-Christos, then the Holy Grail represents the superplanetary interaction of sun and moon. The lunar forces of the silvery moon act as the superplanetary vessel for the Christed, life-giving forces of the golden sun. Interpreted in this way, the unusual sight in the night sky where the dark reddish disc of the moon is seen above the silver-white crescent shape below can also be understood as a superplanetary symbol of the Holy Grail. The round blood-red sphere ("host") of invisible Christ-imbued sun-forces is cradled by the silvery crescent Grail-chalice below. During the daytime, as an even more exalted interpretation, the golden life-giving disc of Christ-light in the sky above (the "celestial host") is esoterically understood to be macrocosmically cradled in the "womb of Nature," in the Grail-vessel of the Logos-Word.

If the Grail-chalice is visualized as a stone receptacle, then the Holy Grail can be microcosmically understood to be the mineralized human skeleton that contains within it the red, blood-producing marrow. By spiritualizing the inner blood-marrow with the life-giving forces of the Risen Saviour, the outer death-dealing forces of skeletal mineralization will also be spiritualized and transformed. Biblically expressed, the "stone will be rolled away from the tomb by the angel of God."

The Grail-chalice as a broad symbol for a vessel or container has also been used to illustrate the "universal principle of manifestation," which states that lower vibrating substance acts as the "vessel" or "container" for the higher vibrating material. So, for example, matter is the Grail-chalice for energy; energy is the Grail-chalice for mind; and mind is the Grail-chalice for spirit. In a similar, physiological application, the body is the Grail-chalice for the blood; the blood is the Grail-chalice for etheric warmth; warmth ether is the Grail-chalice for the ego-forces; the ego-soul is the Grail-chalice for the superplanetary Christ-forces; Christ-consciousness is the Grail-chalice for the macrocosmic forces of the Word; and the Logos-Word is the Grail-chalice for the divine forces of the Son.

The Grail-Lance as another Important Mystery-Symbol

A secondary Christian relic was also associated with the medieval Knighthood of the Holy Grail, the "Holy Lance of Longinus." This was the lance (or spear) that was used by the Roman centurion, Longinus, to pierce the side of Christ-Jesus at the crucifixion. According to Grail-legend, the lance was also safeguarded at Montsalvat, and was purported to miraculously issue a continuous flow of blood from the spear-tip. The Grail-lance has also been used symbolically, together with the Grail-chalice, to convey profound Christian mystery-truth.

Later Rosicrucian teaching used the Grail-lance as a microcosmic symbol for a beam of sunlight and the Grail-chalice as a symbol for the "petalled-cup" of a flower. As the life-generating blood of the Saviour issued from his pierced heart at the crucifixion, so the beam of sunlight that pierces the petalled-heart of the flower stimulates the life-generating forces of the plant. It was also taught, in connection with this particular symbolic interpretation, that within the human body a similar life-process can occur. If the Christ-redeemed generative energy ("spiritualized kundalini") is consciously directed upward along the shaft (the Grail-lance) of the spinal column, thereby piercing the superphysical forces of the cup-shaped larynx (the Grail-chalice), then the powerful life-generating forces of the "creative word" will be released. It was this creative word spoken by Christ-Jesus that healed the sick, calmed the storm, and raised the dead.

Due to the pointed shape of the spear-tip, the Grail-lance has also been esoterically used as a physiological symbol for the pointed, cone-shaped pineal gland in the human brain. Likewise, the curved shape of the Grail-chalice has been used as a symbol for the round, bulbous-shaped pituitary gland. In esoteric Christian development, when the subtle forces of the pineal gland (the Grail-lance) pierce the rarified forces of the pituitary gland (the Grail-chalice), then conscious perception of superphysical realms (of the Risen Saviour) is opened up for the initiate.

Other esoteric interpretations have assigned attributes of gender to the symbols of the Grail-lance and to the Grail-chalice. The penetrative shape and function of the Grail-lance was logically used as a masculine symbol, and the receptive shape and function of the Grail-chalice was logically used as a feminine symbol.[66] The generation of new life in human sexuality could therefore be symbolically understood as the outcome of the sacred forces of the Grail-lance interacting with the sacred forces of the Grail-chalice.

The esoteric purpose of genderizing the symbols of the Grail-lance and the Grail-chalice was certainly not to confuse the sublime details of the Saviour's crucifixion with coarse terms of human sexuality. Rather, it was to "raise up" and spiritualize human sexuality by associating it with the fullness of divine love that was demonstrated by Christ-Jesus on the cross. It was to remind the Christian initiate that the salvation of human nature through the resurrected power of the Risen Saviour also includes the sanctification of human sexuality.

Grail-Personalities as Prototypes of Human

Development

Certain historic individuals associated with the Holy Grail have also been esoterically abstracted, and thereby serve as meaningful representatives, or prototypes, of human development. Take, for example, the virtuous knight, Parzival, who successfully finds the Grail and becomes Grail-king as a result of his devotionally-persistent questioning and searching for the truth. He quite naturally serves as the ideal prototype of the Christian initiate in modern times (the post-Renaissance age of the "consciousness soul")[67] who must acquire supersensible knowledge and union with the Risen Saviour as a result of his own conscious efforts. The modern Christian initiate can no longer depend entirely on prior tradition or religious authority for spiritual truth. Nor can the modern Grail-seeker faithfully and exclusively rely on the hidden forces of subconscious development to successfully result in real union with Christ-Jesus.

The defining characteristic of King Amfortas was the chronic, agonizing wound in his thigh that could only be healed by the power of the Grail-lance in the hands of an exalted Christian knight. Amfortas, then, easily serves as the symbolic prototype of human nature in general, which has been wounded by original sin and which perpetually suffers from incarnation to incarnation. Only the regenerative power of divine love issuing from the resurrected life of the crucified Saviour can completely heal wounded human nature. The "wound of Amfortas" can also be equated with the mortally-injurious "thorn of Sorath" that was nefariously implanted in the corrupted phantom body.

The black magician, Klingsor, serves as an obvious prototypical representative of all the evil forces that occultly oppose the spread and development of Grail-knowledge; that is, knowledge of Christ-Jesus in the superphysical realm. Chastel Merveille, the dark domain of Klingsor, is therefore an apt symbol for the subterranean, etheric realm of Agharti.

5.4   The Rosicrucian-Christian Path to the Risen Saviour

The Demise of the Grail-Knighthood and the Succession of the Rosicrucian Fraternity

For a brief but frightening period in the thirteenth century (around 1250 AD), all clairvoyant perception of superphysical realms abruptly ceased for mankind. During this dark time, the silvery chalice of Grail-knowledge was also eclipsed by this black shadow of supersensible extinction.

Nevertheless, as the dormant seed springs to new life by being planted in darkness, so too from out of this shadowy century, the essence of Grail-knowledge sprang forth anew in the fertile soul of a young, specially-prepared Christian initiate. Though this illustrious initiate died prematurely, anonymously and without worldly accomplishment in that life, in his following fourteenth-century incarnation, he took the symbolic name of "Christian Rosenkreutz" (Christian Rose-Cross), and renewed the stream of esoteric Christianity by establishing the Rosicrucian Fraternity.

With the passing of the medieval age of chivalry and the corresponding demise of the Grail-Knighthood, then, there secretly arose in its place a new, Renaissance form of esoteric Christianity—Rosicrucianism. During Renaissance times, therefore, any sincere seeker of Grail-knowledge would be karmically directed toward the Rosicrucian Fraternity which became the new "guardian" of esoteric Christian wisdom. Moreover, within the hidden confines of Rosicrucianism, Grail-knowledge was slowly transformed from being a visionary, pictorial, imaginative expression of truth into being superphysical knowledge (centred in Christ-Jesus) that was conveyed in clear, objective, intellectual concepts.

While it was certainly difficult in medieval times to gain access to the Knighthood of the Grail, it was equally difficult for the esoteric Christian seeker to make contact with the Rosicrucian Fraternity during Renaissance times. Nevertheless, it is an ancient and inerrant esoteric adage that states, "When the seeker is ready, the teacher appears." Therefore, despite the necessary veil of concealment, the Rosicrucian Fraternity was still accessible to any true and sincere seeker of esoteric Christian knowledge.

As well as learning the fundamental esoteric Christian teachings of the Fraternity, the Rosicrucian student could also undertake an initiatory program to develop wakeful supersensible perception leading to a conscious union with Christ-Jesus. The Rosicrucian-Christian path of initiation was not simply a pale imitation of the practices used in the ancient, pagan Mystery-religions. Since those ancient initiatory practices were no longer effectual, appropriate or progressive, they were supplanted by a Christ-centred system that was specifically designed to satisfy the rigors of intellectual thinking and the clear, self-conscious awareness of modern times.

Anthroposophy as an Independent Branch of the Rosicrucian Fraternity

With the establishment of anthroposophy in 1912 by advanced Christian initiate, Rudolf Steiner, the Rosicrucian-Christian path of esoteric development was made publicly available for the first time in its hidden history. Consequently, for anyone currently desiring to follow the true Rosicrucian initiatory path, it is no longer necessary to directly contact the hidden Fraternity. Moreover, should aspiring Christian seekers be telepathically contacted by Christian Rosenkreutz (in his current embodiment), it is almost certain that they will still be directed to the publicly-accessible information of anthroposophy (at least to begin with).

In conformity with the sacred mission of esoteric Christianity (as established by Christ-Jesus through St. John the Beloved) the original Rosicrucian-Christian path of initiation was *not* a faith-based religion or an emotionally-centred mystical pursuit. Rather, it was the intellectual study and systematic acquisition of superphysical knowledge—particularly in connection to Christ-Jesus. In other words, it was a form of metaphysical, Christian philosophy.

In the twentieth-century hands of Christian initiate Rudolf Steiner, however, Rosicrucian philosophical wisdom was "modernized" and transformed into a science—a "science of the spirit." Moreover, applying the methodology of natural science, Steiner did not merely publicize age-old Rosicrucian knowledge handed down through tradition, but verified and validated all existing Rosicrucian information with his own, independent clairvoyant research. In anthroposophical spiritual science, then, the Rosicrucian-Christian path to union with Christ-Jesus has been carefully adapted to the unique requirements of modern life.

For example, modern initiatory development does not require hierophants (gurus), temples (castles), journeys, seclusion, asceticism, secrecy, rituals, ordeals, vows or blood oaths. The Rosicrucian-Christian path of spiritual science can be undertaken by any and all sincere aspirants, no matter what their particular station in life as regards occupation, gender, age, nationality, religion, geographical location, marital status, education or income.[68]

The Rosicrucian-Christian Initiatory Path of Spiritual Science

The modern-day, Rosicrucian-Christian path of esoteric development (as publicly revealed by Rudolf Steiner) is an intensive, seven-step process, the first phase of which has been traditionally termed the "period of study." During this foundational phase of initiation, the Rosicrucian student earnestly develops abstract, logical thinking. What is most important during this period of cognitive development is not so much the *content* or subject-matter of thinking, but the actual *process* of thinking; that is, the process of generating individual thoughts and then logically connecting them together in a meaningful way.

Though the content in developing "pure thinking" can vary, what is often helpful in this regard are mathematical, geometrical or philosophical concepts that direct the thinking away from familiar sensory perceptions and ideas to more abstract levels of thought. Contemplating existing esoteric subject-matter that has been acquired from *reliable* clairvoyant investigation is also encouraged, since this content also directs thinking away from concrete thoughts to more ethereal ideas in a safe, positive and healthy way.

The intended outcome of the period of study is for the Rosicrucian student to consciously experience "brain-free" thinking; that is, to consciously experience true thinking as an activity that occurs "outside" the grey matter and neurons of the physical brain. This exhilarating experience is usually accompanied by the immediate realization that pure thinking is, therefore, a superphysical (spiritual) process. It is superphysical thinking that generates chemical activity in the brain; not the reverse—it is not chemical activity in the brain that *necessarily* generates thinking.[69] If that were indeed the case, then human beings would be nothing more than chemical automatons; that is, involuntary creatures with no independent will, that are entirely directed by the chemical activity of the brain.

With the conscious awareness and development of brain-free thinking, the Rosicrucian student experiences a preliminary degree of superphysical existence. As such, this fundamental experience can form the basis for developing more advanced perception of superphysical existence, thereby preparing for the next stage of initiatory training, the "development of Imaginative knowledge."

Developing Imaginative Knowledge

The seven steps in Rosicrucian-Christian initiatory training are not strictly sequential; that is, it is not entirely necessary to complete everything possible at one stage to move on to the next. Nor does advancing from one stage automatically lead to the next highest stage. So for example, the Rosicrucian student can advance from the first stage to the fourth stage, or start at the second stage and move back to the first. While exceptions certainly occur due to unique individual differences, for most Rosicrucian students, however, initiatory development proceeds in a predictable, sequential manner. Once brain-free thinking has been experienced (stage one), then it is a logical next step to develop Imaginative knowledge (step two).

Human beings possess the remarkable, often underappreciated faculty of "imagination"; that is, the cognitive ability to freely create pictures or images in the mind. Vague or abstract ideas are thereby given mental form which, in turn, can greatly assist in the formulation of a concept or the expression of an idea in the physical world. Ordinarily, mental images or "imaginations" are entirely subjective; that is, they are generated internally within the mind of a subject-person. Consequently, even though most ordinary imaginations are based on sensory perceptions of people, places and events in the physical world, they don't necessarily conform in every detail to outer, objective reality.

For this reason, most serious thinkers today dismiss personal imaginations as a reliable source of knowledge and truth.

For the Rosicrucian student who has experienced thinking as a superphysical activity, however, the experience of mental imaginations is also to become a superphysical experience. In the case of sensory perception, impressions of the physical world are received and internally processed by the mind, thereby becoming the basis for obtaining reliable knowledge and truth about the physical world. Similarly, in the case of supersensory perception, impressions of the beings, locations and events of the superphysical world can be received and internally processed by the imaginative faculty of the mind, such that a mental image (an "Imagination")[70] is generated. In this case, the mental image was not internally generated by the subject-person, but by the objective impressions of the superphysical world. These objective Imaginations, then, can become the initial, tentative basis for obtaining reliable truth and knowledge of the superphysical world.

It is crucially important at this stage for the Rosicrucian-Christian student to develop "truthful discernment"; that is, the ability to clearly distinguish between a supersensible Imagination and an ordinary imagination. In establishing supernatural truth, this discernment is just as necessary as knowing the sensory difference between an authentic physical perception and a fabricated hallucination or illusion. Unfortunately, not every mental image that "pops into one's head" is a supersensible Imagination. Most involuntary imaginations are simply the subjective picture-creations of the subconscious mind.

Nevertheless, countless painters, sculptors, architects, writers, musicians, inventors, scientists, theologians and civic leaders throughout history have unknowingly received authentic Imaginations from the superphysical world. Truth be told, it has very often been seemingly gratuitous Imaginations from the superphysical world that have repeatedly impelled and guided positive historical change in human evolution.

With sufficient training, it is recognized that true Imaginations have a distinctive transcendent quality and are perceived to enter one's consciousness "from above." Subconscious imaginations are instead perceived to "rise up" in awareness "from below." Moreover, true Imaginations, since they are created by objective supersensible forces, are usually accompanied by an aura of significance; they appear charged with vibrant, life-filled meaning, even though that meaning may not be entirely clear or understandable at first.

It is also important for the Rosicrucian student to understand, at this developmental stage, that even though Imaginations are directly connected to the forces of the supersensible world, they are not direct perceptions of the supersensible world; but rather, symbolic picture-representations. As such, the symbolic imagery is not the full reality; but rather, the picture-image of an Imagination needs to be additionally interpreted in order to uncover the underlying supernatural meaning and truth. Properly understanding an Imagination, however, belongs to higher stages of Rosicrucian-Christian development.

Originally, knowledge of the Holy Grail was received and conveyed in the form of superphysical Imaginations. Likewise, early Rosicrucian wisdom—including the mysteries of Christ-Jesus—was also clothed in the symbolic form of pictorial Imaginations.

Reading the Occult Script

It is one thing to consciously receive a supersensible Imagination; it is quite another thing to gather some meaningful understanding from the Imagination. The same thing can be said for perceptions of the physical world;

simply perceiving something does not automatically mean that it is understood. For example, a man and a woman are observed on a street corner shaking hands. It is not necessarily understood *why* that incident occurred. Is it a first date; are they old friends; is it a business deal; are they having an affair; are they undercover police; are they related?

Simply perceiving individual Imaginations is analogous to seeing separate words on a page. While each word certainly has its own unique meaning, greater understanding can be acquired by connecting the individual words into phrases, sentences and paragraphs. At the third stage of Rosicrucian initiatory training, then, the student learns how to meaningfully connect individual Imaginations together, thereby "reading" the hidden wisdom—the "occult script"—of the supersensible world. For this reason, this developmental stage is termed, "reading the occult script."

While supersensible Imaginations are characterized by a vivid pictorial quality, supersensible knowledge acquired from reading the occult script exhibits more of an interconnecting musical quality. Analogous to arranging individual musical notes into chords, phrases, melodies, tunes and instrumental compositions, reading the occult script combines separate Imaginations into meaningful combinations and associations. Supersensible knowledge achieved in this way is termed "Inspiration" in the traditional Rosicrucian teachings. As with the capitalization of the Rosicrucian term, "Imagination," the Rosicrucian term, "Inspiration," is also capitalized to distinguish this particular supersensible perception from ordinary inspiration.

In the case of ordinary inspiration, the source of the inspired idea or concept is usually the physical world, not the supersensible world. In ordinary life, then, one can be inspired by a television program, or a beautiful sunset, or a political speech, or a religious sermon, or a romantic novel, or an impressive cityscape. As with supersensible Imaginations, authentic Inspirations are not self-generated, but are mentally conveyed by the subtle forces of the supersensible world.

At a certain degree of Inspirational development, the harmonious motions and interrelationships of the sun, the moon, the planets and the cosmos are supersensibly perceived. Beginning with the Mystery-school of Pythagoras in the sixth-century BC, this elevated experience has been esoterically referred to as perceiving the "music of the spheres."[71] In the case of the Christian mysteries, Inspirational knowledge greatly assists in comprehending the superplanetary existence, activity, mission and significance of Christ, as Solar-Christos—the regent of the sun.

Preparing the Philosopher's Stone

The fourth or middle stage of Rosicrucian-Christian initiatory training, rather than developing increased clairvoyant perception, was designed to assist in the long-term development of the physical resurrection body. This inner, transformative process was termed by the esoteric Christian alchemists of the Middle Ages, "preparing the philosopher's stone."

Like most of the publicly-known information connected with the hidden stream of esoteric Christianity, popular knowledge about the philosopher's stone is mainly in the form of distortions, half-truths, misunderstandings, falsifications and exaggerations. For instance, preparing the true philosopher's stone was not a metallurgical attempt to change base metal into real gold. Instead, it was a process of moral development that endeavored to uplift and refine the debased elements of one's nature into the spiritual gold of holy, saintly behaviour.

Nor was the philosopher's stone a magical elixir that would guarantee immortality. Instead, together with the refinement of moral character, preparing the philosopher's stone also involved the purification and transformation of the physical body. Though it was understood, in conventional Christian theology, that the righteous soul would be gifted with an immortal resurrection body by Christ-Jesus at the Final Judgement, it was also esoterically held that the Christian initiate could accelerate this future bodily acquisition through specialized, initiatory training.

In modern-day, Rosicrucian-Christian initiatory training, this bodily transformation is accelerated by specific breathing exercises that have the remarkable effect of gradually transforming the physical heart, from being an involuntary organ of blood circulation, into a life-giving organ under voluntary control. Moreover, with the aid of these special breathing exercises, the physical heart slowly acquires the biological capacity to extract and safely redistribute blood-carbon, which is normally expelled as unusable carbon dioxide through the lungs.

By slowly acquiring the biological capacity to chemically divide unusable carbon dioxide in the blood into usable oxygen and usable carbon, the physical body of the Rosicrucian-Christian initiate also begins to develop the necessary internal forces to transform and incorporate the usable carbon and usable oxygen into self-regenerating living tissue. Since carbon can manifest in a wide range of forms from ultrasoft black powder to superhard clear diamond, the self-regenerating, carbon-based body of the distant future will exhibit a transparent, see-through quality. It is this future "diamond-body" that is the true philosopher's stone.

Preparing the philosopher's stone, then, is the conscious participation with Christ-Jesus in building up one's own immortal resurrection body. Even though the acquisition of a personal resurrection body belongs to the distant future, and will require several incarnations to complete, the esoteric Christian can accelerate the process through Rosicrucian-

Christian initiation. Moreover, as previously indicated, properly preparing the philosopher's stone—the resurrection body—is a combination of moral development and specialized breathing.

In Rosicrucian-Christian initiatory training, great emphasis is placed on combining moral development with cognitive and clairvoyant development. This wise emphasis conforms to the spiritual truth that God is perfect goodness personified. Therefore, the higher one ascends in spiritual development, and the closer one gets to the divine presence of God, the more one is infused and permeated with moral goodness. Unlike the amoral chemical activity of the physical world, the substances and forces of the heavenly world manifest a high moral component. To properly perceive, understand and access the exalted heavenly realms, Christian initiates must likewise clothe themselves in moral goodness.

Since the Rosicrucian-Christian breathing exercises enter deeply into the physical body, and thereby materially transform it, without an accompanying increase in moral goodness, they will instead have a destructive effect on the body. For safety reasons, the details of these exercises have not been freely released to the general public.

At the fourth stage, the focus of Rosicrucian-Christian training moves from cognitive perception in the head to moral and physiological development in the heart.[72] By concentrating initiatory attention on the heart, the Rosicrucian-Christian student unites more fully with Christ-Jesus, since the human heart is the sacred centre of his salvational activity. Since the heart is the bodily organ most intimately connected with the forces of the sun, the Christ-being, as solar regent, works with special concentration in this chest area.

Moreover, within the chest region of the human body is a cube of three-dimensional space that is inaccessible to the forces of Ahriman and Lucifer.[73] Within this impenetrable space, the human ego-self is free from Luciferic and Ahrimanic interference. At the centre of this space is the human heart, wherein is situated a superphysical inner sanctum, a "holy of holies," where none but the divine forces of love can enter in. Through this hallowed gateway in the human heart, the Rosicrucian-Christian initiate is better able to encounter and unite with the Risen Saviour.

Mankind, Know Yourself as Microcosm of the Macrocosm

While increased understanding of the superphysical world is certainly enhanced by experiencing isolated Imaginations in meaningful relationships with each other (Inspirations), there is still a deeper and more comprehensive knowledge of the supersensible world that can by developed in Rosicrucian-Christian training. Once again, this deeper understanding can be analogously compared to the reading of a book; in this case, a murder-mystery. While a great deal of factual information can be gathered in a murder-mystery by the sequential reading of words arranged into sentences, the overall meaning of the details—the complete story—isn't necessarily understood until the very end of the book. Once the murder-mystery is solved, then all the separate sentences are seen to come together into a unified, meaningful solution.

Somewhat similarly, at the fifth stage of Rosicrucian-Christian initiatory training, a deeper, more unified comprehension of the supersensible world is experienced. In Rosicrucian terminology, these penetrating clairvoyant perceptions are referred to as "Intuitions." Once again, the capitalization of the Rosicrucian term, "Intuition," is to distinguish it from ordinary, everyday intuitions. Commonly-experienced intuitions are most often vague, undefined feelings of truth that have not been acquired through conscious reasoning. Most often, these ordinary intuitions pop into our waking awareness from the regions of the subconscious mind; whereas clairvoyant Intuitions shine into our conscious minds from out of the supersensible world.

Characteristically, clairvoyant Intuitions unite separate parts of a truth into a meaningful whole. Since everything in the universe is interconnected, nothing in creation exists in isolation from the rest of the universe. With this truth in mind, the large macrocosmic aspects of the universe can be partially understood by studying the small microcosmic elements of the universe. Likewise, the small microcosmic elements of the universe can be partially comprehended by studying the large macrocosmic features of the universe. For thousands of years, this observable truth has been esoterically known as the Hermetic law of correspondences: "As above, so below; as below, so above." Modern science also applies this universal principle regularly in its empirical research (without necessarily acknowledging its Hermetic origin).

Applying the law of correspondences, the Rosicrucian-Christian initiate can thereby acquire sublime esoteric wisdom concerning the great universe (the macrocosm) by "Intuitively" studying the organs and systems of the physical body (the microcosm). Likewise, elevated knowledge concerning the microcosmic physical body can be "Intuited" by clairvoyantly studying the macrocosmic universe. In this way, the Rosicrucian-Christian initiate comes to realize and experience that mankind is truly created in the image and likeness of God.

In an effort to better understand the nature of a supersensible Intuition, the term "Realization" can also be equally applied. To experience a supersensible Realization (with a capital "R") is to directly and immediately perceive the underlying truth—the essential reality—of something. The experience of a Realization (or Intuition) is often accompanied by a sudden burst of supersensible light as the underlying truth is consciously "revealed."

Authentic Intuitions (or Realizations) are best received when the mind is completely stilled, without active thought, and peacefully receptive to any "messages from above"; that is, messages from the superphysical world. At first, the condition of "mind at rest" seems strange and unusual, even a bit frightening. As intellectual beings living in the modern age, we are so used to the constant din of thought activity in our heads, during waking life, that without it is cause for fear that we might cease to exist. The famous philosophical dictum of René Descartes (1596–1650), "I think, therefore I am," clearly implies that if I don't think, then I am not—I don't exist.

The happy result of "stilling the mind" is that self-awareness continues to exist; and more importantly, once thinking has been experienced as a superphysical activity, then one's selfhood (one's ego-awareness) is also experienced as "something" superphysical. Moreover, the illuminating experience of directly knowing (of "Realizing") that the self exists superphysically is, itself, an authentic Intuition.[74] At this stage of Rosicrucian-Christian training, the initiate comes to Intuitively know that the ego-self exists supersensibly; that it transcends and directs human thought, and that it is intimately connected to the great universe (the macrocosm). However, the full knowledge of the ego-self's relationship to the universe, and also to God, is only unfolded during the sixth and seventh stages of Rosicrucian-Christian training.

Entering Into the Great Universe (Immersion in the Macrocosm)

At this stage of initiation, Rosicrucian-Christian instruction intentionally avoids warm and fuzzy catch-phrases; such as "becoming one with the universe," or "slipping into the cosmic ocean," or "merging with the great I AM." This is to counter the common but mistaken notion, among mystically-minded esotericists, that superphysical union with the great universe involves a return to nascent humanity's primeval condition of semi-conscious, pre-egoic oneness with the natural world. Macrocosmic oneness is mistakenly envisioned as a pleasure-filled melting away of crystallized self-awareness into a dreamy ocean of blissful all-consciousness.

This false vision of cosmic unity is clearly a regressive attempt to return to the nostalgic past and is, therefore, a Luciferically-generated Imagination. In contrast, the Rosicrucian-Christian initiate is trained to unitively enter into the great universe in full conscious awareness. Moreover, rather than a diminishment of ego-awareness, true cosmic oneness involves a universal expansion of self-awareness that reaches out to embrace all of creation.

Entering into the great universe through Rosicrucian-Christian training is essentially an initiatory endeavour to cultivate brief moments of hypostatic union with the Logos-Word—the one life of the cosmos. Only highly advanced celestial beings, such as Christ-Jesus, are able to constantly maintain a conscious union with the Logos-Word. Less-developed humanity (as presently constituted) must remain content with temporary moments of universal "oneness."

Even though human beings regularly undergo an astral expansion into the great cosmos during sleep, the experience is entirely unconscious for the uninitiated. For the sufficiently trained Rosicrucian-Christian initiate, however, the cosmic expansion during sleep becomes increasingly experienced in full conscious awareness. A similar but chronologically longer process of cosmic expansion and universal oneness also occurs after death. Likewise for the uninitiated, the after-death experience is largely semi-conscious; but for the initiated, cosmic consciousness after death is vividly experienced.

For the Rosicrucian-Christian initiate, the safest and surest guide into the wide expanse of the great cosmos is, of course, Christ-Jesus. United with the Risen Saviour, the Christian initiate experiences cosmic oneness as a living interconnectedness of being that is wedded together through the unitive power of divine love. Caution, however, must be exercised in any attempt to astrally expand into the cosmos, since Lucifer also acts as a centrifugal force of universal diffusion. Unfortunately, with Lucifer as cosmic guide, the seeking soul is led regressively into the old cosmos of wisdom and light, rather than progressively into the new cosmos of love and warmth.

Increasingly, the Rosicrucian-Christian initiate carries over the macrocosmic oneness experienced during sleep (and between incarnations) into daily waking life. As a result, the surrounding natural environment becomes suffused with an all-pervading universal life that is intimately united with the initiate's own interior life. Separate daily existence is thereby perceived to be a tiny droplet in an ocean of cosmic existence that flows in and around the Rosicrucian-Christian initiate. This vivid experience of superphysical interconnectedness was biblically conveyed by Christ-Jesus in the Gospel of John (15: 4, 5) where he stated:

"Abide in me, and I in you. As the branch cannot bear fruit by itself, unless it abides in the vine, neither can you, unless you abide in me. I am the vine, you are the branches. He who abides in me, and I in him, he it is that bears much fruit, for apart from me you can do nothing."

Since the conscious experience of cosmic oneness is emotionally supercharged with rapturous joy, exhilaration, amazement, beauty, wonder and love for all, Rosicrucian-Christian instruction for this stage of initiation deliberately de-emphasizes the exalted emotional effects. This perspective avoids the detrimental possibility of pursuing macrocosmic immersion for the euphoric emotional "high" that occurs. The Rosicrucian-Christian principle, regarding initiatory training, is that healthy emotional experience is a complementary after-effect that rightly follows proper cognitive development; emotional experience is never the primary goal of initiatory training.

The Seventh Stage of "Divine Blessedness"

The seventh and final stage of Rosicrucian-Christian training is intended to bring the initiate into more of a conscious union with God, as exemplified in Christ-Jesus. Moreover, this divine union is expected to be fully-conscious and experiential, not simply mystically-vague and theoretical. At this stage, successful Rosicrucian-Christian initiates superphysically stand "face-to-face" in the singular presence of their true self and "Intuitionally know" ("Realize")—with illuminated certainty—that their true self immortally exists as a spiritual reflection of God.[75] They are able to knowingly declare, "I AM one with God." Furthermore, "seventh-stage," Rosicrucian-Christian initiates Intuitionally know that the essential nature of their true self is divine spirit; that is, divine love.

As with the experience of oneness with the macrocosm (the Logos-Word), the transcendent experience of oneness with God only occurs during special, momentary "out-of-body" conditions. Once again, only highly-advanced celestial beings are capable of maintaining a more enduring, conscious union. Nevertheless, in time, the Rosicrucian-Christian initiate is able to carry over the experience of out-of-body union with God increasingly into daily waking life. In this way, an everyday sense of unitively abiding in the all-encompassing presence of God is more lastingly maintained.

At this developmental stage, then, advanced Rosicrucian-Christian initiates look out at surrounding Nature and conceptually see their own spiritual self reflected in the underlying spirit of God. They are able to knowingly declare: "I see my spiritual self mirrored in the spirit of God that underlies the natural world around me." In ancient Vedantic initiatory training, this enlightened declaration was expressed in Sanskrit as "Tat Tvam Asi," and was highly regarded as one of the "Grand Pronouncements" (Mahavakyas). While Tat Tvam Asi literally translates as "That You Are," the initiatory interpretation is "My Self and God are One."

Higher Stages of Rosicrucian-Christian Initiation

While there are more advanced levels of Rosicrucian-Christian initiatory training, these have not, as yet, been publicly revealed. One can be certain, however, that the goal of any further training is to lead the dedicated Rosicrucian-Christian initiate into an ever-deeper communion with the Risen Saviour and the Macrocosmic Word; and thereby into an ever-expanding, spiritual love-relationship with the Trinitarian God.

5.5   The Mystic-Christian Path to Salvation

The Gospel of John as a Path to Salvation

In addition to establishing Rosicrucianism as a modern-day esoteric Christian path to salvation, Christian Rosenkreutz (in his previous incarnation as St. John the Beloved) has also established a complementary esoteric path of "Mystic-Christianity" within the stream of conventional, exoteric Christianity. The foremost guidebook for this particular path of salvation is, not surprisingly, the Gospel of John.

The course of development that characterizes the path of Mystic-Christianity is based on the words of Christ-Jesus himself when he declared: "I am the way, and the truth, and the life; no one comes to the Father, but by me" (John 14:6). In other words, by "walking in the footsteps" of the Messiah, by sincerely striving to imitate his exemplary life on earth, the Christian disciple is led to God through union with Christ-Jesus; thereby attaining personal salvation.

In addition to the Gospel of John, there have been other influential religious texts throughout Christian history that have attempted to assist the devotional Christian in becoming "Christ-like." The *Imitation of Christ*, by the medieval German monk Thomas à Kempis (c.1380–1471), and *Transformation in Christ: On the Christian Attitude*, by Catholic philosopher Dietrich von Hildebrand (1889–1977), are two such examples.

The Gospel of John, however, is much more powerful and effective as an exoteric, initiatory guidebook since it was transcribed from the progressive impulses of the superphysical world by the exalted Christian initiate, Lazarus-John. With the Mystic-Christian path, as outlined in John's Gospel, it is necessary to do more than simply meditate on, or to contemplate, the recorded events of the Saviour's life on earth (though these can certainly be valuable developmental exercises). The Mystic-Christian disciple endeavors to deeply understand, and fervently apply, the sacred truths and the moral principles as taught and exemplified by Christ-Jesus in the Gospel. By striving to embody the moral "way" and the ideological "truth" of Christ-Jesus, the faithful disciple more perfectly conforms his or her own "life" to that of the Risen Saviour.

Following in the Footsteps of Christ-Jesus

By imitating "the way, the truth and the life" of Christ-Jesus, Mystic-Christians logically follow in the footsteps of the Risen Saviour. By doing so, they will inevitably undergo experiences in their own lives that mirror the profound events in the life of Christ-Jesus. So for example, by inwardly surrendering their entire lives to God as a free-will gesture of child-like dependency and trust, Mystic-Christian disciples will experientially mirror the loving sacrifice of the Saviour's crucifixion in their own lives. By directly experiencing the initiatory ordeal of the "mystic cross," the Christian disciple is psychically prepared to experience the "mystic death" and thereby "cross" into the superphysical realm in full consciousness.

The underlying, developmental principle of Mystic-Christianity, which requires that Christian followers personally experience the major transformative life-events of Christ-Jesus, has been succinctly conveyed by mystic poet and German priest, Angelus Silesius (1624–1677):

> Though Christ a thousand times in Bethlehem be born,
> But not within thyself, thy soul will be forlorn;
> The cross on Golgotha thou lookest to in vain,
> Unless within thyself it be set up again.

Since the initiatory path of Mystic-Christianity characteristically involves deep, prolonged spiritual contemplation, it is best undertaken in quiet, peaceful seclusion, such as a monastic environment. This requirement, of course, makes this particular salvational method much more difficult for modern-day Christian aspirants to access, and to effectively apply. In fact, throughout the Christian era there have been very few noteworthy Christian mystics who have successfully followed this difficult path.

Some of the most familiar, Christian mystics known

historically are Justin Martyr (c.105–c.165) Pseudo-Dionysius (c.500), St. Bernard of Clairvaux (1090–1153), St. Hildegard of Bingen (1098–1179), St. Francis of Assisi (c.1181–1226), Meister Eckhart (c.1260–c.1327), Dante (c.1265–1321), Johannes Tauler (c.1300–1361), St. Catherine of Siena (1347–1380), St. Ignatius of Loyola (1491–1556), St. Teresa of Avila (1515–1582), St. John of the Cross (1542–1591), John Donne (1572–1631), Jakob Boehme (1575–1624), John Bunyan (1628–1688) and St. Padre Pio of Pietrelcina (1887–1968).

The Transformative Stages of Mystic-Christianity

In Catholic tradition, the path of Mystic-Christianity is comprised of three stages of soul development: (1) purification, (2) illumination, and (3) mystical union. In Eastern Orthodox tradition these transformative stages are termed: (1) "katharsis," (2) "theoria," and (3) "theosis." In both traditions, the three stages correspond to body, mind and soul (spirit).

The first stage of purification, or katharsis, is focused primarily on disciplining the physical body in order to refine and uplift the passions, desires and compulsions "of the flesh." This has been traditionally accomplished through regular fastidious prayer; periodic fasting and abstinence; self-mortification; vows of poverty, chastity and celibacy; manual labour; and works of social charity, such as feeding the hungry, caring for the sick and sheltering the homeless. The term, "asceticism," most directly applies to this first stage of bodily transformation, though it has also been applied to the entire path of Mystic-Christianity.

The second stage of illumination, or theoria, is focused primarily on enlightening the conscious mind through the infused wisdom of the Holy Spirit. Knowledge acquired at this stage is understood to be a deeper, more profound intuitive comprehension of the spiritual reality underlying sacred scripture and the natural world—a form of "Christian gnosis." At this stage, the life-events of Christ-Jesus, as biblically described (particularly in the Gospel of John), are the primary source material for mystical contemplation and meditation.

To assist in a deeper, more mystical contemplation of scripture, St. Benedict in the sixth century first introduced the monastic practice of "Lectio Divina" (Divine Reading). With this mystical method of study, the Christian contemplative is required to imaginatively immerse himself or herself—together with Christ-Jesus—in the scriptural event being read. In this way, the biblical passage becomes a living, personally-experienced event whereby spiritual insights can arise through the grace of the Holy Spirit. Similarly expressed by St. Padre Pio: "Through the study of books one seeks God; by meditation one finds him."

The third stage of Mystic-Christianity, that of mystical union, or theosis, focuses on the experience of uniting the personal soul with the spirit of God. This mystical union with God may be experienced in a number of ways, ranging from a conscious awareness of God's abiding presence, to a hypostatic oneness with the spiritual nature of God. True mystical union is regarded as a grace, a gift from God, and not as a personal accomplishment that has been justly-earned or self-achieved.

Moreover, in Mystic-Christianity the ultimate attainment of "divinization"—mystical union with God—can only be fully realized by becoming "Christ-like," since the Risen Saviour most perfectly exemplifies the hypostatic union of man and God. In the words of Christ-Jesus: "I am the way, and the truth, and the life; no one comes to the Father [God], but by me" (John 14:6). This role of Christ-Jesus in the divinization (theosis) of humanity has been well-summarized in the

Catechism of the Catholic Church as follows:

> The Word became flesh to make us "partakers of the divine nature": "For this is why the Word became man, and the Son of God became the Son of man: so that man, by entering into communion with the Word and thus receiving divine sonship, might become a son of God." "For the Son of God became man so that we might become God." "The only-begotten Son of God, wanting to make us sharers in his divinity, assumed our nature, so that he, made man, might make men gods." (Paragraph 460)

Within the overall, three-stage path of Mystic-Christianity, finer transformative divisions or developmental stages have also been delineated. For example, St. John of the Cross in his two-volume poem, *Dark Night of the Soul* (c.1578), allegorically described the path of Mystic-Christianity as a "ten step ladder of mystical love." Rudolf Steiner, in numerous lectures (such as "Esoteric Christianity—The Gospel of St. John and Ancient Mysteries"; 27 November 1906) distinguishes seven major stages of initiatory development:

(1) the washing of the feet
(2) the scourging
(3) the crowning with thorns
(4) the crucifixion
(5) the mystic death
(6) the burial and resurrection
(7) the ascension

Anglo-Catholic mystic, Evelyn Underhill (1875–1941), in *Mysticism: A Study of the Nature and Development of Man's Spiritual Consciousness* (1911), postulated a five-stage process to "the way" of Mystic-Christianity:

(1) the awakening of the self
(2) the purification of the self
(3) the illumination of the self
(4) the dark night of the soul
(5) the unitive life

The popular Lenten devotion of the Fourteen Stations of the Cross, observed by the Catholic, Lutheran and Anglican churches, can also be effectively used as contemplative stages of Mystic-Christian divinization. In actual fact, any significant event in the life of Christ-Jesus, such as the annunciation, the nativity, the baptism, or the transfiguration can serve as a contemplative means of drawing closer to the living Saviour, not only in cognitive understanding, but also in direct, first-hand experience.

While the stage of purification (katharsis) in Mystic-Christian development certainly involves disciplining the will in relation to the physical body, and the second stage of illumination (theoria) clearly focalizes on thinking and the spiritualization of the mind, the third and highest stage of mystical union (theosis)—by endeavouring to unite the soul with God through divine love—concentrates primarily on *affective* development; that is, the inner life of feeling and emotion. The true path of Mystic-Christianity is, therefore, essentially a path of the heart, rather than a path of the head, or of the hand.

The Path of Love versus the Path of the Will

The broad diversity of Mystic-Christianity, however, has for many centuries included a well-known developmental system that concentrates primarily on training the will. Rather than a mystical union of divine love, this particular mystical path endeavours to unite the personal free-will of the Christian aspirant with the supreme will of God.

This Mystic-Christian "path of the will" was first established in the sixteenth century by St. Ignatius of Loyola, the founder of the Society of Jesus (the Order of Jesuits). Ignatian will-development is undertaken primarily through a four-stage process known as "The Spiritual Exercises." Each of the four stages is designed to be accomplished in a week's time, with each week focusing on a different theme:

(1) the first week is human sin
(2) the second is Christ's life on earth
(3) the third is Christ's death on the cross
(4) the fourth is Christ's risen life

The developmental exercises are mainly in the form of prayers, meditations and visualizations taken from the New Testament. Moreover, the key technique in applying these Ignatian exercises is the extensive and compulsory use of the creative imagination. Through imaginative prayer and imaginative contemplation, the scriptural events of Christ-Jesus become sensorially tangible and experientially real for the Christian mystic (similar to the practice of Lectio Divina).

The Latent Danger of the Ignatian Spiritual Exercises

In addition to cultivating detailed imaginations based on scripture, however, Ignatius has also included two forceful, non-scriptural imaginations of his own, as an integral part of The Spiritual Exercises. Unfortunately, therein lies the latent danger of the Ignatian path of Mystic-Christianity. During the second week, a non-scriptural imagination is introduced, entitled "The Call of the Temporal King," which pictorially equates Christ-Jesus with a military-style king whose will is "to conquer all the world and all enemies and so to enter into the glory of [God the] Father." Later in the second week, a similar non-scriptural imagination is presented entitled,

"Meditation on Two Standards," which visualizes Christ-Jesus as the leader of an army pitted against the army of Lucifer. As described by Ignatius: "It will be here to see a great field of all that region of Jerusalem, where the supreme Commander-in-chief of the good is Christ our Lord; another field in the region of Babylon, where the chief of the enemy is Lucifer."

Since the visualizations of the Saviour's life that are evoked from sacred scripture (particularly the Gospel of John) act as authentic supersensible Imaginations, the soul of the Christian contemplative is safely transformed by progressive supernatural forces and beings. Unfortunately, vivid, non-scriptural visualizations, such as those presented by Ignatius, can also have a powerful effect upon the soul by arousing regressive supernatural forces and beings. Moreover, to the degree that these regressive forces and beings are permitted to act upon the will, the naïve Christian mystic runs the risk of actually behaving and acting contrary to Christ-Jesus.

Recall, as well, that Christ-Jesus himself soundly rejected the Wilderness temptation to sit upon the temporal throne of King David and amass an invincible army against the enemies of Israel. By whole-heartedly embracing this Luciferically-inspired imagination, as presented in The Spiritual Exercises, the Christian mystic unwittingly opens his or her soul to the infernal influences of the Anti-Christ.

What is here examined concerning The Spiritual Exercises of St. Ignatius is cautionary. It is certainly not implied that every Christian aspirant, or every member of the Jesuit Order who has undergone Ignatian spiritual training, has been corrupted by a couple of false imaginations. Judging by the enormous, positive, world-wide contributions that Jesuits have made throughout the centuries in education, science, the arts and religion, it is clear that Ignatian spiritual training has in general been very positive. Nevertheless, there have also been strong-willed, renegade Jesuits throughout history who have been extreme in their zeal as "soldiers of Christ," and who have therefore acted as destructive influences in human progress. It is not unreasonable to consider that the Luciferic imaginations of "King Jesus and his conquering army," that are contemplated in The Spiritual Exercises, may have contributed to their anti-Christian behaviour.

As previously mentioned, in the second stage of Rosicrucian-Christian initiatory training, it is crucially important for the student to develop "truthful discernment"; that is, the ability to distinguish authentic supersensible Imaginations from purely subjective imaginations. Similarly in Ignatian spiritual training, great emphasis is also placed on "discernment"; in this case, the ability to distinguish divine impulses in the soul from ungodly temptations. No doubt, true Ignatian discernment is also crucially needed to distinguish, and to counteract, any false, unscriptural imaginations that are encountered in Jesuit training as well.

Unusual Transformations of Mystic-Christian Development

Since the salvational path of Mystic-Christianity is essentially a "way of the heart," an initiatory method that focuses on affective development (the spiritualization of feelings and emotions), it is therefore not surprising that practitioners often experience intense and powerful emotional effects at various stages of unfoldment.

For example, after deeply contemplating and imaginatively entering into the scene of the Crucifixion for many years, the Christian mystic may empathize so strongly with the sacrificial suffering of Christ-Jesus that he or she begins to feel intense physical pain themselves. The vicarious pain is predictably most intense in those places of the body where

Christ-Jesus was cruelly pierced: in the hands and feet by nails, in the side by a Roman spear, encircling the forehead by a crown of thorns, and occasionally on the back from being scourged.

On rare occasions, the vicarious pain aroused in the mystic's astral body is intense enough to make deep and lasting impressions in the etheric body which, in turn, cause perceptible changes to the physical body. These psychosomatic effects can range from red blotches on the skin to deep and open sores in the muscle tissue. Very often these painful lesions will resist healing and remain open, resulting in regular discharges of blood and fluid. This mystic phenomenon of vicarious bleeding, in imitation of the crucified Saviour, is termed "stigmata" (from the Greek "stigma," meaning mark or tattoo).

The Mystical Experience of the Stigmata

The Christian mystic, who experiences this unusual developmental effect, is known as a "stigmatic," or "stigmatist." Though rare, there have been a number of noteworthy stigmatists throughout the Christian era; such as St. Paul the Apostle,[76] St. Francis of Assisi, St. Catherine of Siena, Blessed Anne Catherine Emmerich, Therese Neumann, and St. Padre Pio of Pietrelcina. Not surprisingly, most stigmatists have been Catholic, since the path of Mystic-Christianity has been practiced primarily within the monastic orders of the Catholic Church. Even though many saints have experienced the stigmata, the Church does not regard the phenomenon as a divine miracle, or as particular evidence of saintly accomplishment. Moreover, since there have been numerous instances of fraudulent stigmatists, Church authorities have been very careful to authenticate legitimate cases. Due to the often constant pain involved, the chronic inconvenience of tending to open and bleeding wounds, and the public curiosity and notoriety associated with the stigmata, many Christian stigmatists regard the phenomenon as a curse, rather than a blessing, in their lives.

The strong, sympathetic emotions evoked by long-term contemplation of the Crucifixion will predictably be intensified if a replica of the redeemed astral body of Christ-Jesus becomes mystically integrated into the soul of the Christian devotee (refer back to section 5.1, if necessary). Since the redeemed astral body faithfully preserves the desires, feelings, emotions and sentiments of Christ-Jesus throughout his life (and death), the Christian mystic more readily experiences the suffering connected to the Crucifixion. Very often then, the physical manifestation of the stigmata in various saints has been the direct result of the integrated astral body of Christ-Jesus. St. Francis of Assisi is one very good example of this. During the period from the twelfth to the fifteenth centuries, when numerous replicas of the Saviour's redeemed astral body were being mystically integrated throughout Europe, a profusion of saints correspondingly experienced the stigmata.[77]

The Mystical Experience of Supernatural Ecstasy

Another intensified emotional experience that is a common occurrence for those following the path of Mystic-Christianity is "supernatural ecstasy." Supernatural ecstasy is characterized by fervent, all-consuming feelings of pleasure and euphoria; an expanded awareness of supernatural reality; visionary perceptions of superphysical beings and events; an altered sense of time and space; and a transcendent comprehension of spiritual truth. The duration of ecstatic experience is typically short, though some have been recorded to last for several days, or longer. Moreover, to outer observation, the mystical "ecstatic" often appears entranced and paralyzed, seemingly oblivious to physical sensation. Some well-known Christian mystics who experienced periods of supernatural ecstasy are St. Thomas Aquinas, St. Teresa of Avila and St. Padre Pio of Pietrelcina. As with the mystical experience of the stigmata, skeptical investigators have dismissed the mystical experience of supernatural ecstasy as an unhealthy, pathological disorder. There is ample evidence, however, in the lives of ecstatic saints to demonstrate that this particular emotional experience is uplifting, enlightening, positive and health-promoting.

The Mystic Phenomena of Inedia and Incorruptibility

Curiously, Christian mystics who experience stigmata very often demonstrate "inedia," the ability to survive for extended periods of time with little or no food and water; except for the daily consumption of consecrated bread and wine in the Eucharist. St. Catherine of Siena, St. Padre Pio of Pietrelcina and Therese Neumann are three well-known examples of mystics who developed this unusual ability.

Even after death, mysterious and unusual phenomena have been associated with those following the path of Mystic-Christianity. The physical bodies of numerous saints, for example, have inexplicably resisted decomposition and decay, long after death. These are cases that cannot be explained by natural mummification or artificial embalming. Moreover, the incorrupt bodies of many saints, such as St. Silvan (d. c.350), St. Vincent de Paul (1581–1660), St. John Vianney (1786–1859), St. Catherine Labouré (1806–1876), St. John Bosco (1815–1888), St. Bernadette of Lourdes (1844–1879), and St. Thérèse of Lisieux (1873–1897), have been on public display for decades—some for centuries. There are also numerous Eastern Orthodox saints whose bodies are known to be incorrupt.

Though the Catholic Church, up until recently, regarded incorruptibility as a major consideration for sainthood, it no longer maintains this attitude, since the remains of certain disreputable persons have also been found to be incorruptible. In the Eastern Orthodox Church, however, incorruptibility continues to be an important factor in determining sainthood.

Comparing Mystic-Christianity with Rosicrucian-Christianity

As an initiatory "path of the heart," Mystic-Christianity endeavors to achieve union with the divine on an affective, emotional level. Consequently, spiritual development (though often intense) is experienced in a semi-conscious, dreamy manner. Moreover, though powerful, transformative supernatural events are experienced first-hand, they aren't necessarily fully understood or comprehended by the Christian mystic. The stigmatist, for example, most often does not understand the superphysical details of how and why the experience occurs.

In the case of Rosicrucian-Christianity, however, since it is an initiatory "path of the head," union with the divine is to occur at a thought-filled level of mental comprehension. Consequently, spiritual development is experienced in a more wakeful, fully-conscious manner. Moreover, transformative supernatural events are more fully understood and comprehended by the Rosicrucian-Christian initiate. Rosicrucian-Christianity, then, is not a path of the brain-based intellect, which is characteristically cold, abstract and divisive; but rather a path of spiritualized thought that is characteristically warm, authentic and unitive. The comprehension of spiritual truth naturally stimulates and excites profound emotion; whereas the experience of profound emotion is not necessarily accompanied by the acquisition of authentic spiritual truth.

Of the two initiatory paths to salvation—to union with God—it should be clear from the foregoing that Rosicrucian Christianity is the safest, surest, clearest and most direct method for the modern age. No doubt as humanity progresses, in order to better comprehend spiritual truth, the Mystic-Christian will become increasingly interested in Rosicrucian-Christianity. So, for example, it will become increasingly common in the future for Christian stigmatists to balance their mystical development with the clear, illuminating concepts of anthroposophical teaching.

5.6 Yoga: The Ancient Eastern Path to Divine Union

True and False Paths of Initiatory Development

Not surprisingly, various secret societies and mystic organizations offer alternative, non-Christian systems of initiatory development. Unfortunately, most of these systems are psychically dangerous since they knowingly, or unknowingly, arouse harmful atavistic forces and malevolent non-material entities, in connection with initiation. This is because the goal of these non-Christian initiatory systems is not true union with God; but rather the expansion of the worldly-self instead of the divine-self; and the acquisition of personal psychic power instead of the performance of unselfish humanitarian service. In esoteric terminology, these egocentric initiatory systems belong to the "left-hand path," the dark, shadow-side of occultism.

There still exists today, however, an ancient pre-Christian initiatory system which can engender positive spiritual development, since its primary goal continues to be true union with God. That system is the Eastern path of yoga.

The Various Branches of Yoga

The Sanskrit word, "yoga," means to join, to attach or to unite. The word, "yoke," is derived from the same etymological source. Traditionally, yoga has been interpreted to mean, "union with the divine."

To most people today (particularly in Western societies), yoga is little more than a series of physical exercises used for stretching, toning and shaping the body; for minor weight loss; and to promote health and well-being. Little do modern fitness practitioners suspect that many of these yogic postures ("asanas") were developed thousands of years ago as a means of uniting with the divine. Nor do they realize that this system of physical postures belongs to only one particular branch of yoga—hatha yoga—and that there are four other major branches as well.

The branch, known as raja yoga, concentrates on the development of the mind, and can be regarded as "yoga psychology." Jnana yoga is the yoga of knowledge, and can be regarded as "yoga philosophy." Bhakti yoga is a developmental path of devotion, and can be regarded as "yoga spirituality." Karma yoga is known as the yoga of action, and can be regarded as "yogic practical living." There also exist a number of minor branches of yoga that, unfortunately, can be psychically harmful when misunderstood and misapplied—such as tantric yoga and kundalini yoga.

Though each of the five major branches of yoga is an independent path to divine union, a yogic master ["yogi" (male) or "yogini" (female)] is typically knowledgeable and proficient in all initiatory systems.

The Hidden History of Yoga

While the practice of yoga can be archeologically traced back to the third millennium BC in the Indus Valley, and even though some Hindu traditions extend the origin of yoga back to the dawn of creation (to "Hiraṇyagarbha"), esoteric investigation maintains that the initiatory path of yoga was first developed soon after the final sinking of Atlantis. It was during the prehistoric, ancient Indian cultural era, that the specially-appointed messengers of Manu—the seven holy Rishis—instituted the practice of yoga.

From the very beginning, yoga attempted to regain the lost condition of instinctual cosmic oneness that nascent humanity had once possessed before the Fall. While this was not permanently possible due to Luciferic and Ahrimanic corruption, yoga initiates ("chelas") were still able to achieve momentary experiences of mystical, transcendent unity. For the ancient yoga practitioner, the physical world was regarded as an illusionary entrapment ("maya"); only the non-material, transcendent realm was regarded as real.[78]

In attempting to transcend the material world *during life*, the upward path of yoga traditionally combined seven primary areas of personal development:

1. Five abstentions ("yamas"):
   (1) non-violence ("ahimsa")
   (2) non-lying, truth ("satya")
   (3) non-covetousness ("asteya")
   (4) non-sensuality, celibacy ("brahmacharya")
   (5) non-possessiveness ("aparigraha")
2. Five observances ("niyamas"):
   (1) purity ("shaucha")
   (2) contentment ("santosha")
   (3) austerity ("tapas")
   (4) study of God and the soul through sacred writing ("svadhyaya")

(5) surrender to God ("ishvara-pranidhana")

3. Bodily postures ("asanas"): refers to the various physical positions used for meditation. Breath control ("pranayama" from "prāna," = breath, and "āyāma" = to restrain or stop): also interpreted as the control of the life force.

4. Mental abstraction ("pratyahara"): the practice of withdrawing the sense organs from observing external objects.

5. Mental concentration ("dharana"): the practice of fixing the mental attention on a single object.

6. Meditation ("dhyana"): intense mental contemplation of the inner nature of an object or idea.

7. Liberation ("samadhi"): the practice of merging the personal consciousness with the object of meditation.

Final liberation ("videha mukti"), according to yoga teaching, could only be achieved by shedding the physical body *at death*. Once the soul was free from the body, it was able to attain "mahasamadhi," the complete and perfect union with the divine—with the transcendent Self.

Problems with Yoga for Modern Practitioners

In ancient times, the practice of yoga had limited success in positively assisting the East Indian devotee to transcend the material world, and to unite with the divine. However, this was largely due to the fact that the prehistoric practitioner of yoga still possessed residual clairvoyant ability, as well as a tenuous psychic constitution (that is, etheric and astral vehicles that were not strongly attached to the physical body).

Consequently, developmental exercises in yoga, that had a profound and positive impact in ancient times, were no longer effective in later ages; and in some cases, actually became harmful instead. This was particularly true with certain yogic breathing exercises that once had a benign transformative effect but, which later, produced psychic disorientation, mental confusion and bodily detachment (particularly for Western practitioners). For this reason, advanced Rosicrucian-Christian initiatory training has developed different breathing exercises that have been better adapted to modern social conditions and bodily constitutions.

Another major concern with yoga initiatory training is its original, underlying goal. Ancient yoga endeavored to unite with the divine by reacquiring the dreamy, ego-less clairvoyant state of instinctual oneness with Nature that humanity once possessed before the "fall from paradise." Since this goal becomes increasingly more anachronistic in modern times, by seeking to revive the distant past, it now runs contrary to progressive evolution. Yoga's original goal, then, has an unfortunate Luciferic tendency that is incompatible with today's initiatory training.

Progressive Yoga Will Necessarily Lead to Christ-Jesus

Nevertheless, if the vast storehouse of yogic esoteric wisdom is sincerely and selectively applied with undiminished self-awareness and in full waking consciousness, then the ancient Eastern path of yoga can positively assist in achieving an experiential union with the divine. This "modernized" application of yoga will, of course, lead to an eventual encounter with Christ-Jesus. Since Christ-Jesus has established for all humanity the highest level of hypostatic union with God, all progressive initiatory development will in time seek to "follow in the footsteps of the Saviour" in order to truly unite with the divine. As Christ-Jesus himself has clearly stated: "I am the way, and the truth, and the life; no one comes to the Father [God], but by me" (John 14:6).

CONCLUSION

Eternal Life and True Happiness

SINCE THE TRUE SELF of every human being is the one spirit of God reflected in each soul, then initiatory union with God will also unite the spiritual seeker with his or her true self. Likewise, in order to truly understand God, each aspiring soul must seek and find their own true self. Hence the famous dictum of the ancient Mystery schools for those initiates seeking to know God: "O Man, know yourself."

Since God, as supreme being, must logically experience the highest joy in himself, the greatest happiness for the seeking soul must be in union with God through their own true (divine) self. Mankind's search for true happiness, then, is simultaneously the search for God, and the search for each person's true self.

Christ-Jesus as the Doorway to True Happiness

By hypostatically uniting humanity and divinity—the "son of Man" with the "Son of God"—Christ-Jesus has become the "doorway" through which every human being who aspires to God must pass. It is in no way religious sectarianism to declare that Christ-Jesus is "the only way" to God; and who, therefore, stands on the path to true happiness. It is simply an esoteric fact; as objective as saying that in order to drive to San Francisco, one must cross the Golden Gate Bridge.

This is not to say, of course, that non-religious individuals, or that non-Christian believers, cannot experience some degree of personal happiness in life, only that at the gateway to the higher celestial world—the heavenly planes of existence—Christ-Jesus stands as the "greater guardian of the threshold" for all who seek to truly know themselves, and to unite with God. Whether one is Hindu, Moslem, Christian or Jew, all will eventually encounter the person of Christ-Jesus on the path to true happiness.

Choosing a Path of Suffering Instead of the Path to Happiness

Unfortunately, there are individuals who deliberately reject God in order to follow a path of egotistic power instead (thereby rejecting the higher aspirations of their true selves). While they will, of course, never be truly happy with such a course of action, they can instead temporarily satisfy themselves with the perverse "pleasure" of controlling and manipulating others.

From an esoteric perspective, it is puzzling to understand why anyone would deliberately choose a path of pain and suffering for themselves, that is entirely contrary to their own true nature. But such is the enigma of evil; by rejecting God, one is blinded to one's true self, and to what would make one truly happy in life. It seems reasonable to think that a suffering soul would quickly realize the error of its ways and eagerly turn back toward God; but unfortunately, there is the example of recalcitrant beings, such as Sorath, who have rejected God and their own true self for aeons of cosmic time.

The Search for Eternal Life

Once again, since only God is eternal, the search for eternal life is a search for God. Moreover, since the true self of every human being is a reflection of God's spirit, the search for eternal life is also a search for one's true self.

Even though mankind's soul and spiritual vehicles of expression have a long-lasting, enduring quality after physical death (and hence are "immortal"); and even though each person's true self shares in the eternal nature of God, most human beings today are totally unaware of these superphysical facts. Today when death ensues, most individuals slip into a state of deep soul slumber wherein there is diminished self-awareness. This veiled consciousness reduces any sense of continued existence. Likewise, upon entering rebirth, most incarnating souls retain no conscious memory of prior existence. Sadly, then, even though every human being already has eternal life, most do not know it, or experience it.

Eternal Life through Christ-Jesus

Acquiring eternal life, therefore, is not personally gaining a new heavenly attribute, but merely waking up to what one already possesses. Nevertheless, it is still not incorrect to say that "through Christ-Jesus, fallen humanity attains eternal life." As noted above, it is extremely difficult for present-day mankind to retain self-conscious awareness when the soul and spiritual vehicles are separated from the physical and etheric bodies. This difficulty is clearly evidenced during sleep, when there is a partial and temporary separation of vehicles; but even more so after death, when there is a complete and permanent separation of vehicles.

Since the life-spirit is the lowest vehicle of expression of the Solar-Christos (please refer to Figure 7), this germinal attribute in ordinary humanity was particularly enlivened and strengthened through the incarnation of Christ-Jesus. Because of this, the high level of consciousness associated with life-spirit ("buddhic" or "cosmic consciousness") is also esoterically termed "Christ consciousness."[79] Simply stated, Christ consciousness is the certain knowledge and experience that the true self is real, alive, eternal, a reflection of God, and divine love in spirit-nature.

By following in the footsteps of Christ-Jesus, life-spirit and Christ consciousness are awakened and unfolded, thereby strengthening the day-to-day awareness of the true self. In consequence, a continuity of self-awareness is better retained after death[80] (and during sleep), as well as in subsequent rebirths. Through the superphysical forces incarnated in Christ-Jesus (and thereby bestowed upon all mankind), then, the Christian disciple acquires the unbroken consciousness of eternal existence—the seeker attains eternal life.

NOTES

INTRODUCTION

1. The word "theosophy" has a variety of meanings. In this case, theosophy is understood to be a systematic study of spiritual matters (including God), using supersensible methods of investigation and research. Information is presented in clear conceptual form and intellectually comprehensible.

CHAPTER 1

2. Most of the designations used in the Hebrew Tradition section of the chart in Figure 1 are from the *Mishneh Torah* (1170–1180) written by Moses Maimonides. A tenth level of beings, the "erelim" were not included in the chart since they are sometimes considered synonymous with the ishim. Furthermore, although the ten designations of Maimonides were ranked according to the nearness to God (like the other three sections of the chart), they were not originally arranged into three main hierarchies.

3. English translations of Rudolf Steiner's esoteric material

most often use the term "spirit man" for humanity's highest vehicle of expression. Occasionally, the term "spirit body" is also employed, as in the following quotation:

> [T]he internal part of human nature destined to evolve further and further in the future through the three principles of spirit self, life spirit, and spirit body, rested in the bosom of the Godhead. (1907 Lecture on "The Lord's Prayer"; published in *The Christian Mystery*; 1998)

4. In esoteric literature, Lemuria was an ancient volcanic landmass that was situated between the present continents of Asia, Africa and Australia when the earth was still in a fiery, molten condition. Also referred to as the Land of Mu, or Og or Oz, the etheric and astral atmosphere surrounding Lemuria was inhabited by primitive, animal-like, human life-forms.

5. In "Lecture Four" of *Spiritual Beings in the Heavenly Bodies and Kingdoms of Nature* (2011), Rudolf Steiner explains that the group-egos of plants and animals are the "offspring" of the powers, virtues and dominions. More specifically, they are detached self-images that possess life, but not independent self-existence; they remain connected to the beings of the second hierarchy as "a sort of shell or skin." In Steiner's own words:

> We can call what appears instead of manifestation [of a group-ego] in a being of the second hierarchy: a self-creation, a sort of shell or skin. It creates, as it were, an impression of itself, makes itself objective, in a sort of image ... [I]t is shown to occult vision that every time a being detaches such a picture or image of itself, life is stimulated. The stimulation of life is always the result of such a self-creation.
>
> But just as we could say that the beings of the

third hierarchy—the Angels, Archangels, and spirits of the age [principalities]—have offspring who separate from them, so, too, the beings of the second hierarchy likewise have offspring ... Now the spiritual beings who are detached from the beings of the second hierarchy, and sink down into the kingdoms of nature, are those designated in occultism as the group-souls of the plants and animals, the group-souls of the individual beings.

In "Lecture Ten," Steiner goes on to explain that the group-egos of minerals are the "offspring" of the thrones:

These spirits of will belong to the first hierarchy and though their offspring are not so far advanced that they can be reckoned within it [the first hierarchy], these spirits of will or their offspring give forth what becomes the group I of minerals.

6. The vehicle designations associated with the thrones, cherubim and seraphim, given in Figure 6, are recognized to be different than the anthroposophical titles for these beings. There is, however, no contradiction in this. Analogous to the Holy Trinity, where each person of God is separately associated with either divine will, divine wisdom or divine love (even though each divine person equally expresses all three), the triad of thrones, cherubim and seraphim are separately associated with either cosmic will, cosmic wisdom or cosmic love, though they each express all three to various degrees. It is no contradiction, therefore, to associate cosmic wisdom with the seraphim, even though their anthroposophical designation is "spirits of love"; and to associate cosmic love with the cherubim even though their anthroposophical designation is "spirits of harmony."

7. Since Yahweh-Elohim is not an ordinary power, but one who attained that level of development somewhat "later"

in cosmic evolution, he has been given the title of "the Late-born" or "the Last-born" by his fellow progressive beings. This is evidenced in *The Influence of Spiritual Beings Upon Man* (1961):

> "We [the spirits of wisdom] will relinquish it [the human body] to the Late-born, to Jehovah; he is Lord of Form …

> [B]ut in order to form a balance between the Spirits of Wisdom and the Last-born of the old Moon, the Lord of Form, who was the point of departure for the creation of the present moon. (Rudolf Steiner; Lecture 6; 1908).

8. Due to the fact that Yahweh-Elohim was able to embody a transcendent, group-ego consciousness, by uniting with the six planetary spirits of form on the sun, there is a mistaken tendency to conclude that Yahweh-Elohim is *only* this "collective ego-hood" of the elohim, and not a separate *being*. To avoid this error, it is important to keep in mind that Yahweh-Elohim is the *seventh* spirit of form who unites with the others, and the one who became the guiding-spirit (the planetary-ego) of the moon. Rudolf Steiner avoids this confusion by using the name "Jehovah" (as in the note 7 above) or "Jahve," when referring to this particular elohim-being acting individually, and the title "Jahve-Elohim," when referring to this particular elohim-being acting in collective unity. This distinction is clearly evidenced in the following sentence:

> Thus we must think of the process of the moon's separation, and its activity from without, as associated with that Being who represents the Elohim as one undivided entity, with Him whom we call Jahve-Elohim. (1910, Lecture 10; published in *Genesis: Secrets*

of the Bible Story of Creation; 1959)

9. The feminine aspect to Yahweh-Elohim and the moon was touched on by Rudolf Steiner in a lecture given in 1914:

> [W]e have the Ruler of the Earth united with the Earth Mother, whose powers are a result of the Moon period ... Jahve! Hence out of Hebrew antiquity there emerges this mysterious connection of the Moon forces, which have left their remains in the moon known to astronomy and their human forces in the female element in human life. The connection of the Ruler of the Earth with the Moon Mother is given to us in the name Jahve. (Published in *Christ and the Spiritual World and the Search for the Holy Grail*; 2008)

10. Over many centuries, Vishva-Karman has not surprisingly morphed into many different roles, ranging from being the "Carpenter of the Gods" in the *Mahabharata*, to being the "Ultimate Reality" in the *Rig Veda*. Nevertheless, he clearly began as a sun-god, as evidenced in the *Bhavishya Purana*:

> Long ago there was a brahmana named Heli ... He was a worshiper of the sun-god ... Whatever profit he made he used for worshiping the sun-god in the month of Magha by performing sacrifices. Thus the sun-god Vishvakarma (the architect of the gods) became pleased with his sacrifice ... At noon time, Heli offered food to the sun-god according to his desire. In this way he satisfied the three worlds. After leaving his body he entered into the sun-planet.

11. Osirus is usually identified as the god of the afterlife, the underworld and the dead. But since the ancient Egyptians believed that the sun-god spent the night in the underworld, to be reborn the next day, and that in the

afterlife the discarnate soul spent eternity travelling with the sun-god amongst the stars, Osirus was understood in this case to be the hidden sun-god revealed in sleep, death and trance initiation.

CHAPTER 2

12. Concerning the virginal Jesus-being, Rudolf Steiner in a 1910 lecture (published in *From Jesus to Christ*, 1973) stated the following:

> [The ego] substance poured down from the Spirits of Form now flows onward, but that something was held back: an Ego that was now protected from entering into physical incarnations. Instead, this Ego preserved the form, the substantiality, which man had had before proceeding to his first earthly incarnation. This Ego lived on collaterally with the rest of humanity, and at the time of which we are now speaking, when the Event of Palestine was to take place, it was still in the same condition, if we wish to speak according to the Bible, as was the Ego of Adam before his first embodiment in flesh.

From the foregoing statement, it is also clear that this Jesus-individuality possessed an ego (in its pure, uncorrupted form), and that he was a distinct being.

13. One particular statement indicating the association of the virginal-Jesus with the historical figure of Krishna was given by Rudolf Steiner in a lecture in 1913:

> Krishna—that is, the spirit who worked through Krishna—appeared again in the Jesus child of the Nathan line of the House of David, described in St. Luke's Gospel. (Published in *The Occult Significance of the Bhagavad Gita*, 1984)

14. The "Great White Brotherhood" (GWB) takes its name from the order's total dedication to the "pure white light" of the divine spirit. The brotherhood of bodhisattvas is not to be confused, or associated, of course, with the racist American "white supremacist brotherhood" of the Ku Klux Klan. Moreover, the alternate title of the GWB: the "Mother Lodge of Humanity," has no connection, or association, with the shadowy Masonic body in America, the "Mother Supreme Council of the World (aka: the Supreme Council Southern Jurisdiction)

CHAPTER 3

15. In biblical scripture, when Christ-Jesus was referring to his human nature, to himself as a human being, he would often use the term, "son of Man."
16. In attempting to describe the experience of "spiritual oneness," Yogi Ramacharaka has written:

> The highest step in this dawning consciousness of the Oneness of All, is the one in which is realized that there is but One Reality, and at the same time the sense of consciousness that the "I" is in that Reality. It is most difficult to express this thought in words for it is something that must be felt, rather than seen by the Intellect. When the Soul realizes that the Spirit within it is, at the last, the only real part of it, and that the Absolute and its manifestation as Spirit is the only real thing in the Universe ... we realize the Identity of the "I" with the great "I" of the Universe...
>
> The advanced student or Initiate finds his consciousness gradually enlarging until it realizes its identity with the Whole ... And, instead of his experiencing any loss of identity or individuality, he becomes conscious of an enlargement or expansion

of individuality or identity—instead of feeling himself absorbed in the Whole, he feels that he is spreading out and embracing the Whole. (*Raja Yoga or Mental Development*; 1934)

17. The term, "sons of God," when referring to angelic beings (as in Job 1:6— "Now there was a day when the sons of God came to present themselves before the LORD, and Satan also came among them") esoterically indicates that certain celestial beings are also aware that their true selves are reflections of the Son-God.

18. The ordeal of Christ-Jesus in the Wilderness following the baptism in the Jordan is given much greater significance in esoteric Christianity than in mainstream religion. As explained by Yogi Ramacharaka in *Mystic Christianity or the Inner Teachings of the Master* (1935):

> The average student of the New Testament passes over the event of Jesus in the Wilderness, with little or no emotion, regarding it as a mere incident in His early career. Not so with the mystic or the occultist, who knows, from the teachings of his order, that in the Wilderness Jesus was subjected to a severe occult test, designed to develop His power, and test His endurance. In fact, as every advanced member of any of the great occult orders knows, the occult degree known as "The Ordeal in the Wilderness" is based upon this mystic experience of Jesus, and is intended to symbolize the tests to which He was subjected.

19. Interestingly, the esoteric assertion that "turning stones into bread" refers to the economic sector of human affairs was somewhat echoed by the British economist, John Maynard Keynes (1883–1946), when he stated that credit expansion performs the "miracle … of turning a stone into bread." (*Paper of the British Experts*; April 8, 1943)

20. Rudolf Steiner in his lecture series entitled, *The Fifth Gospel* (2007), maintains that both Lucifer and Ahriman were involved with this particular temptation. Since these two beings often cooperate with each other (for entirely different reasons), it is reasonable to conclude that both were probably involved in all three temptations, though one or the other would be the principal instigator.

21. Unfortunately, even though Christ-Jesus thoroughly rejected the Wilderness temptations to become an economic, religious and political world-leader, certain Jewish believers today are still hoping for a Messiah who will fulfill that role. Obviously, any future leader claiming to do so would be a false Messiah—most probably the Anti-Christ. Moreover, certain Christian Fundamentalists similarly envision Christ fulfilling this role at his Second Coming. Once again, anyone claiming to do so would be a false Messiah, and would most probably be the Anti-Christ.

22. This statement conveys the esoteric understanding that physical death was, in fact, established by the *progressive* celestial-beings as a partial remedy for the Luciferic and Ahrimanic damage to mankind's three lower bodies, particularly the physical form. Through death, the human soul was temporarily freed from the stifling restriction of a deteriorated physical body. Moreover, after briefly sojourning in the superphysical realms after death, the rejuvenated human soul could then re-inhabit a newborn physical form to continue its interrupted life on earth.

23. The term, "scapegoat," comes from an ancient Hebrew religious ritual where the high priest, once a year on the Day of Atonement, confessed the entire sins of Israel to Yahweh. These sins were then ceremonially placed on the head of a specially chosen goat, that was led into the desert, pushed over a cliff, and killed. It was believed that the sin of the nation was thereby expiated, or "atoned."

24. This ancient, historical stage is still recapitulated in embryonic development. Cartilage is still the precursor to skeletal structure, and is later replaced by bone during the second and third trimesters.

25. As stated by Rudolf Steiner in a lecture on 7 January 1924:

> How does one know of oneself? Because one has the skeleton inside oneself. It is because of this that one knows of oneself. So if we ask: 'Why does man have self-awareness, what makes him know of himself?' We should not point to the muscles, nor to the soft parts, but we must point exactly to the solid skeletal support. Man knows of himself because he has a solid skeletal support. (Published in *From Elephants to Einstein*; 1998)

26. While brain-based intellection has, up to now, been a valuable tool to understand the sensory world, when thinking becomes entirely confined to the physical realm, it becomes materialistic and destructive to the body and soul. As Rudolf Steiner has expressed:

> The brain is an instrument for purely intellectual apprehension. Intellectualism and materialistic thinking are one and the same, for all the thinking that goes on in science, in theology, in the sphere of modern Christian consciousness—all of it is merely the product of the human brain, it is materialistic ... [T]he materialistic brain really represents a process of decay: materialistic thinking unfolds only through processes of destruction, death-processes, which are taking place in the brain. (Lecture given in 3 April 1920, and published in *The Festivals and Their Meaning*; 2002)

27. In a lecture given on 1 June 1906 entitled, "The Christian

Mystery," Rudolf Steiner similarly remarked:

> Thus do we need to lose all in order to regain all, and this applies to our own existence. In the moment of losing all we appear to die to ourselves and it is in the world around us that we begin to live again. Such is the *Mystic Death*.

28. Concerning the "flash" of life-memory that occurs when one is at the point of death, this should not be confused with a lengthier life-review that lasts for the initial three or four days of the soul slumber. This second review is characterized by being simply an impersonal retrospection of images that pass before the soul. Typically during this time, the phantom body and the etheric body are unconsciously discarded. After the soul has awoken in the astral world, the events of the previous life are experienced for a third, much longer time (about a third of one's life on earth). In this case, the departed soul is emotionally involved in the memory events, acutely feeling all the joy and sorrow caused to others.

Though Rudolf Steiner has often referred to the second and third life-reviews, little is mentioned of the first "flash," except on rare occasions, such as the following:

> The actual instant of death brings a remarkable experience: for a brief space of time the man remembers all that has happened to him in the life just ended. His entire life appears before his soul in a moment, like a great tableau. (Lecture given on 24 August 1906 entitled, "Life of the Soul in Kamaloka," and published in *At the Gates of Spiritual Science*; 1986)

A further esoteric description has been provided by Yogi Ramacharaka in *The Life Beyond Death* (2010):

Another matter that should be mentioned in this

place is that wonderful phenomenon of the review of the past life of the soul, that great panorama which passes before the mental vision of the soul as it sinks into the soul-slumber. This the authorities inform us really occupies but an infinitesimal moment of time—a moment so brief that it can scarcely be spoken of as a point in time. Yet in this brief moment, the soul witnesses the panorama of the life it has passed on earth.

29. The word "asuric" refers to the asuras, a destructive class of regressive principalities (spirits of personality). Since the lowest vehicle of expression for principalities is the ego-bearing soul, the asuras target this vehicle, particularly the consciousness soul, for their corrupting effects on humanity. Their nefarious activity (as mentioned) has also resulted in the degeneration of planetary life ether into subterranean nuclear energy.

30. During the Renaissance and Middle Ages, the Rosicrucian alchemists referred to the transparent human phantom as the "Philosopher's Stone," and the mystical work to purify and perfect it was termed the "Magnum Opus" (the Great Work). As indicated by Rudolf Steiner:

> The alchemists always insisted that the human body really consists of the same substance that constitutes the perfectly transparent, crystal-clear 'Philosopher's Stone.' (From a lecture given in 10 October 1911, and published in *From Jesus to Christ*; 1973)

31. The fact that the corrupt impulses of moral coldness and hatred (particularly hatred of God), which manifest in mankind, have their dark source in the physical body, (the phantom) and not in the spiritual nature, was indicated by Rudolf Steiner in Lecture 12, given on 11 November 1923 (published in *Man as Symphony of the Creative Word*; 1991):

If human understanding and human love are the real impulses upon which communal life depends, how does it come about that the very reverse of human understanding and human love appears in our social order? This is a question with which initiates more than anyone else have always concerned themselves ... Now, if we are unable to look for this lack of human understanding, this human hatred, in the sphere of the spiritual, of the soul, it follows that we must look for them in the sphere of the physical ... There below, in the unconsciousness within us, moral coldness and hatred are entrenched, and it is easy for man to bring into his soul what is present in his body, so that his soul can, as it were, be infected with the lack of human understanding ... [W]e must be able to sustain the knowledge that coldness, moral coldness, lives as physical image in the bones and that moral hatred lives as physical image in the blood.

32. It is important here to understand that the physical phantom does not remain united with the lifeless corpse after death. Under normal circumstances, the phantom is immediately detached and for a short time continues to be occupied by the departed soul. Moreover, the lifeless corpse doesn't instantly fall apart without the phantom, due to molecular inertia; it takes time for the conjoined chemicals to separate and, thereby, decompose the inert cadaver. Regarding the phantom after death, Rudolf Steiner has stated the following:

> Man, however, still possesses his [phantom] form when he goes through the gate of death. One sees it shimmering, glittering, radiant with colours. But now he loses first the form of his head; then the rest of his form gradually melts away. Man becomes completely metamorphosed, as though transformed into an

image of the cosmos. (Ibid)

Christ-Jesus also continued to occupy his purified, but unresurrected, phantom after death. He did not discard it prior to his descent into the underworld.

33. Some anthroposophical readers have the mistaken understanding that Rudolf Steiner denied the existence of gravity. What Dr. Steiner objected to was the scientific notion of a "law of gravity." While there is clearly a force of gravity that can be readily observed, a law of gravity is simply a mental abstraction that has no basis in reality. Concerning earth gravity, Steiner in fact had some very interesting esoteric things to say, such as the following:

> The forces of gravity, for instance, are essentially forces which, in a physical connection, have remained behind from the Moon. The earth would never have developed the forces of gravity had not the residue of what was contained in old Moon been left behind; the moon itself departed. (Given in a lecture on 26 October 1923, and published in *Man as Symphony of the Creative Word*; 1991)

34. Though not identical to what has been indicated here as the centripetal action of the earth on the newly-departed soul, Rudolf Steiner has mentioned similar after-death activity, such as the following:

> By stepping out of the physical world through the East into the spiritual world, the dead person achieves the possibility of participating in the forces which operate, not centrifugally as here on earth, but centripetally towards the centre of the earth. He enters into the sphere out of which it is possible to work towards the earth. (From Lecture 22, given on 21 January 1917, and published in *Karma of Untruthfulness II*; 1992)

35. Many esoteric students are under the false impression that consciously "crossing the threshold" into the superphysical world, whether through initiation or death, is a pleasant "warm and fuzzy" experience. But to authentic clairvoyant investigation, this is definitely not the case. The advanced initiate, Rudolf Steiner, has clearly indicated this in statements such as the following:

> When one crosses the threshold into the spiritual world, the first thing one becomes aware of is something terrible, something which at first it is by no means easy to sustain. Most people wish to be pleasantly affected by what seems to them worthy of attainment. But the fact remains that only by passing through the experience of horror can one learn to know spiritual reality, that is to say true reality. For in regard to the human form, as this is placed before us by anatomy and physiology, one can only perceive that it is built up out of two elements from the spiritual world: moral coldness and hatred. (From a lecture given on 11 November 1923, and published in *Man as Symphony of the Creative Word*, 1991)

36. Concerning the other-worldly origin and alien nature of Sorath, Rudolf Steiner has stated the following:

> This seductive being is of quite a different nature from man. It originates from other worlds; it has acquired the tendencies of other world periods ... This being could only have got something from the Earth by being able to gain the rulership at a certain moment, namely when the Christ-principle descended to Earth. If the Christ-principle had been strangled in the germ, if Christ had been overcome by the adversary, it would have been possible for the whole Earth to succumb to the Sorath-principle. This, however, did not take place, and so this being has to

be content with the refuse of mankind who have not inclined towards the Christ-principle, who have remained embedded in matter; they in the future will form his cohorts. (From a lecture given on 30 June 1908, and published in *The Apocalypse of St. John*; 1993)

37. Ahriman has also been referred to as "the beast," or "the dragon," due to references in the Book of Revelation:

    (1) to a second beast "with ten horns and seven heads" who rises out of the sea (Rev 13:1);
    (2) and to a great red dragon "with seven heads and ten horns" ("called the Devil and Satan") who wages war in heaven with Michael and his angels (Rev 12:3–9).

    The well-known images of St. Michael piercing the heart of the Satanic dragon with his spear, similarly echo the piercing of Sorath's planetary heart of darkness by the divine light-beam of Christ-Jesus.

38. Due to the depraved activity of the fallen asuras, the viscerous core of the earth is further infused with corrupted life ether which manifests as a lurid, dissolute sensuality.

39. Regarding the "thorn" that was implanted by Sorath into the human phantom, Rudolf Steiner similarly stated the following:

    > [H]umanity was given an 'injection' … It was an injection reaching into its actual bodily constitution, and we are born with it to this day … There was injected into humanity that sickness which, in its effect, leads to the denial of the Father God. Humanity—that is to say, civilized humanity—has a 'thorn in the flesh' today … A man today who surrenders wholly to this thorn, to this sickness—for in the physical body this thorn is an actual sickness—becomes an atheist, one who denies God,

who denies the Divine ... His nature was, as it were, mineralized to a certain extent at that time, retarded in its development, with the result that we have within us the sickness which gives rise to the denial of Divinity ... This sickness has many consequences. Through it a bond of attraction is created between the soul of a man and his body stronger than that which formerly existed, stronger than that which arises from human nature itself. The soul is shackled more firmly to the body. (From a lecture given on 16 October 1918 entitled, "How Do I Find the Christ," and published in *Evil*, 1997)

40. Using the allegorical imagery of Genesis, when Adam and Eve (ancestral humanity) consumed the fruit of the tree of knowledge of good and evil (exercised their free-will capacity in an evil, sinful way), seeds from that fruit remained in their bodies, poisoned them, and eventually caused their death.

41. The earth, of course, had a planetary-spirit prior to Christ-Jesus. As with the other planets of our system, the earth's planetary-spirit was an elohim-being operating from the sphere of the sun. In the various ancient mythologies, the earth's planetary-spirit was often regarded as a feminine being: she was Ceres to the Romans, Demeter to the Greeks, Shakti to the Hindus, and Damkina to the Babylonians.

42. The victory of Christ-Jesus over material evil does not prevent beings, such as Sorath, from continuing to *will* evil (which is their free-will choice). What this transmutation of universal matter means is that beings with evil intent will find it harder and harder, over time, to corrupt matter and use it for any evil purpose. This new "spiritualized" matter has a moral component and, as such, will increasingly resist immoral application. There will come a time in the future, for example, when

destructive military weaponry will not operate in the hands of evil individuals.

This process of transmuting regressive elemental matter, through the power of spiritual love (which began with the victory of Christ-Jesus in hell), was also discussed by Rudolf Steiner in a lecture on 24 September 1921 entitled, "The Seeds of Future Worlds—At the Center of Man's Being: II":

> When we are able to penetrate into this inner core of evil in man, and are able also to become conscious of how into this evil, where matter is destroyed and thrown back into chaos, moral impulses can find their way, then we have really found in ourselves the beginning of spiritual existence. Then we perceive the spirit within us in the act of creating. For when we behold moral laws working upon matter which has been thrown back into chaos, we are beholding a real activity of the spirit taking place within us in a natural way. We become aware of the spirit concretely active within us, the spirit that is the seed of future worlds.

43. The following statement by Rudolf Steiner briefly described the extracts of the phantom body, the etheric body and the astral body. Though the ego-bearing soul was not mentioned directly, this was because the "astral body," as Steiner often used the term, included the ego-bearing soul as part of it. As such, the "lower" astral body was discarded prior to exiting the orbit of the moon (the end of Kamaloca), and the "higher" astral body was discarded prior to exiting the sphere of the sun (the beginning of devachan). In Steiner's own words:

> However, today's human beings do not lose their etheric body completely but take an extract or excerpt along with them for all the times to follow. So in this sense the etheric corpse is cast off, but the fruit of the

last life is carried along by the astral body and by the ego. If we want to be quite precise, we will have to say that something is taken along from the physical body as well: a kind of spiritual abstract of this body—the tincture medieval mystics spoke about ... After the etheric body has been cast off, the astral body still contains all the passions, desires, and so on that it had at the end of life; they must be lost and purified, and that is *kamaloca*. Then the astral body is cast off and here, too, the fruit, the astral essence, is taken along; but the rest—the astral corpse—dissolves into the astral world. The human being now enters *devachan* where he or she prepares in the spiritual world for a new life in the future. (From a lecture on 21 January 1909, and published in *The Principle of Spiritual Economy*; 1986)

44. Regarding butterfly substance, Rudolf Steiner has remarked:

> When we look at a butterfly's wing we actually have before us earthly matter in its most spiritualized form. Through the fact that the matter of the butterfly's wing is imbued with colour, it is the most spiritualized of all earthly substances ... From you, O fluttering creatures, there streams out something still better than sunlight; you radiate spirit-light into the cosmos ... streaming out into the universe in the form of rays: a shimmering of the spirit-light of the butterflies. (From a lecture given on 27 October 1923, and published in *Man as Symphony of the Creative Word*; 1991)

45. In clairvoyant research, finally reaching the outer orbit of Saturn (which can take hundreds or thousands of years of earth-time) signals the mid-point of life between death and a new birth. For that reason, this transition event has

been esoterically termed, "cosmic midnight." As the earth-life of Christ-Jesus harmoniously conformed to the astronomical events of the cosmos, so too did his life after death; such that his cosmic midnight was reached exactly at 12:00 midnight on Holy Saturday. As Christ-Jesus had descended to the nadir of material evil on Good Friday at 12:00 midnight, so too he correspondingly ascended to the apex of holiness on Holy Saturday at 12:00 midnight.

46. The fact that the process of transforming the re-united redeemed vehicles, into the new resurrection vehicles, had not been entirely completed when the Risen Saviour first appeared on Paschal Sunday is briefly indicated in the Gospel of John, in the following passage, when Christ-Jesus first appeared to Mary Magdalene in the cemetery garden:

> Jesus said to her, 'Mary.' She turned and said to him in Hebrew, 'Rab-boni!' (which means Teacher). Jesus said to her, 'Do not hold me, for I have not yet ascended to the Father; but go to my brethren and say to them, I am ascending to my Father and your Father, to my God and your God.' (John 20:16, 17)

47. This esoteric understanding of the discarded phantom and etheric bodies hovering within the sealed tomb prior to the resurrection of Christ-Jesus, explains the intuitive, traditional notion that there were two shining angels within the sealed tomb awaiting the Saviour's resurrection.

CHAPTER 4

48. In certain instances, Rudolf Steiner clearly indicated that the visual appearance of the Risen Saviour for St. Paul on

the road to Damascus, and for St. John as the "Son of Man" referred to in the Book of Revelation, was more than just an etheric manifestation. In a lecture on 9 May 1909 (published in *Reading the Pictures of the Apocalypse*; 1993), Steiner stated the following:

> For this reason Paul knew that what appeared to him before Damascus in human form could be none other than the Christ. The writer of the Apocalypse describes the same thing to us when he speaks of the "Son of Man" ... [H]e saw the "Son of Man" as the spiritualized, purified form of the physical body, not only the etheric body, but the spiritual-physical form of "Man," the human being, now purified and sanctified.

The fact that there is a unique physical component to the etheric appearances of the Risen Saviour was also indicated by Steiner in a lecture on 1 October 1911 entitled "The Etherization of the Blood" (published in *The Reappearance of Christ in the Etheric*; 2003), where it is stated:

> A certain number of individuals will see the etheric Christ and will themselves experience the event that took place at Damascus. This will depend, however, upon such human beings learning to observe the moment when Christ draws near to them ... [H]e may become aware that suddenly someone has come near to help him, to make him alert to this or that. The truth is that Christ has come to him, although he believes that what he sees is a physical man. He will come to realize, however, that this is a supersensible being, because it immediately vanishes.

49. Regarding this future time when advanced human beings inhabit their own resurrection vehicles, in a lecture on 14

March 1908, Rudolf Steiner has similarly stated:

> The Christ worked in Jesus' blood from age 30 on.
> Before that Jesus had worked on his physical, etheric
> and astral bodies. Then Christ took hold of the blood
> and purified it during the three years. That's why
> blood had to flow. When we've purified our four
> bodies in the same way [and developed our own
> resurrection vehicles] we'll then have the four-fold
> philosophical fire that belongs to the Vulcan period.
> (Published in *From the Esoteric School: Esoteric Lessons
> 1904–1909*; 2007)

Moreover, during the future Vulcan Period any further
indwelling by the Solar-Christos would no longer be
logically necessary, since the earth itself will then have
become a sun and all its inhabitants will have become
sun-beings (like Christ is today). As once again explained
by Rudolf Steiner:

> We look back to three previous embodiments of our
> Earth: to the immediately preceding embodiment
> which we call the Old Moon (not to be confused with
> our present moon); then to that of the "Sun"; and still
> further back to that of "Saturn." And looking forward
> we see prophetically that our Earth will be
> transformed into a "Jupiter," a "Venus" and a
> "Vulcan" …
>
> During the stage of Earth-existence itself, the
> Earth will reunite with the Sun, just as during the
> same phase of evolution it separated from the Sun.
> But during the Jupiter stage there must again be a
> separation. The Earth beings must again be separated
> from the Sun during the Jupiter condition. Again
> there will be a reunion, and during the Venus-
> condition our Earth will be united permanently with
> the Sun, will have been taken up for all time into the

Sun. During the Vulcan-condition our Earth will itself have become a Sun within the Sun and have contributed something to the Sun evolution. (From a lecture given on 27 January 1908, and published in *The Influence of Spiritual Beings upon Man*; 1961)

50. One typical example of the many statements made by Rudolf Steiner that have not been comprehensively understood, in the light of more accurate information that he conveyed, is the following:

> When Jesus of Nazareth had reached about the thirtieth year of his age, his Ego, having purged, purified, and ennobled his physical, etheric, and astral bodies, was able to renounce these, so that a threefold bodily sheath was left—a most pure and refined human envelopment, consisting of a physical, an etheric, and an astral body. At the Baptism by John this threefold bodily sheath received into itself that Being who had never before descended to earth nor passed through former incarnations. This is the Christ-being, who up to that time could only be found in the universe beyond our earth. At the Baptism by John this individual Being united Himself with a human body and dwelt therein for a space of three years in order to accomplish in that time the work [of redemption]. (From a lecture given on 3 July 1909 entitled, "What Occurred at the Baptism by John," and published in *The Gospel of St. John in Relation to the Other Gospels*; 1982)

51. Some students of Rudolf Steiner also entertain the mistaken idea that what was "held back," from Luciferic corruption during Lemurian times, was simply virginal etheric and astral substance that was not associated with any particular human being. To clearly see that this horrid notion was not supported by Rudolf Steiner, please refer

back to Chapter 2, note 12.

52. In a lecture given on 15 November 1913, and published in *Jesus and Christ* (1976), Rudolf Steiner clearly stated that the repeated emphasis on the Christ-being, in spiritual science, was not to minimize or ignore "the man Jesus," but rather to develop a deeper understanding and appreciation of the historical Jesus. In his own words:

> Spiritual research thus leads us to Christ, and through Christ to the historical Jesus. It does this at a time when external investigation, based upon external documents, so often questions the historical existence of Jesus ...
>
> Indeed, it is possible to indicate with mathematical precision when Christ must have lived in the man Jesus, in the historical Jesus ... That Being who lived in Jesus from his thirtieth to thirty-third years gave the impulse humanity needed for its development at a time when its youthful forces were beginning to decline ...
>
> Spiritual science not only tries to lead us to Christ; it *must* do so. All the truths it advances must lead from a spiritual contemplation of man's development to a comprehension of Christ. Men will experience Christ in ever greater measure, and through Christ they will discover Jesus ...
>
> In future, Jesus will be found on that path we may characterize with the words, *through a spiritual knowledge of Christ to a historical knowledge of Jesus.*

53. Regarding the relationship of the Christ-being to the twelve bodhisattvas, Rudolf Steiner in a lecture given on 21 September 1909 (published in *The Gospel of St. Luke*; 1990) stated the following:

> If you were able to look into the great Spirit-Lodge of the twelve Bodhisattvas you would find that in the

midst of the Twelve there is a Thirteenth—one who cannot be called a 'Teacher' in the same sense as the Bodhisattvas, but of whom we must say: He is that Being from *whom wisdom itself streams as very substance*. It is therefore quite correct to speak of the twelve Bodhisattvas in the great Spirit-Lodge grouped around One who is their Centre; they are wrapt in contemplation of the sublime Being from whom there streams what they have then to inculcate into Earth evolution in fulfilment of their missions. Thus there streams from the Thirteenth what the others have to teach. They are the 'Teachers,' the 'Inspirers'; the Thirteenth is himself the Being of whom the others teach, whom they proclaim from epoch to epoch. This Thirteenth is He whom the ancient Rishis called Vishva Karman, whom Zarathustra called Ahura Mazdao, whom we call the Christ. He is the Leader and Guide of the great Lodge of the Bodhisattvas.

54. In describing the dual function of the Christ-being as regent of the sun *and* regent of the earth, Rudolf Steiner stated the following in a lecture given on 13 December 1907 entitled, "Christmas":

> Through the Mystery of Golgotha he then became the Spirit of the Earth, but as Earth Spirit he nevertheless still remained Sun Spirit; he has transferred his work to the Earth and through this act drew the Earth into the work of the Sun ... and in the Spirit of the Earth we find the Christ-Ego, the Sun Ego. The initiate is henceforth able to see in Christ himself the Sun Spirit which formerly, at the time of Christmas, was only to be seen at the midnight hour of the Sun in the holy places of the ancients.

55. Concerning the end of Kali Yuga, and the reappearance

of Christ-Jesus in the etheric realm, Rudolf Steiner stated the following in a lecture given on 25 January 1910, entitled "The Event of Christ's Appearance in the Etheric World" (published in *True Nature of the Second Coming*; 1961):

> Kali Yuga began approximately in the year 3101 B.C ... And because in this Dark Age, in Kali Yuga, man could no longer go forth from the physical into the spiritual world, it was necessary for the Divine Being, Christ, to come down into the physical world—Christ's descent into a man of flesh, into Jesus of Nazareth, was necessary in order that through beholding the life and deeds of Christ on the physical plane it might become possible for men to be linked, in the physical body, with the kingdoms of heaven, with the spiritual world ... Kali Yuga came to an end in the year 1899 and we have now to live on into a new age. What is beginning is slowly preparing men for new faculties of soul ... A new epoch is at hand when the souls of men must take a step upward into the kingdoms of heaven ... it will be possible for men to acquire the new faculty of perception in the etheric world ... the souls of men must advance to the stage of etheric sight and therewith to vision of Christ in the etheric body ... To a man in whom natural clairvoyance has developed this will be like a Second Coming of Christ Jesus.

56. The migration of black magical practices from west to east in pagan Europe is briefly touched on, in the entry on "Black Magic," from the *Gale Encyclopedia of Occultism & Parapsychology* (2000):

> In medieval magic may be found a degraded form of popular pagan rites—the ancient gods had become devils, their mysteries orgies, their worship sorcery ...

Some historians have tried to trace the areas in Europe most affected by these devilish practices. Spain is said to have excelled all in infamy, to have plumbed the depths of the abyss. The south of France next became a hotbed of sorcery, branching northward to Paris and the countries and islands beyond, southward to Italy.

57. While Pentecost is commonly understood to be the "birth of the Christian Church," the actual inception of the Church was at the Crucifixion. As stated in Paragraph 766 of the *Catechism of the Catholic Church*:

> The Church is born primarily of Christ's total self-giving for our salvation, anticipated in the institution of the Eucharist and fulfilled on the cross. "The origin and growth of the Church are symbolized by the blood and water which flowed from the open side of the crucified Jesus. For it was from the side of Christ as he slept the sleep of death upon the cross that there came forth the wondrous sacrament of the whole Church." As Eve was formed from the sleeping Adam's side, so the Church was born from the pierced heart of Christ hanging dead on the cross.

CHAPTER 5

58. Even though discarded vehicles typically deteriorate and disappear after death, there have been noteworthy exceptions throughout post-Atlantean times. The vehicles of the ancient Persian religious leader, Zarathustra, are one such historical example. According to the clairvoyant research of Rudolf Steiner, Zarathustra's etheric and astral bodies persisted for many centuries; and were later integrated and used in the reincarnated lives of two

important pupils. The pupil who later incarnated in Egypt, as Hermes, integrated Zarathustra's discarded astral body; and the pupil who later incarnated in Egypt, as Moses, integrated Zarathustra's discarded etheric body.

While the discarded vehicles of highly advanced human beings may persist for many centuries, they do not have the power to replicate, to form exact copies of themselves. It is only when discarded vehicles have been temporarily indwelt in life by an advanced celestial being (such as Christ) that they are able to replicate.

Prior to Christ-Jesus, however, there have been rare instances in human history where discarded vehicles have both endured and replicated; for example, the etheric body of Shem, the son of Noah. In this special instance, since Shem was destined to be the ancestral forefather of the entire Semitic bloodline, his etheric body was infused with the forces of an advanced celestial being (an "avatar"). As a result, the countless after-death replications of Shem's discarded etheric vehicle were, for centuries, integrated as an etheric prototype into all direct Semitic descendents; thereby uniting them into one, large tribe of peoples.

59. Various versions of Holy Communion are also celebrated by other Christian denominations. Baptists, for example, do not regard Holy Communion as a sacrament, but rather as a remembrance of the Saviour's atonement. Calvinists, on the other hand, believe that the ceremonial bread and wine establish an efficacious connection to the spiritual presence of Christ-Jesus. Furthermore, Lutherans believe that the body and blood of the Saviour are present in Holy Communion, but exist separately "in, with, and under" the bread and wine.

60. Through the hypostatic union of man and God in Christ-Jesus, all the temporal events of the Saviour's earthly life, from the baptism to the ascension, are thereby "stamped"

with the eternal quality of divine existence; that is, they continue to endure throughout earthly time in the ever-present NOW. As such, the Saviour's previous life-events are much more intensely real and alive than the typical akashic records of past occurrences. Moreover, divine power continues to radiate seemingly undiminished from these events.

Therefore, each time the consecrated bread and wine is transubstantiated during Holy Communion, the priest-celebrant, acting "in persona Christi Capitis" (in the person of Christ-Jesus, head of the Church), "re-presents" the original crucifixion and resurrection events. The divine power eternally radiating from these original events transubstantiates the sacramental bread and wine. The crucifix (Christ-Jesus on the cross) is displayed in the sanctuaries of the Catholic and Orthodox Churches as a visible sign that the mystic death is re-presented during Holy Communion.

61. An accurate Greek adjective for resurrected substance is "epiousios," meaning "supersubstantial." In the original Greek wording of the Lord's Prayer, what has been prosaically translated as "daily" in the sentence, "Give us this day our daily bread," is the word "epiousios." This sentence should more accurately read, "Give us this day our supersubstantial bread," as it does in the Douay-Rheims Bible (Matt 6:11). In the sacrament of Holy Communion, then, the consecrated offerings become "supersubstantial bread" and "supersubstantial wine."

62. As expressed in the *Catechism of the Catholic Church* (paragraph 1374):

> In the most blessed sacrament of the Eucharist "the body and blood, together with the soul and divinity, of our Lord Jesus Christ and, therefore, *the whole Christ is truly, really, and substantially contained.* This presence is called 'real'—by which is not intended to exclude the

other types of presence as if they could not be 'real' too, but because it is presence in the fullest sense: that is to say, it is a *substantial* presence by which Christ, God and man, makes himself wholly and entirely present."

63. Some esotericists have alleged that the Knights of the Holy Grail were initially established in France, around 1750, by Charibert of Laon, the maternal grandfather of Charlemagne (742–814 AD). While there is some deep, underlying truth to this assertion, it needs further clarification.

In the thirteenth century romantic poem, "Floris and Blanchefleur" by Konrad Fleck, the Grail Knight Floris is regarded as one of the grandparents of Charlemagne (that is, Charibert of Laon). Rudolf Steiner, however, has stated in a lecture given on 6 May 1909, entitled "The European Mysteries and Their Initiates," that Floris and Blanchefleur were not actual historical figures but were instead legend-symbols of initiatory union:

> The event recorded in the legend of the Holy Grail is also described in the legend of Flor and Blancheflor. Flor and Blancheflor must not be thought of as outer figures—the lily [Blanchefleur] symbolises the soul which finds its higher Egohood [Floris].

Further in the lecture, Steiner also states:

> But among the Initiates it was said: The same soul who lived in Flos or Flor and of whom the legend tells, was reincarnated in the thirteenth and fourteenth centuries as the founder of Rosicrucianism, a Mystery-School having as its aim the cultivation of an understanding of the Christ Mystery in a way suited to the new era. (Ibid).

The true hidden meaning to this esoteric information

is that Charlemagne, and certain French knights who joined the already-existing Order of the Holy Grail, were hereditarily inspired and nurtured by a supersensible figure—Floris—the individuality of Christian Rosenkreutz (not the historical Charibert). Since the entire stream of esoteric Christianity is under the aegis of St. John the Beloved, then it is quite correct in this case to consider Floris as the underlying "founder" of the Grail Knighthood.

Moreover, Fleck's "Floris and Blanchefleur" lends poetic support for the Spanish, not French, origin of the Grail Knights, since Charibert is described as the son of Felix, king of Spain. As well, Charibert himself becomes king of Spain with the death of his father.

64. This is not to say that there is no conceptual component to Holy Communion. In fact, there are very sublime theological ideas (such as the concepts of "transubstantiation" and "re-presentation") associated with the Blessed Sacrament. Moreover, there was also an experiential component to the Holy Grail as well. Before becoming increasingly allegorical and symbolic, it was originally necessary that worthy Grail-seekers *behold* the sacred relic with their own eyes, and that they *perceive* the supernatural contents with their own clairvoyant sight.

65. The term, "initiate," when used in the context of esoteric Christianity, differs significantly from the term that was used in the ancient, pagan Mystery-religions. The Christian initiate has a developed sense of self-awareness and clear powers of intellectual thinking. Knowledge of superphysical life is acquired in full consciousness, and in connection with Christ-Jesus. Superphysical knowledge ("mystery-wisdom") is not intentionally kept secret, but is always shared when safe and progressive to do so.

The ancient Mystery-initiate, on the other hand, acquired superphysical knowledge in an artificially-induced trance condition, and was strictly bound under penalty of death to keep this knowledge secret. Moreover, this initiatory process was not guided directly by Christ-Jesus but, instead, by the human hierophant of the Mystery-temple.

66. The pot of manna and the rod of Aaron, that were sealed inside the ancient Hebrew Ark of the Covenant, can likewise be interpreted in symbolic gender form.

67. In the overall esoteric scheme of human development, Egypto-Chaldean civilization (3000 BC–747 BC) focussed on developing the sentient soul; Graeco-Roman civilization (747 BC–1415 AD) concentrated on developing the intellectual, or mind, soul; and modern Euro-American civilization (1415–3500 AD) is currently developing the consciousness soul.

68. In the words of Rudolf Steiner:

> All that is connected with our culture and the life we lead and must lead, is lifted up, raised into the principle of initiation through the [Mystic-]Christian and through the Rosicrucian[-Christian] training. The purely [Mystic-]Christian way is somewhat difficult for modern man, hence the Rosicrucian[-Christian] path has been introduced for those who have to live in the present age. If someone would take the old purely [Mystic-]Christian path in the midst of modern life he must be able to cut himself off for a time from the world outside, in order to enter it again later all the more intensively. On the other hand the Rosicrucian[-Christian] path can be followed by all, no matter in what occupation or sphere of life they may be placed. (From a lecture given on 6 June 1907 entitled, "The Nature of Initiation," and published in *Theosophy of the Rosicrucian*; 1981)

69. Unfortunately, there is a lazy, somnolent form of brain

activity, somewhat akin to "daydreaming," whereby thoughts are involuntarily generated without much conscious volition. This involuntary thinking is much more brain-based and chemically influenced. Moreover, by cognitively denying the existence of anything spiritual, dedicated materialists increasingly reduce their own pure, superphysical thinking into more of a brain-dependent activity. Tragically, harbouring the erroneous assumption that thinking is entirely brain-dependent will, in time, become a physical reality, a "self-fulfilled prophecy." Over time, then, hardened materialists will increasingly become robotic creatures tossed about in life by their own brain chemistry.

70. When referring to a mental image that has been generated by the objective forces of the supersensible world, it is customary in Rosicrucian teaching to capitalize the term, "Imagination." When referring to an ordinary, subjectively-created mental image, the uncapitalized term, "imagination," is used instead.

71. Concerning the third stage of Rosicrucian-Christian initiatory training, and the "music of the spheres," Rudolf Steiner has stated the following in a lecture given on 6 June 1907 and entitled, "The Nature of Initiation," (published in *Theosophy of the Rosicrucian*; 1981):

> The third stage is *Reading in the Occult Script*, that is, not only seeing isolated pictures but letting the relationship of these pictures work upon one. This becomes what is called occult script. One begins to coordinate the lines of force which stream creatively through the world forming them into definite figures and colour-forms through the imagination. One learns to discover an inner connection which is expressed in these figures and this acts as spiritual tone, as the sphere-harmony, for the figures are founded on true cosmic proportions.

72. Regarding the connection of morality with the human heart, Rudolf Steiner stated the following in a lecture given on 26 May 1922 and entitled, "The Human Heart":

> The real fact is that all that happens in the moral life, and all that happens physically in the world, are brought together precisely in the human heart. These two—the moral and the physical—which run so independently and yet side by side for modern consciousness today, are found in their real union when we learn to understand all the configurations of the human heart.

73. To clairvoyant perception, the conflicting forces of Lucifer and Ahriman press into the physical body from all directions of three-dimensional space. The will forces of Lucifer press into the body from above, while those of Ahriman press in from below. The feeling forces of Lucifer press in from the front, while those of Ahriman press in from the back. The thought forces of Lucifer press in from the left, while those of Ahriman press in from the right.

The counter-forces of progressive celestial beings, however, have prevented Lucifer and Ahriman from completely extending their influences into the central chest area of the body. It was into this free space that Yahweh-Elohim "breathed" the gift of independent selfhood. As Rudolf Steiner described in a lecture given on 21 November 1914 and entitled, "The Balance in the World and Man, Lucifer and Ahriman":

> We are told in the Bible of the breath of Jehovah which was breathed into man. But into what part of man was the breath breathed? ... [T]he region into which the breath was breathed is the intervening region that is in between the onsets [of Lucifer and Ahriman] from before and behind and from above

and below—there, in the middle, where Jehovah created man, as it were in the form of a cube. There it was that he so filled man with His own being, with His own magic breath, that the influence of this magic breath was able to extend into the regions in the rest of man that belong to Lucifer and Ahriman. Here in the midst, bounded above and below and before and behind, is an intervening space where the breath of Jehovah enters directly into the spatial human being. (Published in *The Balance in the World and Man, Lucifer and Ahriman*; 1948)

74. The joyous, light-filled experience of quieting the mind, and Realizing (Intuiting) the superphysical nature of one's ego-self, has been wonderfully described by the Beatles in the song, "Tomorrow Never Knows":

> Turn off your mind relax and float down stream;
>   It is not dying, it is not dying.
> Lay down all thoughts, surrender to the void;
>   It is shining, it is shining.
> Yet you may see the meaning of within;
>   It is being, it is being.
> Love is all, and love is everyone;
>   It is knowing, it is knowing.

75. The "illuminated certainty" of knowing the reality of one's God-self is a truth not obtained as an "Intuition" of the celestial world, but rather as a "revelation of the Holy Spirit"—as a direct communication from the heart of God. This experience is a clear demonstration that spiritual truth can be conveyed to human consciousness directly by God, and not necessarily through the intermediation of the natural world, or by another created being (however exalted).

76. The assertion that St. Paul experienced the stigmata is based on remarks he made in his Letter to the Galatians:

But far be it from me to glory except in the cross of our Lord Jesus Christ, by which the world has been crucified to me, and I to the world ... Henceforth let no man trouble me; for I bear on my body the marks [in Greek, "stigmata"] of Jesus." (Gal 6:14, 17)

Since there was no other reported historical evidence of physical wounds, his remarks could also be taken figuratively, rather than literally.

77. Clearly the redeemed phantom body of Christ-Jesus is not the cause of stigmata (as some esotericists have alleged), since numerous medieval mystics experienced the stigmata (such as St. Francis of Assisi) without having integrated a redeemed phantom replica.

78. As stated by Rudolf Steiner in a lecture given in 1906 entitled "The Post-Atlantean Cultural-Epochs (published in *At the Gates of Spiritual Science*; 1986):

Now there are various ways of finding the Godhead. The Indians, who were the first sub-race of the Aryan race, took the following way. Certain God-inspired messengers of Manu, called the holy Rishis, became the teachers of the ancient Indian culture. No poetry or tradition tells us about this, it is known only through what has been handed down orally in the occult schools ... The ancient Indian felt in his heart that external nature as he saw it was unreal, and that behind it the Godhead was concealed. The name he gave to this Godhead was Brahman, the hidden God. The whole external world was thus for him an illusion, deception, Maya ... Yoga was the name of the training he had to undergo in order to penetrate through illusion to the spirit and the primal source of being. The profound Vedas, the Bhagavad Gita, that sublime song of human perfection, are only echoes of that ancient divine wisdom.

CONCLUSION

79. Unfortunately, it is common in New Age spirituality to separate "Christ consciousness" from any connection to the person of Christ-Jesus. It is not correctly recognized and understood that until the incarnation of Christ-Jesus, the consciousness of life-spirit (buddhi) only existed as a germinal potential in ordinary humanity. Christ consciousness is, in fact, a high degree of self-awareness that was first brought to earth and made available to mankind by the person of Christ-Jesus. Any effort to truthfully unfold Christ consciousness will inevitably unite one with the person of Christ-Jesus. Correspondingly, if the seeker does not encounter the person of Christ-Jesus on the path of Christ consciousness, then he or she is on the wrong path.

80. The crucial importance of Christ-forces in retaining self-awareness after death was explained by Rudolf Steiner in a lecture on 14 April 1914 entitled, "Pleasures and Sufferings in the Life Beyond":

> If the Christ-impulse had not entered the earth, an interruption would have occurred, a break, in the middle of the period between death and rebirth which would have made our existence inharmonious. Long before the Midnight Hour we should have forgotten that we were an 'I' in our last life; we should have felt connection with the spiritual world, but we should have forgotten ourselves. We have to develop our Ego so powerfully on earth, that we gain this Ego-consciousness ever more and more. This has become necessary since the Mystery of Golgotha. But because on earth we attain to an ever great consciousness of our Ego, we thereby exhaust the forces we have need of after death in order that we should really not forget ourselves up to the Midnight Hour of existence. In

order to be able to retain this remembrance, we have to die in Christ. For this the Christ-impulse is necessary. It preserves for us up to the Midnight Hour of existence the possibility of not forgetting our 'I'.

SELECT BIBLIOGRAPHY

(in alphabetical order)

- *Catechism of the Catholic Church* (Our Sunday Visitor, Publishing Division, 2000)

- Dietrich von Hildebrand, *Transformation in Christ: On the Christian Attitude* (Ignatius Press, 2001)

- Holy Bible, *RSV-CE* (Ignatius Press, 2006)

- Levi H. Dowling, *The Aquarian Gospel of Jesus the Christ* (De Vorss & Co., Publishers, 1980)

- Magus Incognito, *The Secret Doctrine of the Rosicrucians* (Yogi Publication Society, 1949)

- Rudolf Steiner, *An Outline of Esoteric Science* (SteinerBooks, 1997)

- Rudolf Steiner, *Christ and the Spiritual World and the Search for the Holy Grail* (Rudolf Steiner Press, 2008)

- Rudolf Steiner, *From Jesus to Christ* (Rudolf Steiner Press, 1973)

- Rudolf Steiner, *Genesis: Secrets of the Bible Story of Creation* (Anthroposophical Publishing Co., 1959)

- Rudolf Steiner, *Life Between Death and Rebirth* (Anthroposophic Press, 1978)

- Rudolf Steiner, *Man as Symphony of the Creative Word* (Rudolf Steiner Press, 1991)

- Rudolf Steiner, *Spiritual Hierarchies and their Reflection in the Physical World* (Anthroposophic Press, 1970)

- Rudolf Steiner, *The Christian Mystery* (SteinerBooks, 1998)

- Rudolf Steiner, *The Christ Impulse and the Development of the Ego-Consciousness* (Kessinger Publishing, 2010)

- Rudolf Steiner, *The Fifth Gospel* (Rudolf Steiner Press, 2007)

- Rudolf Steiner, *The Gospel of St. John and Its Relation to the other Gospels* (SteinerBooks, 1982)

- Rudolf Steiner, *The Gospel of St. Luke* (SteinerBooks, 1990)

- Rudolf Steiner, *The Gospel of St. Matthew* (Kessinger Publishing, 2003)

- Rudolf Steiner, *The Influence of Spiritual Beings Upon Man* (Anthroposophic Press, 1961)

- Rudolf Steiner, *The Occult Movement in the Nineteenth Century*

(Rudolf Steiner Press, 1973)

- Rudolf Steiner, *The Occult Significance of the Bhagavad Gita* (Anthroposophic Press, 1984)

- Rudolf Steiner, *Theosophy* (SteinerBooks, 1994)

- Rudolf Steiner, *Theosophy of the Rosicrucian* (Rudolf Steiner Press, 1981)

- Rudolf Steiner, *The Principle of Spiritual Economy* (Anthroposophic Press, 1986)

- Rudolf Steiner, *The Reappearance of Christ in the Etheric* (SteinerBooks, 2003)

- Rudolf Steiner, *The Spiritual Beings in the Heavenly Bodies and the Kingdoms of Nature* (SteinerBooks, 2011)

- Three Initiates, *The Kybalion: A Study of the Hermetic Philosophy of Ancient Egypt and Greece* (Yogi Publication Society, 1949)

- Yogi Ramacharaka, *Mystic Christianity or the Inner Teachings of the Master* (Yogi Publication Society, 1935)

- Yogi Ramacharaka, *Raja Yoga or Mental Development* (Yogi Publication Society, 1934)

- Yogi Ramacharaka, *The Life Beyond Death* (Cosimo, Inc., 2010)

OTHER BOOKS BY

RON MACFARLANE

THERE IS a puzzling and pervasive misconception in present-day thinking that the existence of God cannot be intellectually determined, and that mentally accepting the existence of God is strictly a matter of non-rational belief (faith).

As such, contemplating God's existence is erroneously regarded as the exclusive subject of faith-based or speculative ideologies (religion and philosophy) which have no proper place in natural scientific study.

The fact is, there are a number of very convincing intellectual arguments concerning the existence of God that have been around for hundreds of years. Indeed, the existence of God can be determined with compelling intellectual certainty—provided the thinker honestly wishes to do so. Moreover, recent advances and discoveries in science have not weakened previous intellectual arguments for God's existence, but instead have enormously strengthened and supported them.

Intellectually assenting to the existence of God is easily demonstrated to be a superlatively logical conclusion, not some vague irrational conceptualization. Remarkably, at the present time there are only two seriously competing intellectual explanations of life: the existence of God (the "God-hypothesis") and the existence of infinite universes (the "multiverse theory"). The postulation of an infinite number of unobservable universes is clearly a desperate attempt by atheistic scientists to avoid the God-hypothesis as the most credible and logical intellectual explanation of life and the universe. Moreover, under intellectual scrutiny, the scientifically celebrated "evolutionary theory" is here demonstrated to be fatally-flawed (philosophically illogical) as a credible explanation of life.

In this particular discourse, five well-known intellectual arguments for God's existence will be thoroughly examined. In considering these arguments, every attempt has been made to include current contributions, advances and discoveries that have modernized the more traditional arguments. Prior to examining these particular arguments for God, the universal predilection to establish intellectual 'oneness'—"monism"—will be considered in detail as well as the recurring propensity to postulate the existence of one supreme being—"monotheism."

Once intellectual certainty of one Supreme Being is established, a number of divine attributes can be logically deduced as well. Eleven of these attributes will be determined and examined in greater detail.

This book is available to order from Amazon.com

The Son of Love
and the Birth of the New Mysteries

Ron MacFarlane

FOR COUNTLESS esoteric students today, the Mystery centres of ancient times have retained a powerful and fascinating allure. Moreover, there is often a wishful longing to revive and continue their secretive initiatory activity into modern times.

Unfortunately, this anachronistic longing is largely based on an illusionary misunderstanding of these Mysteries and the real reasons for their destined demise.

The primary reason for the disappearance of the ancient Mysteries is that they have been supplanted by the superior new mysteries—the mysteries of the Son. These new mysteries were initiated by Christ-Jesus himself. In order to better understand these Son-mysteries in a spiritually-scientific way, Rudolf Steiner (1861–1925) established the Anthroposophical Movement and Society.

Unfortunately, anthroposophy today has become unduly influenced by members and leaders who long to transform spiritual science into a modern-day Mystery institution. Moreover, contrary to his own words and intentions, Rudolf Steiner is even claimed to be the founder of some new "Michael-Mysteries."

By carefully establishing a correct esoteric understanding of the ancient pagan Mysteries, as well as a better appreciation of the new mysteries of the Son, this well-researched and readable discourse convincingly shows that all current and past attempts to revive the ancient pagan Mysteries regressively diverts human development backward to the seducer of mankind, Lucifer, rather than progressively forward to the saviour of mankind, Christ-Jesus.

Moreover, by additionally tracing the intriguing historical development of esoteric Christianity (particularly the Knights of the Holy Grail and Rosicrucianism) alongside Freemasonry, the Knights Templar and Theosophy, this important and necessary study illuminates the correct esoteric position and true significance of anthroposophical spiritual science.

This book is available to order from Amazon.com

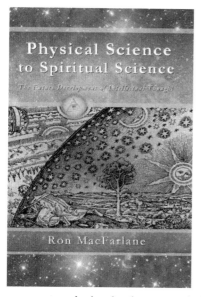

THE PRIDE OF civilized mankind—intellectual thinking—is at a critical crossroads today. No doubt surprising to many, the cognitive capacity to consciously formulate abstract ideas in the mind, and then to manipulate them according to devised rules of logic in order to acquire new knowledge has only been humanly possible for about the last 3,000 years. Prior to intellectual (abstract) thinking, mental activity characteristically consisted of vivid pictorial images that arose spontaneously in the human mind from natural and supernatural stimuli.

The ability to think abstractly is the necessary foundation for mathematics, language and empirical science. The developmental history of intellectual thought, then, exactly parallels the developmental history of mathematics, language and science. Moreover, since abstract thinking inherently encourages the cognitive separation of subject (the thinker) and object (the perceived environment), the history of intellectual development also parallels the historical development of self-conscious (ego) awareness.

Over the last 3000 years, mankind in general has slowly perfected intellectual thinking, and thereby developed complex mathematics, sophisticated languages, comprehensively-detailed empirical sciences and pronounced ego-awareness. Unfortunately, all this intellectual activity over the many previous centuries has also exclusively strengthened human awareness of the physical, material world and substantially decreased awareness of the superphysical, spiritual world.

That is why today, intellectual thinking is at a critical crossroads in further development. Thinking (intellectual or otherwise) is a superphysical activity—an activity within the soul. Empirical science is incorrect in postulating that physical brain tissue generates thought. The brain is simply the biological "sending and receiving" apparatus: sending sense-perceptions to the soul and receiving thought-conceptions from the soul. All this activity certainly generates chemical and electrical activity within the brain; but this activity is the effect, not the cause of thinking.

The danger to future intellectual thought is that increased acceptance of the erroneous scientific notion that thinking is simply brain-chemistry will increasingly deny and deaden true superphysical thinking. Future thinking runs the risk of becoming "a self-fulfilled prophecy"—the more people fervently believe that thought is simply brain-chemistry, the more thought will indeed become simply brain-chemistry. As a result, future human beings will be less responsible for generating their own thinking activity and more involuntarily controlled by their own brain chemistry. The artificial intelligence of machines won't become more human; but instead human beings will become more like robotic machines.

Presently, then, empirical science is leading intellectual thinking in a downward, materialistic direction. Correspondingly, however, true spiritual science (anthroposophy) is also actively engaged in leading intellectual thought back to its superphysical source in the soul. *Physical Science to Spiritual Science: the Future Development of Intellectual Thought* begins by examining the historical development of intellectual thinking and the corresponding rise of physical science. Once this has been discussed, practical and detailed information is presented on how spiritual science is leading intellectual thinking back to its true soul-source. It is intended that upon completion of this discourse, sincere and open-minded readers will themselves come to experience the exhilarating, superphysical nature of their own intellectual thought.

This book is available to order from Amazon.com

THE DIVINE TRINITY—the greatest of all Christian mysteries. How is it that the one God is a unity of three divine persons? Christ-Jesus first revealed this mystery to his disciples when on earth. Later, around the sixth century, the Trinitarian mystery was theologically clarified and outlined by the formulation of the Athanasian Creed. Conceptual understanding of the divine Trinity has changed very little in Western society since then. Similarly with the theological understanding of the Logos-Word, as mentioned in the Gospel of St. John. The traditional understanding, that has remained essentially unchallenged for centuries, is that the Logos-Word is synonymous with God the Son. As for creation, the best that mainstream Christianity has historically provided is an ancient, allegorical account contained in the Book of Genesis.

Out of the hidden well-springs of esoteric Christianity, and as the title indicates, *The Greater Mysteries of the Divine Trinity, the Logos-Word and Creation*, delves much more deeply into the profound mysteries of the Trinitarian God, the Logos-Word of St. John and the creation of the universe. The divine Trinity is here demonstrated to be the loving union of Heavenly Father, Holy Mother and Eternal Son. The Logos-Word is here evidenced to be the "Universal Man," the primordial, cosmic creation of God the Son. Universal creation itself is here detailed to be the "one life becoming many"—the multiplication of the Logos-Word into countless individualized life-forms and beings.

The depth and breadth of original and thought-provoking

information presented here will, no doubt, stimulate and excite those esoteric thinkers who are seriously seeking answers to the deeper mysteries of life, existence and the universe.

This book is available to order from Amazon.com

Also check out the authour's website:

www.heartofshambhala.com

A Site Dedicated to True Esoteric Christianity